# FOREIGN

## THE SECRET LIFE OF

## ROBERT MAXWELL

# FOREIGN BODY

THE SECRET LIFE OF
## ROBERT MAXWELL

## RUSSELL DAVIES

BLOOMSBURY

Grateful acknowledgement is made to Faber and Faber Ltd
for permission to reprint the lines from
'In Time of War' VIII by W. H. Auden,
from *The English Auden: Poems, Essays and Dramatic Writings 1927–1939*
by W. H. Auden, edited by Edward Mendelson.

First published 1995
This paperback edition first published 1996
Copyright © 1995 by Russell Davies

Bloomsbury Publishing Plc, 38 Soho Square, London W1V 5DF

A CIP catalogue record for this book
is available from the British Library

ISBN 0 7475 2937 X

Typeset by Hewer Text Composition Services, Edinburgh
Printed in Great Britain by Cox & Wyman Ltd, Reading

He turned his field into a meeting-place,
And grew the tolerant ironic eye,
And formed the mobile money-changer's face,
And found the notion of equality.

And strangers were as brothers to his clocks,
And with his spires he made a human sky;
Museums stored his learning like a box,
And paper watched his money like a spy.

It grew so fast his life was overgrown,
And he forgot what once it had been made for,
And gathered into crowds and was alone,

And lived expensively and did without,
And could not find the earth which he had paid for,
Nor feel the love that he knew all about.

W. H. Auden,
'In Time of War,' VIII

# Contents

# Illustrations

After page 86

# Foreword

There is no single 'story of Robert Maxwell'. It is in the nature of the case that many versions of his life will be circulated, and all of them will have their insights to add to our knowledge of a secretive man. Oddly enough, the process has some features in common with the 'creative accounting' that Maxwell practised, or caused to be practised. Creative accounting is an important modern-art form, which has gathered into itself many of the other eccentric style-movements which have fascinated the twentieth century: Cubism, for example, where the same object seen from many angles seems to resemble a multiple of itself (very useful in dedicating the same funds to a number of purposes simultaneously); and Surrealism, where the sane observer is made to feel mad by a conjunction of impossibilities that presents itself serenely as a form of the truth. What is unnerving about Robert Maxwell's career is that so many of its most Surrealistic conjunctions are now proving to be not just authentic but, in Maxwell's own terms, normal.

Other histories have concentrated on Maxwell's life in newspapers – journalists will always jump at the chance of writing about their working lives – and on his business career, many details of which have probably already disappeared for ever into the shredder. I hope it will come as a relief to many readers that this account treats those topics as part of Maxwell's domestic background, his habits of life. He was a businessman, and businessmen do move money about. Maxwell may have invented some new movements of his own, but that

1

is for the business community to marvel at, or condemn, or probably both at once. I do not pretend to follow every one of Maxwell's fiscal mystifications and sleights-of-hand. Still less do I understand why some of the manoeuvres I *do* follow were allowed to proceed, under the regulatory systems of the British and European financial worlds.

But this is not the story of Maxwell's business – with which, in any case, he was becoming, at the end of his life, increasingly bored and lax. To juggle resources, even if some of them were phantom resources, had simply become a kind of reflex with Maxwell. Employing people, from the beginning, had rarely been a pleasure, and usually amounted to a stressful tussle with the obtuseness and incompetence of subordinates, not to mention their baffling adherence to correct and conventional methods. Yet his business status had to be maintained, for buying-power was the measure of Maxwell's international presentability, the excuse for his travels, and a passport far more influential than the one tucked into his capacious jacket.

'I only want to be of service,' Maxwell used to say. But he had no masters. His life might almost have been an experiment set up to determine how far an individual can be taken by his incorrigible will. Brought up not just in the severest poverty but with what he experienced as a sense of animal-like insignificance, Maxwell made himself prevail. 'I happen,' he said in his last days, 'to be a well-known figure across the world.' His many enemies could not deny it: they had helped to make it true. Maxwell's power was limited, but he spread his influence with ferocious persistence through the councils of the world. Yet his international ambitions were the ones he most privately pursued.

The British public in his lifetime was content with its idea of Maxwell as a merely local tyrant. He was the fat football chairman lolloping grotesquely across a field to celebrate his team's success, the buffoonishly self-advertising newspaper publisher who could not understand why his readers disliked seeing the controller of their pleasures paraded within the homely pages of the *Daily Mirror*. (He had not realised that the British actually dislike the idea of newspaper ownership altogether, preferring to think of their reading matter as something that grows organically, like the trees from which the newsprint is made.) That Maxwell had courted foreign tyrants was vaguely known, and vaguely connected with his own foreign origins. It was assumed that some sort of Eastern European nostalgia was at work in him; or perhaps something more sinister. By the end of his life, Maxwell had begun to boast of his interference in world affairs; but nobody took it too seriously. There was probably nothing to it – just the international dimension of his megalomania.

But his international dimension was the serious part of Maxwell. His 'Executive Telephone Directory: Chairman's Private Edition (Strictly Confidential)', of which I have the July 1989 edition, contains a section of eighty-six blue pages detailing the 'Chairman's Contacts'. They range from the Aga Khan to Leonid Zamyatin, the Russian Ambassador of the day, taking in Senator Howard Baker, Dr Henry Kissinger (four numbers, including personal fax), the Secretary of the Cabinet (three numbers), Yitzhak Shamir (personal fax) and Shimon Peres (three numbers), Hans-Dietrich Genscher and Chancellor Helmut Schmidt. Senator John Tower, a big earner on the Maxwell payroll, appears in the yellow 'Staff' pages, as Chairman of *Armed Forces Journal International*. (No fewer than eleven numbers are given, incidentally, for Mr Rupert Murdoch.) Maxwell's many Eastern European contacts include publishers of several kinds; his Moscow office representative, Felix Sviridov; and a variety of Soviet and Bulgarian staff not identified by role. Among these names, for sure, is the head of the KGB's London operation, with whom, on Ambassador Zamyatin's own evidence, Maxwell was then in private contact. Maxwell's personal collection of telephone numbers is as fat a volume as the directory supplied to most of us by British Telecom. Even in its official version, this is not the contact-file of a dilettante in international affairs; and it is reasonable to speculate that there were other important numbers which Maxwell would not commit to any printed document, however restricted its circulation. His sometime 'equerry' and *Daily Mirror* Foreign Editor, Nicholas Davies, says that there was a red phone in Maxwell's office which 'never rang'. Maxwell identified it jovially as his hot line to Moscow.

Of all Maxwell's secret tasks, the pursuit of worldwide political influence was the one that took precedence. He dropped everything when a political call came through, ignoring his present company, or even shooing distinguished visitors out of his presence, to the mortification of the staff whose job it was to undo the offence. Even the creation of the 'global communications empire' Maxwell predicted was only a means of imposing his influence on the world – a job he really preferred to do himself, in person. So this Maxwell story concerns itself, as exclusively as is possible without leaving too many practicalities unexplained, with the man's attempt to exercise the power not only of a broker and negotiator but virtually of a small, independent world-force. Other individuals organised pressure groups: Maxwell was more like a one-man republic. Roy Greenslade, the former *Daily Mirror* editor, in his memoir *Maxwell's Fall*, jokingly refers to his ex-boss as 'the President of Maxwellia'; but in truth, no private citizen ever came closer to creating such a status entirely out of his own self-belief.

His fortune, however, was not entirely self-made. New evidence shows how Maxwell, an information addict from his youth, was deliberately financed by the British at the outset of his career, as a two-way trafficker of knowledge; and how he took that opportunity and developed it, over decades, into a freelance political role designed to suit himself. Maxwell wanted to matter in the world – not among his terrorised minions, whose opinion counted for nothing, but among the world's great leaders. (And all leaders, in Maxwell's eyes, were great, for as long as they led.) In his early days as a British citizen, he had worked up an ambition to be a political leader himself, knowing as he did that while foreign-born persons are debarred from the American Presidency, a Prime Minister of Ruthenian birth is a possibility in Great Britain. In securing election to the House of Commons, he took the first essential step towards the goal of conventional high office, but discovered that he was once again a stranger in a strange land. He would never be 'preferred'. I believe that, in his later engagement with international diplomacy and the play of power, there was a component of revenge upon his British hosts, and their stupid inability to perceive and use his talents.

Many of us, in his lifetime, thought it best to stay well out of Maxwell's way, and generally managed to do so. I saw the man in action only twice – or rather once, for on the other occasion, he saw me. This was in March 1990, when I presented Granada Television's *What the Papers Say* Awards Ceremony, before its traditional audience of editors and scribes, in the Lincoln Room of the Savoy Hotel. At Granada, ever since its founding by Sidney Bernstein and development under Sir Denis Forman, there has been something of a tradition of cheerful Northern Labourism, by no means incompatible with the ethos of the *Daily Mirror*, at least in its pre-Maxwell guise. But by 1990 several glum years had gone by, during which it would have been ludicrous to give an award to the so-called 'Daily Maxwell'. It was not so much the well-known glut of stories about the Publisher's own activities that had disfigured the paper, as the evidences of the brutally clumsy bingoid populism he had forced upon it. A few semi-independent parts of the paper, however, were still functioning well, and Paul Foot's campaigning column had scored several loud victories in the course of 1989. It was determined that Foot should be Journalist of the Year – but at the same time, that no opportunity to dissociate Foot's achievements from Maxwell's disfigurements should be spurned. In the event, the citation for one of the other awards gave me the opportunity to draw this distinction.

As recording began, the sight of the 'Mirror Publisher' himself, scoffing greedily at the top table right in front of the dais, was discouraging. Over the lunch that traditionally precedes the annual gong-giving, somebody from the production team had even floated the theory that, when his name came up in the script, Maxwell would either get up and walk out, or stand and make a noisy intervention from the floor – possibilities we considered good for the notoriety of the programme (but not, I privately felt, for the equanimity of its presenter). Fortunately, as the show got under way, the huge blue suit of the magnate was almost obscured by my lectern, so that I had forgotten he was there by the time I found myself reading the citation justifying the award of Commentator of the Year.

The year referred to was 1989, when the Berlin Wall had fallen and the Communist bloc crumbled, so that the European political analysts had enjoyed a particularly competitive season. 'This writer,' I said, referring to the award-winner, Timothy Garton Ash, 'has issued some almost satirically barbed reflections of his own – ' the cue for Granada's team of 'voices' to follow up with a quotation from an article Garton Ash had written for the *Spectator*. It described a period when Erich Honecker, former East German Head of State, had been removed from office, and temporarily replaced by a man scarcely less compromised by his role in the old Communist GDR, Egon Krenz:

> Meanwhile, in that extraordinary villa colony north of Berlin where most of East Germany's top leaders (including Krenz) live behind a high wall – when a friend and I asked the guard at the gate what this compound was, he replied, '*Ein Objekt*' – there sits a sick old man who suddenly has time on his hands. What does he do? Lovingly he turns the pages of a large, expensively produced, red-bound volume, *Erich Honecker: From My Life*, in the 'Leaders of the World' series. ('Already published: Leonid Ilyich Brezhnev ... In preparation: Nicolae Ceauşescu, Kurt Waldheim.) Tenderly he recalls his conversations with the series publisher and General Editor, Robert Maxwell MC.
>
> But will Robert Maxwell come to visit him now? Or is it 'In preparation, Egon Krenz'? If so, Maxwell had better hurry, otherwise he might again find himself puffing yesterday's man.[1]

Receipt of the award by Timothy Garton Ash followed immediately, and during the applause, I sneaked a look at Maxwell, as did everyone else within range. He was pretending, with no great measure of success, to be asleep, a sight which brought me disappointment and relief in just about equal measure.

I had seen Maxwell himself in the podium role at a magazine-award lunch I attended, as Deputy Editor of *Punch*, on 30 March

[1] The observation proved truer than the writer can have hoped, for Krenz lasted only six weeks in office, before he, too, was deposed and Free Elections announced.

1988. As usual, he wore a brilliant-red bow-tie, a white shirt, and a suit of that peculiar blue, radiant but poisoned, which is otherwise attempted only by cheap after-shave lotions – the overall colour scheme of red, white and blue being, of course, Maxwell's attempt to wrap himself in the flag, as he had been doing since his usurpation of the 'I'm Backing Britain' campaign of the Sixties.[1] His speech was extraordinary. Of the ceremonial purpose of the occasion, he said almost nothing, devoting himself instead to the revelation of the trades he had made that morning in the international publishing market. Looking now at the Maxwell Group of Companies' Index of Press Releases, prepared by his Press Officer Bob Cole, I see that the Group issued three statements on that day: the preliminary profit announcement of the Maxwell Communications Corporation; the same Corporation's 'acquisition of Home and Law magazines from Ladbroke Group'; and the impending launch of three new colour magazines for Mirror Group Newspapers.

These evidences of corporate progress Maxwell managed to brandish at us while simultaneously implying a) that we should be flattered, as journalists, to be the first to hear of such developments, and also grateful that jobs were being created for us even as we sipped our coffee; b) that, however, such coups were so routinely brought off by Maxwell companies that the morning had not, in fact, been an exceptional one for the proprietor; and c) that, indeed, the excitement-level of the Maxwell day had dipped a good deal, now that he found himself with nothing better to do than to address a gathering of people who either already were, or surely soon would be, his employees.

That particular lunch had been struggling for dignity and a sense of occasion all along. Maxwell's contribution scuppered it completely. Not since playground days had one seen and heard such simple and sonorous boasting; and yet it was not only braggadocio that made Maxwell's performance that day unacceptable. One further sensed an alienness in him that had

[1]The 'I'm Backing Britain' campaign of 1968 had been launched with an advertisement in *The Times*: Maxwell responded with his own 'Think British – Buy British' slogan.

nothing to do with the complexities of his origins, but everything to do with the culture of personal self-aggrandisement – a term to be taken, in Maxwell's case, as literally as you like. By 1988, he was a huge man, and getting bigger. It was as if he had allowed his body to swell commensurately with his private notion of his possibilities; and the process had begun to make him look unreal. Maxwell was his own theatrical presentation; his confidants have since reported how deeply he dreaded being parted from his powder-puff. But in putting such a distance between himself and the normal, he had miscalculated badly. The bloated degeneration of his body no longer matched the ink-black, double-dyed hair and eyebrows dominating his face (which would have made him ideal casting for Dracula's fat brother). The result was an embalmed look we had all seen before, in the faces of the 'Leaders of the World': those same ageing tyrants of the Eastern bloc whose lives he had celebrated in the Pergamon biographies.

Maxwell, at that moment, was not senile, except perhaps in a business sense. That spring of 1988, he was about to allow his mercantile instincts to slip out of control. In August came the beginning of the battle to take over the vast American empire of Macmillan Inc., a process that was still unresolved when, at the end of October, Maxwell's Pergamon Group Holdings Ltd announced it was to buy Official Airline Guides from Dun & Bradstreet for $750 million cash. The acquisition of Macmillan went through (at the cost of $2.6 billion in borrowings) a fortnight later, followed by the usual stream of peanut deals: the $3.7 million acquisition of Stanley Davis Services Group; a Maxwell Foundation sugar-daddy grant of £2.5 million over five years, for basic research in Molecular Sciences at Leeds University; and at the end of November, a Europe-wide distribution of seven million preview copies of Maxwell's new paper, the *European*, with the assistance of twenty-odd leading European journals. The *Daily Mirror* claimed its highest-ever advertisement revenue on 2 December. Six days later, Robert Maxwell was elected President of State of Israel Bonds (UK). The acquisition of Official Airline Guides was finally ratified just before Christmas, a week after the launch of the Armenia Relief Operation launched by the *Mirror* and the

*European*. It had been a huge year for Maxwell – much too huge. Macmillan Inc. was already shedding its saleable subsidiaries, and the end of empire was beginning.

Two years pass. If one knew nothing else about Maxwell beyond what the loyal Bob Cole put out in his Press Releases, it would be sufficient to consult the Index of those documents to sense what a change had come over Maxwell's world by the beginning of 1991. The Maxwell Communications Corporation's first three statements of the year offered nothing but: the closure of Wheaton Publishers; the opening of an 'Information-Age' AIDS Treatment Centre by the Princess of Wales (Maxwell had seemed to take an avuncular interest in this cause, and its patroness, but had resigned from the post of Chief Fund-raiser); and a notification that the sale of Panini, an Italian manufacturer of stickers and 'decals', and one of the big buys of 1988, had failed to go through after last-minute disagreements over terms. (Bob Cole in his Index marked this release simply 'PANINI', without signalling that the reference was to an ignominious sell-off that hadn't even worked.) Then, on 16 January, an upbeat item: 'Maxwell Communications and BBC Enterprises sign agreement to make Noddy TV series'. So this now counted as a reportable triumph. For Noddy's chum, Big Ears, there might have been a job in Maxwell's offices that very month, when Maxwell personally appointed John Pole as Director of Group Security – a sign of the times, and the mood of the man at the top. Pole's task was to collect information, notably through the bugging of telephones, on the private utterances of Maxwell's subordinates, including members of his family. Within months, pictures of the devices used would be appearing in Maxwell's own newspapers. Probably the best thing that happened to his companies as his last winter expired was the acquisition of the *Correspondent* by the *European*: a starving troutlet swallows a dead minnow.

In mid-April, 1991, came the Press Pack announcing the Flotation of Mirror Group Newspapers. Documents outlining the proposed sale of Pergamon Press – the company whose name had been synonymous with Maxwell's, in good times and bad, for forty years – followed a week later. Some small acquisitions were still being made, but the autumn was a tale of sell-offs: 'Maxwell Communications Dispose of Professional Reference Publishing Unit for US $56.5 million'; 'Maxwell Communications Corporation plc Divests the Macmillan Directory Division for US $146 million Cash'. The story was almost over. Late in October, Maxwell issued writs against the publishers Faber & Faber; their author Seymour Hersh, the American journalist; and the MPs Rupert Allason and George Galloway, who between them all had sought to connect him with illegal arms trading. Maxwell's last, wan attempt at an upbeat statement came on 25 October, when Robert Maxwell Estates Ltd was 'pleased to announce the successful completion of the re-financing of properties': a deathly formulation to anyone who was making a close study of Maxwell's finances – such as the BBC *Panorama* team who reported on his business and accounting methods in September. Once the President of the Macmillan Publishing Company had 'relinquished his post' on 30 October, there were to be no more statements authorised by Robert Maxwell. On 5 November, Maxwell Communications Corporation made it known that its boss was 'reported missing at sea'.

We know now that the state of Maxwell's empire had become much more desperate even than these evidences imply. It may be, as Maxwell's former secretary and aide Jean Baddeley insisted, that his making off with the Mirror Group's pension funds was an emergency measure, to be reversed and repaired before the world had realised it had happened. But Maxwell, accustomed though he was to making enemies in the financial community, had never in all his years of dealing risked such a blatant redistribution of wealth in his own direction. There had been many deals of which City insiders would have (and had) disapproved; but this was a move which, if discovered, would not simply alienate potential financial partners, but reveal Maxwell to the entire nation as a plunderer and a thief. If the disappearance of the pension funds were made public knowledge, then even the least numerate observer would perceive Maxwell's elementary, unforgivable guilt.

When Maxwell retired to his yacht, effectively alone, to consider his position in the early days of November 1991, he was faced with a horrible future. A man unused to contemplating what are euphemistically called 'financial difficulties' could easily have given way at such a moment. And by the standards even of Maxwell's own previous funding crises, this was a big one. It might be tempting to believe that the strain of the moment killed him – that he suffered the beginnings of a heart attack, staggered out on deck to get some air, and fell overboard. But not even a man of such top-heavy bulk would have found it easy to fall from the deck of the *Lady Ghislaine* outside Maxwell's stateroom. You can't fall into the sea thereabouts; you have to climb into it.

It is certainly possible that Maxwell's energy, his resistance, his outrageous self-propulsion subsided at last in the early morning hours of 5 November, and that he slipped quietly and deliberately into the Atlantic, leaving the world to explain to itself a mess too big even for Captain Bob to bluff out. But this theory does not convince many who knew Maxwell. His debts were colossal, his transgressions criminal, but he was not, at that moment, powerless. His biggest investment, throughout his life, had been in information, and he was personally the repository of huge amounts of compromising testimony. Had he returned to face his problems, as most of his former intimates believe he would have sought to do, there is no doubt that Maxwell would have parlayed his knowledge shamelessly into as many degrees of immunity as he could obtain. Not all interested parties would have welcomed the revelations that were likely to emerge from such a process. More than one onlooker, indeed, realising that Maxwell was about to be exposed, would have wished him to go down silently, in the way that he did, rather than noisily in the British courts.

If he was murdered, then the usual questions of motive and opportunity arise. Those two traditional factors are almost comically imbalanced in this case. Practically anybody known to Maxwell, across his almost limitless field of influence, had a reason for wishing him dead. But the opportunity was available to few; and it takes experts to stage a death as debatable as Maxwell's. Such experts exist, however, and they are not all employed by wicked tyrants in far-off lands.

# CHAPTER ONE

# A Travel Agent

Although Robert Maxwell appeared to live his life under the perpetual glare of the spotlights he had paid for and the flashbulbs he had invited, he truly belonged to the Forties, most shadowy of all twentieth-century decades. It was in those shadows that he had constructed the persona he would later sell the world, along with his goods and services. The shifting identities of his early adult years remind one vividly of some of the century's other re-inventors of self, many of whom came, like Maxwell, from Eastern Europe. It is characteristic of such men to have been born in towns in disputed territories, places with two or even three names, according to the requirements of the dominant authority of the day. The writer B. Traven, for example, author of *The Treasure of the Sierra Madre*, who seems to have been born Otto Wienecke (later Feige) in Schwiebus (or Swiebodzin), later travelled the world as Ret Marut, Traven Torsvan and Hal Croves, among other names. Remarkably, Traven (as Marut) acted as a censor of the press in Munich shortly after the First World War, just as Maxwell would in Berlin in the aftermath of the Second World War. It may be one of the unwritten rules of communication that the most secretive individuals end up in charge of other people's information.

Even more striking are the parallels between Maxwell and an earlier figure, Trebitsch Lincoln, born as Ignácz Trebitsch in Hungary in 1879. Having converted from Judaism to Christianity, Lincoln spent some time as a missionary in Canada before making his way to Britain, achieving naturalisation, and finding himself elected to Parliament, as Liberal Member for Darlington, in 1910. As with Maxwell's election, half a century later, xenophobia and anti-Semitism were not excluded from the campaign, and the win was a narrow one. Lincoln then made premature and over-eager contributions to House of Commons debates, which were received, like Maxwell's, with dismay and ridicule. That Parliament, however, was one of the shortest on record, and by the time Lincoln came to present himself for re-election, his finances were in such public disarray that he could not be re-adopted. His speculations in oil failed, and during the Great War, he became a German agent – perhaps a double agent. His later years as a right-wing revolutionary and international spy terminated in the bizarre period he spent as a Buddhist monk in Shanghai, under the name of Abbot Chai Kung. The former MP died in hospital there, but it is by no means certain whether his death was due to natural causes, suicide, or the murderous intervention of some former Nazi associates.

Even in Maxwell's own time, there were figures at large in British public life who seemed to be providing the template upon which he would pattern his procedures and ambitions. The name of Sidney Stanley is forgotten now, but in his day, he was responsible for precipitating one of the most entertainingly detailed examinations of commercial finagling (and alleged government corruption) ever undertaken by a public body in this country. In the years after the Second World War, amid the deprivation and rationing of an exhausted Britain, Stanley had privately advertised himself as the wielder of special influence with certain figures in government, the Civil Service and the Bank of England. The Lynskey Tribunal – whose reported proceedings were followed by every politically aware adult at the time, including, for a certainty, Robert Maxwell – was set up to determine the facts of the matter. But the extent of the possible corruption was difficult to assess without first establishing the narrative of Sidney Stanley's life and methods. His interrogator was Sir Hartley Shawcross, the Attorney-General, who would later question Robert Maxwell on behalf of the Take-Over Panel during Maxwell's dispute with the American company Leasco; and what emerged under Mr Justice Lynskey's chairmanship was a kind of cheeky-chappie, spiv-era parody of the *modus operandi* we have since come to associate with Maxwell himself.

Stanley had been born in Poland, and for reasons not always connected with commercial subterfuge had been known at different times as Solomon Kohsyzcky, Schlomo Rechtand, and Sid Wulkan. He had also used the somewhat prescient name of Blotts. In the grandiosity of his post-war operations he was a Maxwell in the making. Stanley habitually claimed acquaintance with famous persons, and represented himself as a potential catalyst in the reviving of worldwide trade. It was clear that he had offered to apply whatever influence he had, at a price, in the procurement of trading licences and permits – in the Austerity era, the business community faced a daily obstacle-course of restrictions – though he had often priced himself too high, and killed a possible deal. Stanley had undoubted connections in America; and his real friends in government, at sub-Cabinet level (as opposed to the Cabinet ministers whose forged testimonials he carried around in his pocket), did for a time regard him as a likely source of vital transatlantic trade.

Sidney Stanley was in fact a small-scale juggler, a kiter of cheques, and a fantasy philanthropist: with the proceeds of the book he would write in commemoration of the Lynskey experience, he announced, he would found a Children's Trust in his own name. But in his big talk, and his political ambition, there are strange pre-echoes of Maxwell. Stanley was never prosecuted, and in 1949 he disappeared, to resurface again in Tel Aviv. Questioned by researchers in the early Sixties, he still claimed a wide political acquaintance, and stated that he had played some part in the unfolding of the Suez Crisis. Clearly he was a fabulist, but the nature of the fable, it seems, goes to the heart of certain rootless or uprooted personalities. They need to feel needed where they cannot feel welcomed, and influential where the basis of their influence is perhaps least secure.

Most of all, perhaps, they desire – because a 'refugee mentality' obliges them to withhold some degree of confidence in their host country, just in case – to live in the interstices between nationalities, as a kind of political lubricant. Sidney Stanley became indignant when described as a 'contact man', but

14

that was what, in his comically inefficient way, he was. Robert Maxwell, a much more gifted and effectively ambitious individual, was able to realise some of the dreams in which Stanley had briefly wallowed. He also came up against the two forms of anti-Semitism to which Stanley had been exposed: the pseudo-friendly caricatural impulse, expressed in cartoons and jokes, and that deeply embedded, would-be aristocratic disdain which caused Maxwell, in later years, to mutter darkly about 'the Establishment'. He never really seemed to know who they were, probably because they never told him. There were secrets on both sides.

Maxwell's beginnings, like those of all these bizarre prototypes, were extremely obscure. He was born on 10 June 1923, his natal place going variously by the names of Slatinske Doly, Szlatina, Aknazlatina, and Solotvino. Formerly passed around among the Hungarians, Czechs and even Poles, the town was absorbed by the Soviet Union after the war, and today finds itself well inside the border of the Ukraine, where it has come to be known (according to the *Times Atlas of the World*) as Solvotvin. That Maxwell's true family surname was Hoch is not disputed, though in 1923, even that 'fact' was of fairly recent invention. The name had been dispensed to the Hochs in the most arbitrary manner possible, when some visiting bureaucrat decided that the outstanding family trait was tallness. The German for 'high' or 'tall' is '*hoch*' – although the official doling out of these appellations appears to have been Hungarian rather than German. Jews, evidently, qualified only for names with a 'foreign' tinge. Maxwell's own given name may have been Lev, though within the family circle he was called Abraham Leib after a grandfather, and Leiby, or Lajbi, for short. In 1919, however, the area around Solvotvin came under Czech administration, which encouraged or enforced a change from Lajbi to Ludvik, and the addition of the standard Czech name 'Jan'. Maxwell showed some attachment to this monosyllable, which eventually became 'Ian' in English, or Scottish, although the name still did not settle down until Maxwell had finally decided in which order to place 'Ian' and 'Robert'.

In the meantime, several other identities had been briefly worn. It is very likely that there were some we shall never hear about, for Maxwell's improvised route through early wartime Europe cannot now be reliably retraced. His story changed from decade to decade, though it would appear that he left Hungary with some Czech volunteers and headed south. In a House of Commons debate in 1968, he gave credit, in passing, to 'the Yugoslavs . . . who helped us across Europe with false papers and money'. In the long journey down to Asia Minor, across the Mediterranean and north again to France and Britain, Maxwell must surely have undergone several narrow escapes, though not necessarily the ones he specified, which featured such picaresque details as one-armed guards, flights from condemned cells, and contacts with the French Foreign Legion. By the time he had reached England in 1940, at any rate, it is safe to say that a sense of 'personal identity', for Ludvik Hoch, must have been bound up much more in what he had done, or said he had done, and what he now intended to do, than in the name any man might call him by, or any nationality he might ultimately adopt. He had characteristics, but not yet a character.

That Maxwell should have joined Britain's infantry under the name of Private Ivan (or Leslie, or both) du Maurier now seems absurdly melodramatic. A packet of du Maurier cigarettes – quite believably – inspired the change, but the surname also belonged to three generations of du Mauriers (George, Gerald, Daphne) who were so well known in the world of the arts as to make the alias dangerously attention-getting. It was also not an obviously English name; and non-Britons fighting with the British army – especially those from Eastern Europe – were known to be treated ruthlessly by the Germans if captured. No doubt it was in search of some welcome anonymity that 'du Maurier' next took the names of Leslie Smith and Leslie Jones, which then, at last, were abandoned in favour of I.R. Maxwell. More than one explanation for the choice was later supplied by the nominee himself. The last version, which appeared in *Playboy* just before his death, has Maxwell insisting, 'The army chose it for me.' It would not be in the least surprising if these stories proved to have been embroideries covering the fact that Maxwell had simply reverted to the 'du Maurier' methodology, and taken the brand-name from an American coffee tin. This would turn his later adoption of Maxwell House as the name of his business headquarters into an agreeably circular joke, instead of the bathetic mistake some of his British underlings took it to be – though in view of Maxwell's eventual fate, it might give the old slogan of Maxwell House coffee, 'Good to the last drop', a slightly macabre edge.

Maxwell's distinguished service in battle will always count in his favour. There were moments in later years when, under verbal attack, he would seem to cite it too optimistically as unimpeachable evidence of his universal good faith; but the day when General Montgomery pinned the MC on his chest was, surely, the day when Maxwell became, to the extent that he could, British in his heart. It may also have been the day when he first realised the usefulness of having one's moments of achievement photographed, a precaution he took to excess in later life. His moment with Montgomery was immortalised, at all events (the photographer was Monty's), and decades later, Maxwell was happy to have that evidence to hand when political opponents actually went so far as to doubt whether he had been decorated at all. (The fact was that some of the fiercest fighting in which Maxwell engaged took place after his citation for the Military Cross.)

Unfortunately, no parallel recording of Maxwell's voice has survived from that early time, so that it is only by the impressionistic memories of acquaintances that we are able to judge now how remarkable his progress had been in speaking the English language. That he was not a native English speaker was still evident – to the ear of a fairly harsh judge – in the Sixties, when Maxwell addressed Labour Party conferences. It seems to be a rule of English speech that, when it is not generically 'posh', it must offer some sort of identifiable regional or class tinge instead; and Maxwell, even at his most fluent, somehow fell between these categories. But by every standard short of perfection, he was an admirable English speaker, and probably an impressive enunciator of any language, in his deep brown voice. How his other non-native languages compared, we may never know, for we can judge only by piecemeal evidence gathered from scattered sources. Maxwell never seems to have run into the professional polyglot who might have tested him –

and may have avoided the type on principle, for fear of exposing his limitations.[1]

His commonest claim was to the mastery of nine languages. It is not, regrettably, difficult to impress the English with even a smattering of a foreign tongue, but clearly the military authorities had researched which of their man's languages were indeed smatterings, and which he could deploy extensively. For it was at this point that Maxwell's knowledge of German secured him a job in Intelligence, interrogating prominent Nazis at the internment camp at Iserlohn, (where one of his colleagues was the future historian Hugh Trevor-Roper, now Lord Dacre of Glanton). What Maxwell had not already deduced about the Intelligence world was about to be divulged to him, partly through the Allies' own activities and requirements, and partly through the evidence he was taking from the Germans in his charge, especially Hermann Giskes, who had been Hitler's counter-espionage chief in the Netherlands and Northern France.

Giskes, in that role, had been directly in charge of the German effort to resist the ruses of the Special Operations Executive, set up by the British Government in 1940 to incubate resistance wherever the Nazis ruled. In Holland, SOE was penetrated, and its operations used to send false reports back to London, though there is a strong possibility that London knew its Dutch agents to have been eliminated and 'impersonated' by the Germans. It is now believed that SOE continued to send agents into Giskes' area, knowing they would perish, but justifying the sacrifice by giving the agents misleading information to convey, especially about the forthcoming D-Day invasion. The fact that the Germans did indeed keep forces in reserve, north of Calais, suggests that they still expected the onslaught to come in that area, and that SOE's sacrificial double-bluff had worked.

According to his 'official' biography *Maxwell* by Joe Haines,

---

[1]The one exception here would be his 'Foreign Minister' of the late Eighties, Sir John Morgan, who, according to Peter Jay, was 'a genuine ex-diplomat unlike myself and an immensely gifted linguist, and for every language Robert Maxwell almost spoke, he spoke five genuinely, both East Asian as well as East European'. Of course, it was better for Maxwell to employ such a person than to risk facing him in the wider world.

Captain Maxwell drew up a report on the Giskes interrogation which declared that this double-bluff theory corresponded to the truth. Maxwell's superiors rejected this assertion derisively. But it is interesting that Giskes was later brought to London for further questioning, and eventually released by the Dutch in 1948, without having faced any war-crime charge. No such charge could have been brought, of course, without exposing SOE to the accusation that it, in turn, had acted with criminal inhumanity, by sending its own operatives into the waiting arms of the Germans, knowing that only torture and death could follow. Thus Maxwell had not only come to a most unwelcome conclusion about SOE's tactics, but was actually in possession of information that incriminated the organisation. It may have become desirable at this point to come to some arrangement with Maxwell, making him 'one of us'. Certainly the moment was not far off when some former senior SOE personnel, in their post-war role as representatives of M.I.6, did in fact decide that Maxwell was worth taking on board.

The task of interrogating Nazis was particularly distasteful to Maxwell, in that the collapse of Germany had now exposed the machinery of the Final Solution, among whose victims had been both Maxwell's parents, three siblings, and a very large number of more distant family members. It had taken him a while to discover this fact, though he must long have feared it. Fragments of letters written at that time reveal a hatred of Germans, but one that Maxwell had determined to sublimate into an ambition to administer their affairs. With a view to joining the Control Commission in Germany, he was taking daily Russian lessons in order to add formal structure to one of his 'smatterings'. With English and French already in the bag – Maxwell had by now married a French wife – the addition of reliable Russian would give him the full set of languages with which to deal with the ruling Allies in post-war Berlin. When he duly joined the Control Commission in the summer of 1946, it was at the most temporary and junior grade, and yet one which immediately gave him powers of censorship over the press in Berlin, from which any lingering totalitarian traces were to be expunged. This appointment, says Maxwell's best-known biographer Tom Bower (*Maxwell The Outsider*), 'represented the end of his association with any British Intelligence activities and his introduction to a profession which would shape the rest of his life'. Only the second half of the statement is true.

Maxwell's business career was effectively kick-started by the Control Commission when it instituted a Joint Export-Import Agency which would provide the utterly bereft German economy with a kind of basic starter's kit of comestibles, raw materials and staple items. To show a man like Maxwell what this range of stuff looked like was to invite him to engage for himself in its logic of supply-and-demand. The bartering instinct with which he had been brought up in Carpo-Ruthenia, where his father had been a jobbing cattle dealer, had no doubt sustained him throughout the war. (It is known that he induced a Czech officer to search for information on his missing sisters by supplying him with petrol.) For a time, he became one of the Sidney Stanleys of the immediate post-war world, prepared to trade in any commodity: a firm called Low-Bell (founder Arnold Lobl) gave him a working basis for these transactions even while he was still serving as a Control Commission officer and facing a number of potential conflicts of interest.

But what Maxwell had learned, above all things, both from his ragged peregrinations over Europe and from the stripped-down army life, is that the most tradable of all commodities is knowledge. Everyone wants information, nobody has as much as he requires, and it need not even be written down. Maxwell, in fact, would rather have written nothing down at all. The whole process of handwriting irked him, because he had received no education commensurate with his talents, and feared again to expose his deficiencies. He was almost ahead of science in his preference for instant communication, by the spoken word. It is doubtful whether anyone in Maxwell's lifetime relied as extensively on the telephone as he did, or used the instrument to such aggressive effect. He called his approach 'telephone terrorism', and he perfected it in the rubble of Berlin.

A Maxwell born fifty years later could not have failed to become a computer wizard. In the Austerity era, computers were still called 'electronic brains'; each one filled a room, and few European civilians had seen one until the Festival of Britain put an early prototype on display. Knowledge too complex to be communicated down a telephone had to be committed to paper, and built into books; so it was into the book and journal trade that Maxwell moved. He never showed more than a conversational interest in fiction or the aesthetic impulse in writing (which made him a somewhat ludicrous prosecution witness when, in 1966, obscenity charges were raised against the publishers of Hubert Selby's *Last Exit to Brooklyn*). From the start, it was scientific publishing – knowledge as power – that obsessed Maxwell. From his debriefing of selected Nazis, and the Control Commission's work in cleansing German institutions of Nazi influence, he must have emerged with a very strong sense of Germany's strength in scientific research and development; and individual publishers who applied to him on a more mundane level – in search of supplies of paper, for example – will also have left him in no doubt that some of their stock was of possible benefit to the West, in the anticipated struggle against the Communist bloc.

Maxwell had been in just such a contact with the firm of Ferdinand Springer, who had some claim to being considered one of the world's most productive scientific publishers. At the time, however, Springer was completely becalmed amid the social wreckage inside Germany. No trade links with any European partners could be established. Maxwell undertook to put this right, and thus laid the foundations for his future business empire in publishing, certainly in the field of scientific tracts and periodicals. Until now, it has been believed that Maxwell generated and sustained this business entirely unaided. But the fact is that the start of his collaboration with Springer Verlag coincided with a bankrolling project initiated by the Secret Intelligence Service in London. Desmond Bristow, then a serving officer with M.I.6, was present when the subject came up, and his highly circumstantial account shows Maxwell and Military Intelligence working together.

It happened, Bristow says, in the autumn of 1947: 'I was then a "P" Officer, which is a sort of administrative type looking after the Iberian Peninsula. And a friend of mine, an older chap than me called Count Van Den Heuvel – who we used to call Fanny – rolled up in the morning and said, "Look, I want you to be on a committee." ' Van Den Heuvel had been working as a senior intelligence officer in Switzerland during the war. Bristow remembers two other colleagues as having been present at the committee meeting, which was held at the Passport Control Department (which was allied to SIS) in Queen Anne's Gate. Van Den Heuvel explained that the object of the meeting was 'to get blanket approval to finance Bob Maxwell', on whom he then gave a 'brief', explaining who this Maxwell was, where he had come from, and what he had done.

'Fanny' then got to the point. The object of the finance was to set Maxwell up to initiate an exchange of published scientific information with Russia, in order to break what was, at the time, practically an information blackout: 'Nothing was coming out of Russia,' Bristow says, 'neither then nor for a very long time later. How were we getting information – I suppose we were getting it largely through the press! We had no agents in Russia itself, at that time – nor did anybody else, for that matter, so far as I know.' Yet the same need was felt on both sides: 'It mustn't be forgotten that the Russians felt themselves very behind scientifically, although they pretended to themselves not to be. It was sort of squeezing something out of the red orange which we weren't able to get any other way.'

There were no objections to Fanny's proposal, and Bristow doesn't see how there could have been: 'We really weren't in a position to comment much, I mean Van Den Heuvel had worked for the firm for donkey's years and it was nice to be chaired by somebody who'd been very successful in the field.' Fanny thanked the meeting, which dispersed, except that Bristow himself hung around afterwards to ask, 'What the hell is all this about?' Here Van Den Heuvel was a little more specific: 'He said, "Well, the fact is that he's been involved with some German publisher in Germany who has already got access to Russian stuff." And the idea would be for him, Maxwell, to start getting in on that basis and see if he could in fact establish a relationship with some Russian publishing organisation. Which in fact he did.'

The initial application of the finance was perhaps surprising. It went not into publishing but into a front organisation of a different kind: 'Well, they bought Marshall's, the travel agent, first,' Desmond Bristow remembers, 'which in fact sort of became a kind of M.I.6 travel bureau as far as I can remember. I know after I left, I was invited to do a job for them in Tangier and they wanted to book me through Marshall's, and I said no bloody fear, the whole world knows that Marshall's is the sort of M.I.6 travel agent. That was an exaggeration.'

It would appear that the 'firm's' representatives, perhaps especially those who had been SOE personnel, wanted to keep a fairly close eye on Maxwell's movements at first. 'Then later, as I recall,' Bristow says, 'I'd left the country then, but I heard that they in fact went on and bought some firm . . . Butterworth's, which was a publishing company.' The result was Butterworth Scientific Publications, which had a limited life of its own, and soon merged with an offshoot of Springer.

The question arose of how the Maxwell financing should be raised and paid, but that proved to be a simple matter: 'Obviously it had to be paid through a bank, and of course Hambro's was chosen, for obvious reasons. Charles Hambro had been a member of the Special Operations Executive. So it was done through him, which would be a guarantee of complete discretion and secrecy.'

Bristow today is not completely sure of the sum originally involved in the Marshall's manoeuvre, but thinks it was probably £30,000. He is certain that it was a surprising sum in the economic climate of the time: 'Money was very scarce after the war, so scarce that we left a lot of agents high and dry.' Indeed, since average weekly pay in Britain had crept up only to £6.8s by 1951, one can judge that £30,000 was an immense sum – perhaps the better part of half a million today.

It was, as ever, Maxwell's languages that had impressed the firm, according to Bristow:

I think the feeling was that here's a chap, he speaks these languages, he got himself to Britain, he got himself into the Pioneer Corps, from the Pioneer Corps he got himself transferred to the army, somebody picked him out thinking, well, here's a hell of a character, which he was. And speaking all these languages – we didn't have any agents or anybody with that linguistic capacity around the place. There was an old boy in the War Office called Major Clark who allegedly spoke thirty-two languages, but whether he spoke them well or not, I wouldn't know. But here was Max who was a sort of gift of the gods, really. He did speak very well all those languages. Even in those days he was speaking English pretty, pretty well.

Such a view does rather suggest that Britain not only undervalues language-teaching, but undervalues it at the nation's peril (and at unnecessary cost). It does not take a xenophobe to point out that a country which relies on foreign-born messengers for its intelligence must, from time to time, be taking a risk.

A former senior intelligence officer, who cannot be named, confirms that, in the Sixties, he was told by George Kennedy Young, the future Deputy Chief of M.I.6, that he, Young, had been responsible for 'running' Maxwell, while based in Vienna. When Young left his Vienna posting in 1950, Max, the 'gift of the gods', was already hard at work. 'He started supplying – from our point of view – pretty spurious stuff to the Russians,' Desmond Bristow recalls. At no stage was Maxwell equipped with sufficient scientific knowledge to influence the detail of what was published or exchanged, but he knew enough to sense the importance, or otherwise, of a body of information. From the beginning, Maxwell travelled, making contacts himself. He became one of the earliest 'frequent flyers', and reputedly the first customer of the British Overseas Airways Corporation to cover one million miles. Evidences of prosperity were offered to the public gaze well before Maxwell's business was truly prospering. One Sidney Stanley touch was the large Dodge automobile in which Maxwell travelled the British roads. He must have pulled several strings, not only to import the car from Berlin, but to keep it on the road in the Austerity years, gas-guzzler that it was.

At first, Maxwell managed to stay close enough to the plan that British Intelligence had devised for him. 'Not to start with, but after a year or so, they were beginning to get some change out of this,' Bristow states, though he is unsure how deeply Maxwell's operation was penetrating into the secrets of Soviet science. 'But it must have been successful, because I know he was kept on very sort of – how would we put it? – *discreetly* by M.I.6 for quite a long time. Probably, in fact, till the end of his days.' To detach oneself wilfully from an intelligence connection is commonly reckoned a difficult and perhaps inadvisable course. Even Dr Betty Maxwell, in her memoir of life with husband Bob, *A Mind of My Own*, admits to being haunted by the phrase 'Once a spy, always a spy'.

As it happens, Dr Maxwell, in her sometimes disconcerting way, has supplied an anecdote which constitutes one of the clearest indications we have that Maxwell's relationship with British Intelligence did remain alive. She tells of a sunny morning in a Moscow hotel bedroom – the year was 1958 – when Maxwell burst in with what he claimed was a list of book titles available for publication. Had those been the real contents of the documents, they would scarcely have needed to be photographed, in emergency fashion, with a movie camera borrowed from Professor Fred Whipple and his wife, who were also on the trip.

In fact, as Betty Maxwell noticed, the documents actually listed 'Firms whose plant was to be dismantled and sent to the Soviet Union' – an operation that had been undertaken more than a decade before, when the Russians first got their hands, virtually unobstructed, on the ruined Berlin and its environs. Maxwell had known of this plundering campaign, but had been unable to convince his Intelligence bosses of its extent or importance. Now, at last, he had been supplied with the evidence (one wonders what quid pro quo Maxwell himself had offered for it), and felt it was worth his while to go through this photographic manoeuvre in order to convince a contact at home that he had been right. The suggestion is that the old relationship with British Intelligence chiefs was still in place, that Maxwell was reporting what he could to them, and that their give-and-take was lively enough for him to feel that these belated proofs of his rightness were worth producing. Maxwell was also keeping a regular attendance at atomic-power conferences during these years, and may well have spotted details that were still of current interest.

He had not been allowed to operate unobserved. Heavily reliant on his secretary, Anne Dove, who is credited with putting much of the social gloss on Maxwell during his early business years, he was also monitored by the lady. During the war, she had been an SOE secretary in London, the Middle East and Italy, and it is scarcely credible that her old colleagues in Intelligence should not have used her unparalleled proximity to Maxwell as a means of keeping him under the departmental eye. Only one instance of such checking has reached the public domain. Maxwell's journey to Moscow in 1954, when he first put forward proposals for the translation and publication of Russian scientific papers, is known to have caused British Intelligence to call Anne Dove in to the War Office, where they secured from her a formal corroboration of his fidelity to British interests. But that degree of trust in her powers of judgement suggests that this was no once-for-all assessment, but a moment of on-the-record severity in a continuous process of observation.[1] There was a potential conflict here between M.I.6, who had merrily sent Maxwell out into the world in search of information, and M.I.5, with its responsibility for security. M.I.5 took a special interest in 'East-West traders', any or all of whom might be targeted by the KGB for 'turning', though their fears in regard to Maxwell would not approach a climax of speculation until the middle Seventies.

By 1958, Maxwell had cut loose from one of the restraining influences that had kept him close to the original operating pattern, as outlined by his early paymasters at M.I.6. The moment of change came when Dr Paul Rosbaud left Pergamon, the company under which Maxwell had grouped his output of international scientific journals. Rosbaud had joined the business at the time Butterworth and Springer had formed their partnership – a step which had coincided with another large input of money from Hambro's – and had supervised the orderly production of scholarly periodicals through the early Fifties. It was Rosbaud who suggested that Butterworth-Springer should

---

[1] Anne Dove, tellingly, did not rate a single mention in Joe Haines's biography of Maxwell, *Maxwell*, the 'definitive' account of his life to which the subject himself contributed.

take the name of Pergamon Press. His interest in the journals was confined to the scientific soundness of their content, not their profitability. It was when Maxwell began to move in on Pergamon in the mid-Fifties, with a heavily expansionist and publicitarian hand, that Rosbaud began to feel a draught. He had been in scientific publishing since the Thirties in Germany, and now began to realise that much of his accumulated effort was being hijacked and re-directed by Maxwell.

Rupert Allason, MP, who writes on Intelligence matters under the name Nigel West, and has pursued researches into Rosbaud's career, once had an appointment with Maxwell to discuss the relationship between the publisher and his partner-in-science; but at the last moment, Allason was turned away. 'Maxwell was in the building, but he wouldn't see me. And I thought this was really a quite extraordinary way to behave.' It was this cancelled meeting that first gave Allason the interest in Maxwell which culminated in his being the recipient of one of the tycoon's last writs for libel. And for the Rosbaud connection, Allason gives it as his interpretation that Maxwell had seen:

> . . . a golden opportunity, huge potential in a vast warehouse of scientific literature that Rosbaud had accumulated as an editor during the Thirties, when scientific data weren't being circulated or published outside the Third Reich. Rosbaud owned the rights, and Maxwell took full advantage of that, exploited all the material to the full, published it around the world, and then cut Rosbaud out of the deal. Absolutely classic Maxwellian tactics.

This is a spicy story in itself, but more than a dash of extra pepper is added by the fact that Rosbaud himself had Secret Intelligence connections which considerably predated those of Maxwell. 'Rosbaud of course had a very well-developed relationship with SIS, because after all, he'd been supplying scientific information to SIS virtually all the way through the war. The evidence for that is overwhelming.' Allason sees it as likely that M.I.6 would have taken an early opportunity to bring these two suppliers of scientific information together: Rosbaud, the generator and refiner of the information itself, and Maxwell, the 'contact man', to use the term Sidney Stanley so deeply despised. 'My suspicion,' Allason says, 'is that, in the background, that key introduction between Maxwell and Rosbaud was engineered by an Intelligence intermediary.'

Indeed, it seems likely from what Rosbaud-researchers have produced so far that Count Van Den Heuvel had had Dr Rosbaud very much in mind from the start, well before he invested in Maxwell's future as a publisher. His scheme to out-exchange Russia in the matter of scientific information may well have been a secondary 'experiment' launched on the back of a more surely productive plan to bring Rosbaud's full panoply of ex-Nazi knowledge (Rosbaud was of course a campaigning anti-Nazi, hence his SIS connections) into the West, using Maxwell's eagerness as the conveyance. What all parties reckoned without was Maxwell's ambitious independence, his skill in juggling his businesses behind his back, and his ruthless willingness to find a reason to dispense with a colleague like Rosbaud, once the end of his usefulness could be seen approaching.

One doubts whether Rosbaud, with his long record of service to the SIS throughout the dangerous years of the war, will have taken very kindly to being ditched by Maxwell – a junior creature of M.I.6 – with nothing more than a once-for-all compensation payment of £2,500. It would have been natural for Rosbaud to complain at this point to M.I.6 themselves, who had wished this painful and ultimately almost profitless partnership on him. But if Rosbaud did complain, it is doubtful whether he got more than a sympathetic shrug out of 'the firm'. They must long have realised that Maxwell had taken their money and run, into a wider world of business. He maintained a sentimental attachment to Sir Charles Hambro, but no more disbursements from that source were to be forthcoming.

I think it became clear very quickly [Rupert Allason says] that he was really far too difficult to handle. I think to start off with, of course, he was regarded as probably a useful, perhaps even a valuable asset with tremendous potential. I think latterly he was regarded with a considerable amount of hostility and trepidation. And I suppose in the middle period there must have been quite a lot of doubt about his bona fides: what kind of relationship had he struck up with hostile intelligence agencies. Certainly it was known within British Intelligence that he had created and cultivated contacts both in the Israeli intelligence and security services, and the Soviets'.

Israel would come later. But the Soviet connection was always live, just waiting to be plugged in.

# CHAPTER TWO

# Very Much 'Up'

It was always a habit of Robert Maxwell's to take an interest in the outcast: to move towards his position of isolation and make him an offer. Any nation in a weakened or ostracised condition could expect a visit from Maxwell. Partly, no doubt, this was an instinct that grew out of his own lonely estrangement from his origins. He was merely doing as he would be done by, in a grudging world. But few of Maxwell's instincts failed to coincide with an excellent business rationale. The gratitude and relief of the outcast, thus approached, could be relied upon: he would give you a good deal, sometimes for no better reason than that he was enabled to say that a deal existed. Such was the basis of Maxwell's early dealings with Moscow.

It was sometimes hard to remember that the Soviet Union could be as vulnerable as that – especially when the May Day Parade rumbled by in Red Square, showing off rank after rank of missile-carriers and rocketry. Desmond Bristow recalls watching the film coverage in much the same apprehensive mood that afflicted the uninformed civilian: 'You'd think, good God, what's *that*, you know, what's the third thing on the left down there? We'd better find out.' Public display in the USSR seldom suggested anything but square-jawed, implacable self-sufficiency. But Robert Maxwell sensed needs beneath the armoured carapace, and catered to them.

How early in his career he began to do this is still a question in search of an answer. It is now clear that M.I.6 in late 1947 established Maxwell as an information conduit and an agent of exchange, an arrangement which necessarily meant that certain kinds of information would be passed, via his publications, to the Russians: remembered by Desmond Bristow as 'pretty spurious', but, as he says, convincing and meaty enough to retain the recipients' interest. But it is possible that M.I.6 co-opted Maxwell in this unusual fashion not only because of his linguistic talent and mania for communication, but because they knew he had already made a political contact with Russian representatives in Berlin.

A rumour persists that 'at one stage' during his Berlin postings, Maxwell fell into the arms of the KGB – probably with alcoholic encouragement – and undertook to provide assistance on demand, at some future time. It is, indeed, by no means inconceivable that a young officer whose parents had so recently succumbed to the Nazis' industrial programme of murder should have been drawn to the Russian position, on the basis of anti-Nazism alone. As the well-known double-agent Oleg Gordievsky points out:

Many Jews, particularly of his generation, regarded the Soviet Union as a country sacrificing quite a lot, losing millions and millions of soldiers in the Second World War. It saved Europe and it saved the remaining Jews of Europe from the Nazi annihilation, and that's probably why he wanted to be helpful to the Soviet Union in one or another way.

Maxwell did not allow his feelings about the Holocaust to show until the last half-decade of his life, but the fact that they were still strong enough, at that stage, to reduce him to public tears suggests that identification with the Jewish victims' fate had been, all along, his emotional core.

Another curious narrative, related by Leonid Zamyatin, has Maxwell actively considering a life within the Soviet Union itself. Zamyatin, a Member of the Politburo since the Sixties, and the former Chief of the Communist Party of the Soviet Union (CPSU) International Committee, served between 1986 and 1991 as Moscow's Ambassador in London. During that time, he saw a great deal of Maxwell, conversing on matters both great and small. One of the seemingly smaller ones, discussed by the two men in Maxwell's Holborn eyrie, concerned a house in Cambridge which had been occupied in the pre-war years by the internationally known Soviet physicist, Pyotr Leonidovich Kapitsa, a sometime colleague of Ernest Rutherford at the Cavendish Laboratory. (In his early Cambridge years, Kapitsa had been awarded, oddly enough, the 'Clerk Maxwell Studentship', named after the nineteenth-century Scottish physicist, James Clerk Maxwell.) Zamyatin told Maxwell that Kapitsa's house had remained in his family name after his return to the Soviet Union in 1934, and had been used in latter years as a lodging house for students. After so many years, however, the place 'was falling into ruins,' and in need of restoration. It was in hopes of getting a grant from the benefactor Maxwell that Zamyatin had brought the matter up.

> Maxwell then told me a surprising story [says Zamyatin]. He said he would pay for the restoration of the house because Kapitsa, this scientist, had played an important role in determining the path of his own life. He told me that, when he was a captain in the army, at a time when he was situated on Russian territory – I believe that he bore the rank of Captain – he met Kapitsa, who was at that time also in Russia. This was during the war, and Maxwell was interested in new developments in Russia, in the Soviet Union, and in him arose the desire, as in all young, romantic men, to live under the new order in Russia. To see what will become of it all. He shared these feelings at his chance meeting with this academic, whose name in those days was already famous. According to Maxwell's words, Kapitsa told him in confidence that, in his opinion, he should not stay in Russia, as he could end up in one of Stalin's camps. He advised Maxwell to leave, the sooner the better. Maxwell told me that he heeded this advice and that now, as I could see, he was alive . . . so when the question of restoring the house was mentioned, this story came up. The house was then restored.

Though it is difficult to situate in both time and place, this anecdote is interesting in many ways. Kapitsa's alleged advice certainly sounds plausible, since he had already suffered greatly from Stalin himself. In the middle of his Cambridge work, in 1934, Kapitsa had paid what was intended to be the latest in a series of short visits to his homeland, but had been prevented from leaving again on the express orders of the dictator. Stalin had created a new 'Institute for Physical Problems', of which Kapitsa was to be the Director. Having little choice in the matter, Kapitsa began this new life, and naturally disappeared into the shadows of Soviet science during the Second World War. Although he was nominally occupied in developing industrial applications for liquid oxygen, it is widely assumed that his expertise was also devoted to the development of atomic weapons: indeed, a novelettish, mid-Fifties account of his life, first published in German, was translated into English under the title *Kapitsa: the Story of the British-trained Scientist Who Invented the Russian Hydrogen Bomb*.

The nominal head of the Russian atom-bomb project in those years was Lavrentii Beria, who of course doubled as the Chief of the Secret Police. Kapitsa was unable to coexist harmoniously with Beria, an impasse which in the case of dispensable citizens usually resulted in their early disappearance. But Kapitsa was too valuable an asset. The fact that he won the Moscow Defence Medal in 1944, the Order of Lenin in 1943, 1944 and 1945, and in this last year was made a Hero of Socialist Labour as well, suggests that his contribution to the war effort was of huge significance. After the war, however, Beria did prevail, and Kapitsa was dismissed not only from his low-temperature oxygen project but also from the Directorship of the Institute of Physical Problems. Kapitsa wrote to Stalin on 6 August 1948: 'It is now two years since I was deprived of doing serious scientific work.' Kapitsa was not actually reinstated as Director of the Institute for Physical Problems until 1955.

Stalin died in March, 1953, so Maxwell's story of Kapitsa's advice would have to date from before that. Zamyatin's placing of these events 'during the war' does not seem to accord with Maxwell's known movements – and it is overwhelmingly unlikely that a valuable scientific resource like Kapitsa, with his suspicious 'British past'[1], would have been allowed near such a dangerous international centre as Berlin. Only an unrecorded visit by Maxwell to Moscow – a city to which Kapitsa was virtually tied, first by his work, then by a form of house arrest – would easily explain an exchange of views between the two men at a time when Maxwell was still free enough to consider moving East.

Evidence of such a visit comes second-hand. The memoir *The Unknown Maxwell* (notoriously unsourced) written by Maxwell's *Daily Mirror* henchman Nicholas Davies says this:

> Files inspected in Moscow in the summer of 1992 reveal Maxwell's name in a hitherto secret document of the Strict Regime Office Number 32 of the USSR Foreign Affairs Ministry that registered arriving individuals suspected of being spies. He was given the name 'Bob Hoch' and the document revealed that Maxwell in fact first visited Moscow some time between 1947 and 1949. He stayed three days.

Those dates coincide most acceptably with Kapitsa's estrangement from Stalin, and his inner exile from his scientific responsibilities. As for the practicalities of such an unusual visit, the Marshall travel agency would presumably have minimised the fuss.

But if Maxwell was able to speak to such a prestigious and well-guarded figure as Kapitsa during a visit of only three days – on what was allegedly his first and only visit to Moscow under Stalin – then it speaks extremely well of his progress in establishing the desired links with Soviet science, given that no help would have been forthcoming at that stage from British Intelligence sources within the Soviet Union. It also strongly suggests the influence of Dr Paul Rosbaud, who had known Kapitsa in Cambridge. Maxwell's wife, Betty, for her part, records in *A Mind of My Own* that Bob and his local commanding officer, Major George Bell, 'went off together in blizzard conditions to visit the first post-war Leipzig Book

[1]During the Cold War, Kapitsa continued to appear in the British *Who's Who*, as though a light were being kept burning for him in the West.

Fair' ... which took place late in 1946. 'It was,' she asserts, 'the first time Bob ever went to the Russian zone; he was not to go behind the Iron Curtain again until 1951.' Not that she knew, at any rate.

That Kapitsa and Maxwell would have had a great deal to talk about emerges with striking clarity from the physicist's published letters.[1] In 1937, three years into his semi-enforced work for Stalin, he was writing to the dictator, in a letter full of sub-headings which detailed his concerns:

> Scientific journalism. Our newspapers publish scientific material only incidentally and it is often completely garbled. Neither *Pravda* nor *Izvestiya* has a scientifically literate journalist who could put together an interview on a scientific theme independently. When I ask why this is so, I am told it is because there wouldn't be enough work for such a person. But I have met very good journalists of the leading English and American newspapers with whom it is both pleasant and interesting to talk, since they are well informed on scientific topics. However, our own newspapers are very poorly and inadequately informed about scientific life both here and abroad.

Had Count Van Den Heuvel wished to draw up a manifesto upon which Maxwell should act, the text of this letter would have served very well.

In spite of the succession of oppressive regimes under which he worked, Pyotr Kapitsa remained wedded to an internationalist and co-operative notion of scientific progress. Much later in life, he had seen a translation of his book *Science – An International Activity* published in Italy, with the agreement of VAAP, the authors'-rights protection unit (which was under the thumb of the KGB). When Kapitsa received his copy, he discovered that the first thirty pages – a chapter entitled 'Pyotr Kapitsa: Humanist, Scientist, and Practical Revolutionary' – had been torn out. Wasting no effort, Kapitsa complained directly to

---

[1] *Kapitsa in Cambridge and Moscow*, Edited by J.W. Boag, P.E. Rubinin, and D. Shoenberg. North-Holland, 1990.

Yuri V. Andropov, head of the KGB, who gave this comically self-defeating reply:

> Deeply respected Pyotr Leonidovich,
> Referring to your letter about the circumstances of your receipt of your author's copy of your book from Italy, I have to inform you that the organs of the KGB do not engage in the activity you speak of. I enclose a new copy of the Italian edition of your book containing the complete text.
> With best wishes,
> Yu. V. Andropov.

Kapitsa does figure in one of the accounts of Maxwell's life, but at a later stage. Joe Haines (*Maxwell*), working here presumably from an account supplied by Maxwell himself, says that Kapitsa, newly restored to favour, numbered among the Soviet scientists Maxwell met in 1956, when at the invitation of the Academy of Sciences he visited Moscow with a view to examining the publication possibilities there. Maxwell told Haines it was this visit that convinced him 'that we in the West were making a grievous mistake in underestimating the value of Soviet research in many fields, and I resolved to start a major five-year programme of translation of their books and journals'. The idea of Maxwell's five-year plan may have been new, but the conviction that Soviet research was worth collecting can hardly have been. Why else had M.I.6 brought Maxwell and Rosbaud together, some seven years previously?

The effect of Zamyatin's story, in the end, is to reinforce the suspicion that young Captain Maxwell, in the post-war confusion, did go through a brief but perhaps intense period of political self-examination, during which the possibility of moving to the USSR was seriously considered. The clinching detail that gives authenticity to this fifty-year-old happenstance is Kapitsa's Cambridge house. The address he gave when writing to congratulate Rutherford on his sixtieth birthday in 1931 was 173 Huntingdon Road. This house was indeed used for some time as a lodging by the students of the nearby Churchill College. Title to the premises belonged, at that stage, 'to the Soviet People'. Since the break-up of the Soviet Union, responsibility for the house has been placed jointly in the hands of the Russian Embassy and the Russian Academy of Sciences. The Embassy of the Russian Federation is unable to advise on the matter, but recommends consulting the present occupier of 173, Huntingdon Road. No word has so far been received from the person in question – Dr Andrei P. Kapitsa, the physicist's son.

If Captain Maxwell's flirtation with post-war Russia was momentarily serious, and more particularly if he was reckless enough to place his recently won status among the British security forces at the disposal of the KGB, one of two sequences of events must have followed. Either British Intelligence remained in ignorance of this contact, and later financed Maxwell, in all innocence, as simple believers in his talents; or the British got wind of Maxwell's indiscretion and faced him with it, threatening to expose him at the very outset of his commercial career if he did not agree to exploit the confidence of the KGB to British advantage. Such negotiations between Secret Intelligence and Maxwell would have preceded the Count Van Den Heuvel meeting which Desmond Bristow attended, and indeed would help to explain it. Bristow's account of the meeting exudes a sense of surprise that it was necessary at all for Van Den Heuvel to obtain a 'blanket approval' from members of the firm considerably junior to himself. The assembled men, according to Bristow, did not fully understand why their view was being formally canvassed in this way. 'Well, we looked at each other, thinking to ourselves, how can we deny this? Or why should we deny it? Who were we to say whether he was worth whatever he was worth?' The whole event has an air of show, a deliberate parading within 'the firm' of a version of Maxwell which had been pre-agreed by senior personnel, with a view to discouraging the asking of further questions about Maxwell's existing connections.

In a sense, however, it does not matter greatly which of the opposing intelligence communities was the first to believe that it had Captain Maxwell on its books. By the time his international business interests were developing out of the initial failure of Butterworth's, both sides were obviously taking an interest in him. Business travellers from West to East were rare and conspicuous creatures in those days. Almost anything they might say, to either party, would be heard with interest. As Stephen Dorril, a private researcher into 'parapolitics', an area which includes the activities of all manner of secret agencies, remarks:

> You have to remember that, in that period, M.I.6 had very few contacts in Eastern Europe. They did not have agent sources in the Soviet bloc. They were desperate to recruit people, anybody in fact who was going abroad into the Soviet Union, so they began to recruit businessmen, journalists, students, and these were being debriefed when they came back. One of these almost certainly was Robert Maxwell. He was going into the Soviet bloc, buying up Soviet publications, writing biographies, publishing material from the Soviet bloc, building up contacts. Now these might be open sources, but they were all that British Intelligence had at the time. He would come back and then give information to people like Dickie Franks, who was running M.I.6's research production unit which was responsible for contacts with the Soviet Union.

Such a programme had probably been followed by Maxwell since his Marshall-Butterworth days. That, certainly, was the view of the KGB, as given now by its one-time operative, the defector Oleg Gordievsky. Speaking in his comfortable English lair, Gordievsky confirmed that:

> . . . in the KGB, many people thought that Robert Maxwell was working for the British Intelligence. They knew his biography very well, they knew that he used to be in the British Military Intelligence after the war, and in the KGB, they believed 'Once a spy, always a spy'. If he hadn't been an officer, so he was an agent of the British Intelligence Service, working for them unofficially, running errands for them, going abroad and talking to the people like important East European leaders and then writing reports, sending them to the British Intelligence Service.

Informed speculation, plus a mass of circumstantial evidence, would have been enough to bring the KGB to this conclusion. But there may have been no need for speculation at all. We are dealing here with an era of Burgess, Maclean and, above all, the notorious Kim Philby, through whom an imponderable amount of operational detail leaked into Soviet hands during the Fifties. By way of emphasising how clandestine Count Van Den Heuvel's original Maxwell briefing had been, Desmond Bristow, quite unprompted, has raised the possibility that Maxwell's involvement with M.I.6 had been passed to Philby directly from that meeting. The occasion says Bristow, 'was completely and utterly secret, nobody knew anything about it. There must have been the chief; Walters, who was the paymaster, although he probably didn't know the reason; [it was just] something signed by the chief – hand over, you know.' There was one figure present, Bristow recalls, who was friendly with Philby and might conceivably have talked to him about it. 'And if he had done, of course, then Maxwell would be in a way blown. But I don't think the Russians would have minded too much about that. They like playing double and triple agents. They enjoy it.'

There was also plenty for Maxwell himself to enjoy in such an arrangement. Too large, loud and identifiable to be credible as any sort of spy, he could still make a virtue of his obviousness on both sides of the Iron Curtain and make both sides work for him. Straightforwardly bankrolled by Britain, he could take his Soviet recompense in kind – permissions, access, publishable materials – thus deriving commercial advantages from both directions of the trading traffic. There are some indications that the sheer shamelessness of this operation was taken by hard-line elements of the KGB as a kind of insult to their professionalism. Gordievsky recalls that:

... my boss, Colonel Svetanko, was absolutely convinced that he was a spy. I remember him writing on a telegram, a cable received from London, signed by the ambassador – some report about conversation with Robert Maxwell – and he wrote on the telegram, 'Look! This arch-spy again!' So yes, he believed it firmly, that Robert Maxwell was a British spy.

But by that time, Maxwell had ingratiated himself with Communist Party figures who outranked the KGB in the Soviet hierarchy, so Svetanko's spluttering protests were in vain.

Common sense suggests that Maxwell's rare immunity from KGB interference within the USSR stems partly from the visibility of his enterprise. He was too garish to be a threat. Even the likes of Gordievsky – who admittedly came to consider the matter somewhat later – found it hard to believe that such a multi-media personality could be acting upon the most hidden of agendas: 'Already I felt, oh, it can't be true, it can't be true, he has been in the Parliament, an MP, he is a big businessman, he is getting on in age, he can't be a member of an intelligence service, what nonsense. And yet, yes, many people in the KGB believed he was a spy.' But, most unusually, the KGB felt discouraged to interfere in this meddlesome foreigner's case.

Maxwell had deliberately bypassed them, a fact they resented, but were powerless to rectify: 'I know that in many countries,' Oleg Gordievsky says, 'people who wanted to get to the heart of the Soviet bureaucracy, of the Soviet hierarchy, they would use the channels of the KGB, believing that the KGB channel was the shortest and the best – and it was a mistake, because it was not true.' Maxwell was one of those who avoided this error: 'He understood the Soviet system very well. The KGB was important, he knew it, but the Central Committee was the real boss in Soviet society, the KGB was just one of the servants of the Central Committee. So he went directly to the Central Committee, to the International Department and other departments of it. Probably he knew people from the Ideological Department as well.'

In this way, Maxwell reached members of the Politburo, the ruling body, and spoke directly to them; and because of the similarity of the hierarchies in various parts of the Communist bloc, this availability of senior personnel reproduced itself all over Eastern Europe: 'Each time he went to Moscow, to Sofia, Warsaw, East Berlin,' Gordievsky explains, 'he would be able to speak either to the number one, General Secretary of the Party, or at least number two or three, which was still very high and very important for him.'

Much of this diverting personal history had still to be assembled when Maxwell made his big move into the Soviet 'market'. An important witness to the amassing of goodwill by Maxwell in Moscow is Felix Sviridov, formerly a senior official in VAAP. Sviridov latterly became the head of Maxwell Communications Corporation's operation in the Soviet Union, and as such, Maxwell's own 'man in Moscow'. He is also alleged by prominent Soviet intelligence veterans to have been a practitioner in that area himself: Mikhail Lyubimov (sometime head of the KGB British section) identifies him as a KGB operative, Oleg Kalugin (former KGB General) as a member of the GRU, the Soviet military intelligence operation. Sviridov first met Maxwell during the winter of 1960–61. Having spent over five years in the United States (not without incurring there a suspicion of intelligence connections), Sviridov had returned to the Foreign Relations Department of the Soviet Academy of Sciences. 'Bob Maxwell came to sign an agreement on cover-to-cover translations of some 150 or 200 Soviet scientific journals, translations into English.' (It was this sort of expansion into bulk trading that had driven Paul Rosbaud out of Pergamon Press.) 'Since then,' Sviridov says, 'the number of journals increased, and finally reached, I think, a figure of 370 to 400 titles of scientific Soviet journals being translated by Bob Maxwell.'

At that stage, Sviridov maintains, Maxwell was already regarded very favourably in Soviet academic circles:

The man who actually was running the Academy of Sciences in those years was the first Vice-President, Academician Dobchev, a world-renowned scientist in the field of polymer science. He was speaking about Mr Maxwell only in positive terms, as extremely dynamic, and a very pragmatic man who understood that he could make a substantial fortune in bringing the Soviet science to the West and the Western scientific community. In other words, killing two birds with one stone: a) contributing largely to the dissemination of scientific knowledge, and b) earning substantial money with it.

As memories of the Cold War recede, it becomes difficult

mentally to recreate the atmosphere in which the Soviet authorities could have believed that there was much in this deal for them. 'Propaganda', however, was the key term. Just as the Soviet system relied internally on the power of propaganda to convince their own people of the progress in which they were supposedly participating, so the evidence of Soviet scientific achievement was held, by the Soviets themselves, to exercise a persuasive force in the outside world, in emphasising the viability of Communism and suggesting a depth of resource which has since been revealed as illusory.

> Actually, this propaganda aspect [says Felix Sviridov] was playing an important part in negotiations conducted by Mr Maxwell, because when he was trying to get better terms for a deal, he was usually saying, 'Look, Comrades . . .' Whenever he was in the Soviet Union, he was addressing all Soviet representatives putting the word 'Comrade' before the name, just as we all were doing here – and he was saying, 'Look, Comrades, after all, I am not hiding that I am making money, but I'm doing a very effective propaganda for your science.'

Under Victor Louis, Sviridov's predecessor as Maxwell's Moscow representative, the publication rights to scientific journals had been ceded to Maxwell at extremely modest rates: in fact, Soviet publishers were under instructions not to press for particularly advantageous contracts, but to take Maxwell's terms. Such was the keenness of the Russian scientific establishment to receive credit for its work, plus a little hard currency on the side. With the Space Race adding its own urgency to the existing Arms Race in the late Fifties, Maxwell's early investments in published research material would later bring pleasing returns.

But with time, there grew in Maxwell a desire to speak to the Soviet Union at levels higher than those implied by the exchange of mere publishing contracts. Felix Sviridov believes that 'first traces of this appeared at the final years of Khrushchev'; and indeed, Maxwell's own contributions to his Russophile publications of that era do show him putting a political construction on his efforts. A notable example occurred in 1962, when he inaugurated Pergamon's 'Countries of the World' series (which, he stated with typical bravado, 'will eventually cover all the countries of the world') with a volume entitled *Information USSR*. This was a boil-down of the *Great Soviet Encyclopaedia*, prepared 'with the editorial advice and assistance of the editors' of that work.

'In publishing this volume,' Maxwell declared, 'I am expressing neither agreement nor disagreement with the opinions in it.' He did, however, take the opportunity to rebuke the compilers of the *GSE* for some of the opinions that appeared in the full-home-grown edition of the encyclopaedia, and which he had strenuously excluded:

> It is unfortunately true [Maxwell wrote in his Editor's Preface] that in the past, the leaders, intelligentsia and general public of the USSR have been most inadequately informed about the actual conditions in, and the intentions of, the peoples of the Western world. For example, the articles in the *Great Soviet Encyclopaedia* concerned with Great Britain and the USA and other Western countries are notoriously tendentious and inaccurate, and surprisingly they have not yet been withdrawn (for instance, an article in the *Soviet Encyclopaedia* about Great Britain calls the philosopher Bertrand Russell 'an obdurate enemy of the Soviet Union and a cynical war-monger'). Many other similar absurd statements could be quoted.

Russell at that time, in fact, was one of the leading proponents of nuclear disarmament in Britain, and was briefly imprisoned for that belief, just as he had been in the First World War on account of his pacifism.

There was certainly a case for saying that 'cynical war-monger' failed to catch the flavour of Russell's political ideology, but Maxwell may have attracted some hostility in Moscow official circles by making such freelance comments on an official publication. Valery Rudnev, a functionary who first came across Maxwell's name in a secret report to the Central Committee in 1962, the year of publication of *Information USSR*, has stated that Maxwell was regarded with great suspicion at that time, partly because of the competition afforded by Pergamon to the home-grown Sputnik publishing house, and partly because of the 'unacceptable ideological content' of a series of educational books he had published. Maxwell's semi-belligerent Preface to *Information USSR* cannot have failed to count against him in this secret assessment.

Such chiding of the Soviets by Maxwell was naturally not innocent of self-interest. 'Ignorance is the worst enemy of peace,' he argued, in the same prefatory piece. 'By presenting in a handy format essential basic information about the USSR, I hope to have made a contribution to peace and mutual co-operation. But there is need for a reciprocal gesture . . .' This would naturally come, he recommended, in the form of a similarly encyclopaedic treatment of the cultures of Britain and America, to be distributed among the Soviets – the assembly and publication of which enlightening tome, it was heavily implied, Robert Maxwell would be only too pleased to undertake, should the offer of a realistic contract be forthcoming.

Yet for the moment, Maxwell's trading impulses seemed almost to have been subordinated to his political message. By 1962, he had developed a notion of internationalism which he was keen to publicise. In this Editor's Preface, he characteristically used both encouragement and threat to recommend it:

> The time has definitely come [he advised, in encouraging mode] when every intelligent individual must learn to think globally, beyond the horizon of a narrow, nationalist point of view . . . This does not at all imply that you need to stop being as patriotic or as staunch a nationalist as you like, but patriotism which does not acknowledge the patriotism and sincerity of others is a rather sterile form of motivation in the second half of the twentieth century.

Now Maxwell addressed his Moscow hosts directly, the mood darkening:

> The most important step the USSR Government can take to assure the Western peoples of its peaceful intentions is

to encourage the dissemination of objective information about itself and the people it governs; and to allow the dissemination within the USSR of similar information about the Western world. I gladly pledge all my resources [this became a very typical Maxwell formula in his later tycoon years] to encourage such a mutual exchange because I believe that the alternative is nothing less disastrous than the devastation, within a matter of five years, of Russia, Europe and the USA.

This looks, in hindsight, a melodramatic pronouncement, but its date (May 1962) shows Maxwell to have been exaggerating sadly little. The Cuban Missile Crisis, bringing the world as close as it has been to nuclear-age confrontation, took place less than six months later (and in its aftermath, incidentally, it was the 'war-monger' Bertrand Russell who stated that the human race owed a large debt of gratitude to the Soviet leader, Khrushchev). Where Maxwell was wildly unrealistic was in supposing that an elephantine production like the *Great Soviet Encyclopaedia*, however skilfully abridged, could possibly have made the significant contribution to international understanding that he claimed for it. One might as well have put *Whitaker's Almanac* on sale in the Soviet Republics, and expected its buyers to derive from it an eye-opening impression of the British way of life.

For the next decade, Maxwell's progress in Moscow was to be delayed, if seldom truly thwarted, by a number of changes in the ruling cadre of the Soviet Union, each of them necessitating a certain wariness as the new personnel took control. Nikita Khrushchev was ousted from the General Secretaryship of the Communist Party in October 1964. It happened the day before the British General Election which sent Maxwell to Parliament. The superimposition of a House of Commons timetable upon his usual agenda meant that Maxwell's international activities, at least in so far as he was able to pursue them in person, were limited for a time. On the other hand, as a new Parliamentarian, he immediately became of much more pressing interest to Soviet personnel stationed within Britain.

Mikhail Lyubimov, who came to England in 1961 as a young

Political Intelligence officer, was given the task of collecting information about the political situation inside Britain, and about external relations with other countries. 'I had to penetrate the Conservative Party and the Labour Party as well,' Lyubimov says today, 'although the Conservatives were my main task – and of course at that time, we worked very actively against the American bases in South Ruislip, and so on.' Lyubimov was expelled from Britain for espionage in 1965, but not before he had made the acquaintance of Robert Maxwell, MP. 'We shook hands and introduced each other. When I came to the Chief of Station I reported to him about Maxwell, because Maxwell was interesting for us as a man who could cover some relations inside the Labour Party.' Lyubimov's chief, nonetheless, offered some warning words. ' "Oh Mikhail Petrovich," he said, "you see this man is an M.I.6 spy – M.I.5 spy to be exact – and you should be very careful." '

Apparently the KGB's London station had met with moments of unsuccess in approaching Maxwell. 'Inside the station,' Lyubimov relates, 'we had a Political Intelligence line, a Counter-Intelligence line, and other lines; so the Counter-Intelligence line tried to contact him – but unfortunately they had, you see, no resources. I mean there were two fools, I suppose, who knew very bad English . . .' Scientific Intelligence then took a turn at Maxwell – but no less warily than the others. 'He was considered at that time to be a spy,' Lyubimov insists, 'a man who's closely connected to the British Intelligence, and a man who you should not meet because he will get you into a provocation – though we knew he was very successful in his publishing affairs.' Summing up his London efforts, before the sudden deportation, Lyubimov says, 'I tried to get him into the service. But it failed, because he was too dangerous.'

During the Khrushchev era, Maxwell had made little progress within the Soviet Union, and yet at home, the Political Intelligence officers were circling round him. It might seem that mutually contradictory attitudes to Maxwell were maintained at the same moment, in Moscow and in London; but the fact really is that the commercial preoccupation was uppermost in Red Square, and the political accent was the first to be heeded in London. Yet Maxwell would soon be getting his political points across in Moscow, too. 'Important things in this part of the world,' Sviridov confides, 'are never done in a sort of cavalry attack. But with Brezhnev in power there, this aspect of Bob Maxwell's activity increased, and actually became one of the major, if not the major area of his activities in the Soviet Union.'

One of Maxwell's chief contacts on the borderline between the scientific community and the political echelons above was Academician Dzhermen Mikhailovich Gvishiani, a philosopher and sociologist who had spent ten years on the State Committee for New Technology – always a subject to attract Maxwell. Gvishiani emphasises that, in Khrushchev's time, the Central Committee of the Communist Party was not the active body it later became:

> The divisions of the Central Committee were not actively involved. They were judging policy; executive work was done by governmental bodies. Gradually, when people were changed after Khrushchev, Brezhnev became Secretary-General, Kosygin became Prime Minister – at that time, gradually, the Central Committee began to be involved. Some assistants were involved in contacts. It was a time when for instance Armand Hammer, the American businessman, was very frequently in the Central Committee, being received by one of the Secretaries.

Hammer was a figure who had escaped the investigative impulses of the contemporary news media to a remarkable degree. Throughout his long life – he had known Lenin himself – Hammer demonstrated an ability to divide his money-making and money-distributing instincts between East and West in a way that only rarely attracted an inconvenient notoriety. There is no doubt that Hammer's personal style in dealing with the post-Stalinist Soviet bureaucracy provided Maxwell with a pattern that he was keen to follow. Gvishiani, for example, recalls a visit from Hammer when the American's purpose proved to be:

> . . . to give to Brezhnev Lenin's letters, which he by chance

obtained in the United States. He was mentioning the cost, $250,000; and after all, he decided to give it free of charge to the Central Committee, so it was done. I was present at this meeting; and it seemed that, when Armand Hammer came, he was asking telephone numbers of the staff of the Central Committee, Secretaries and so on. And Robert Maxwell was doing the same later, when he started to be a publisher of books.

Gvishiani still judges the approach of Maxwell, probably quite rightly, in tactical, Cold War terms. 'I think it was a correct approach by Maxwell. He took a very businesslike topic to begin with, but I think one could soon see, with the effects, that he was ending up political.'

As an acquaintance of Dzhermen Gvishiani's, Maxwell had a very good chance to 'end up political', since the Academician was at that stage the son-in-law of Prime Minister Kosygin. And the influence of simple human compatibility should not be left out of account. 'Mr Gvishiani,' says Oleg Kalugin, a former KGB General (who managed to serve under four successive chiefs of that organisation), 'is a jovial character, I mean a Georgian, always in a good mood, you know, always friendly. And Maxwell, apparently, partly due to his own good-natured character . . . made friends and made good.' Subordinates of Maxwell in his British operations might be surprised to see him described in such terms, but it seems clear that Maxwell for the time being was presenting himself in Moscow as the sunniest of creatures, and a stranger to wrath.

Spared the obvious harassments to which the capitalist visitor was traditionally subjected at that time, he could afford to relax. His friendship with Gvishiani, with the latter's family connection to the top echelon of Soviet rule, put Maxwell out of bounds when it came to the disciplinary interference of the security forces. 'It was simply forbidden to interfere with the relations between Mr Maxwell and Mr Gvishiani,' said Mikhail Lyubimov. 'We were advised, and we knew ourselves, that if we do not want any troubles, better to keep it off [sic], you know. We decided, as we did many times before – like for instance, you remember Armand Hammer, who was in close touch with our leadership – we decided not to interfere at all.' Gvishiani, for his part, must have found Maxwell a fruitful object of study, not only in the fields of philosophy and sociology but in a discipline new to Gvishiani, and indeed to most of us. In 1969, he accepted the improbable post of head of the Laboratory for Research into Complex Problems of Management at the Institute of Concrete Social Research. Maxwell was certainly a Complex Problem of Management.

What the Soviets withheld from Maxwell in the way of personal pressure they tended to reapply from time to time through the clumsiness of their foreign policy. In all his years of developing his Moscow connections, Maxwell faced no trickier moment than the late August of 1968, when Russian troops occupied Czechoslovakia in order to undo and discredit the reforms of Alexander Dubçek, who had been seeking 'Communism with a human face'. However insecure the allegiance of his natal territory, Maxwell had at least nominally been born a Czech, a fact he acknowledged at the beginning of his contribution – a contribution he could scarcely have avoided making – to the Emergency Commons Debate of 28 August. Maxwell had been an MP since 1964, elected ('by a comfortable margin,' Dr Betty Maxwell has written, 'for a marginal seat') to serve the constituency of Buckingham in the Labour interest. Throughout the House, he was held to have failed to exude the proper humility of a new Member, and, having begun badly (that is, too confidently), he had subsequently acquired the reputation of an egotistical windbag. On this topic, however, he was heard with unusual tolerance and even appreciation.

The line he took was not an easy one to promote, though Maxwell got away with it. He hoped, he said, that the (Labour) Government would not be panicked – especially not into extra spending on defence:

Is it not a fact that whereas we, together with most of the world, condemn the Russians for their dastardly act in invading by trickery this defenceless country in the way they did, that invasion has not altered the status quo? The position as between East and West remains the same. It would be utterly wrong to give up the *détente* for which we have all fought, worked and made sacrifices [a serious cynic, no doubt, would substitute 'I' for 'we' in this passage, and even 'profits' for 'sacrifices'] merely because of this ghastly Russian invasion.

Maxwell managed to characterise the invasion as 'ghastly' three times in the course of his speech, but insisted that acts of protest should be undertaken not by governments, but by individuals.

Among the symbolic or cosmetic protests he recommended was the withdrawal of visas for the touring Red Army Choir, and the cancellation 'or postponement' of holidays to the Soviet Union or its assisting allies. Finally taking up 'a suggestion made by the *Sunday Mirror*' (a paper which, later in life, Maxwell would own, and controversially manipulate), he proposed that '. . . if people can think of nothing better to do, they should send a postcard to Mr Brezhnev telling him how they abhor this ghastly act of oppression against this friendly country. Such steps would prove extremely helpful and encouraging to the long-suffering Czech people.'

This mention of Brezhnev as a possible recipient of British postcards was the only allusion Maxwell made to the ruling General Secretary, a figure whose acquaintance he had already made considerable efforts to cultivate, and whom he would later flatter extensively through the medium of Pergamon Press's English-language publications.

Though there was a passage in the speech where Maxwell spoke movingly by adopting the voice of the Czechs themselves ('Certainly you have occupied us, but you do not own us. You cannot command us and you will not control us. We will take instructions only from our legal Government'), the effect of the whole was to seek a reason why the ordered progress of his own developing relationship with the USSR should not be disturbed. Maxwell rebuked the London Chamber of Commerce, with its policy of 'business as usual', contrasting its behaviour with that of the 'splendid examples of the TUC', who had cancelled some fraternal visits to the Soviet bloc. But there is little evidence that Maxwell, as the months went by, did not himself pursue the same policy as the Chamber. In this, he was behaving more like a government than an individual.

Where he did display his knowledge of the Russian governmental mind was in his analysis of the reasons why the Prague Spring had been crushed. For most observers at the time, the idea that Russia might actually be afraid of the developments in Czechoslovakia – the fear being that the new appetite for democratic socialism might be communicable to Soviet society, like a disease – could be seen only as an excuse for the Soviet tyranny, and not a real reason for the invasion. If this line was heard at all, it was simply an argument put forward by Soviet apologists to justify a brutal defence of the Communist monolith. Yet Maxwell had perceived in his dealings with the Soviets that the fear was real, and his speech drew attention, in a way unnoticed at the time, to the Canute-like aspect of Brezhnev's military manoeuvre. 'They were afraid to let the shaft of light into their own party,' he told the House. 'They may have gained for themselves a few years' respite, in which their kind of dictatorship can prevail and their way of democracy can continue. That is for them to judge.' Twenty-one years were actually to pass before the Berlin Wall fell, and Dubçek returned to Prague, but Maxwell's suggestion that Communism had bought only a 'respite' was sound enough.

His own political ambitions, in so far as they had centred on the possibility of high office within a British government, were now waning. Shortly after the 1966 election which had returned him to Parliament with a slightly increased majority, Maxwell had let it be known privately that he had made himself unavailable 'for junior office, not because I am big-headed, but because I have considerable commitments to Pergamon and to our export drive, and I have not been long enough in Parliament to deserve senior office. Therefore, you can rest assured that the result of this massive win for Labour will be that I shall once again be able to devote the bulk of my time to Pergamon'. In effect, this meant that Maxwell's political effort was once again to be applied abroad, through his business and publishing connections and his personal charm and clout, rather than in the representation of the people at home.

His time in the Commons had been frustrating in many ways. From the start, the selection process had brought Maxwell uncomfortably close to the xenophobia and even racism of some provincial Britons, and within the Commons chamber itself, he must have been able to detect more than a whiff of the same foul air. His own party clearly did not trust him. (If M.I.5 at this stage was circulating negative reports about Maxwell, his leader, Harold Wilson, was of the temperament to take them seriously.) The Chairmanship of the House of Commons Catering Sub-Committee, Maxwell's only office, must have been experienced by him as a humiliation. He had an interest in food, to which his obesity would soon be attesting, but it did not extend to argufying with piqued Tories over the non-availability of their favourite hors-d'oeuvres. Yet Maxwell was bound in tightly to his Commons work, at first by the size of Labour's majority, which at one stage dwindled to a single vote. He was able to keep up an appearance of commitment to constituency matters, though his successes in this line were largely due to the efforts of his wife.

If, by the end of his Commons service in June 1970, Maxwell had concluded that he was simply taken more seriously abroad – which was a fair conclusion – he was about to be driven even more forcefully into the arms of his foreign contacts by the British government's official evaluation of his business methods. The Department of Trade and Industry Reports of 13 July 1971 and 11 April 1972 were based on investigations begun in 1969, under the auspices of the old Board of Trade, before Maxwell's loss of his Parliamentary seat. One of his first, and repeated, tasks after that loss was to give evidence to the Board's investigators. Both in terms of morale and influence, this was a low point Maxwell had not reached before. Too much of his energy was taken up in simple self-defence.

The first DTI report was longer than this book, but all that is ever remembered of it is the conclusion 'that, notwithstanding Mr Maxwell's acknowledged abilities and energies, he is not in our opinion a person who can be relied on to exercise a proper stewardship of a publicly quoted company'. Maxwell took this adjudication, perhaps not without cause, as the Establishment's attempt to kill him off as a commercial operator. Whatever clandestine support he had received in the past – and Hambro's Bank had decided as early as 1953 that it was unable to justify further subventions to Maxwell – he seemed unable to call upon it now. His recent attempts to broaden his British power-base had included attempts to acquire newspapers, but these had failed. Unseated in Parliament, he was destined to fail in two more elections, both held in 1974. The following year, he managed to get a new paper, the *Scottish Daily News*, briefly off the ground, but the venture foundered. Two more attempts to secure adoption as a Labour candidate met with rebuffs. It did not seem possible that Maxwell could ever be a political force again.

From his foreign activities, however, he remained strangely undeflected. Thanks to his quick resumption of control over Pergamon, which remains to this day one of his most astonishing coups, Maxwell was able to remain a continuously credible presence in international publishing, especially in the Soviet Union. A couple of twists of history had also brought him back into fashion, as it were, with Soviet observers. After the invasion of Czechoslovakia, it was perceived that Maxwell had signalled, albeit in a manner hedged around with expressions of dismay, that he personally was not to be considered as one of those whose feelings for the USSR had been frostbitten by this new Cold War development. Then came the diplomatic crisis of 1971, when the British government ordered the expulsion of 105 persons identified (correctly) as KGB officers. Relations between the two sides were already tense, and would further worsen when Moscow responded by expelling five Britons on its own account, and blocking the admission of a dozen more. Maxwell, at that moment, standing between DTI reports, was nearing his weakest, yet his usefulness as an intelligence bridge, available to both Britain and the USSR, had been restored to something like the potential it had enjoyed in 1954.

Whether either side facilitated Maxwell's remarkable recovery from the commercial trough of the early Seventies must remain, for now, an open question. Knowing what we know now of his compartmentalisation of business, and the methods of accountancy he encouraged, it does not seem at all unlikely that money was laundered into his enterprise by an ally who was determined to keep him commercially viable; and from the quick re-growth of Pergamon's Russian business, and the spectacular expansion of Maxwell's Moscow contacts, the natural deduction is that the ally was the Central Committee of the Communist Party.

Boris Pankin, who in the aftermath of the anti-Gorbachev coup of 1991 was to become, briefly, Foreign Minister and then Moscow's Ambassador to London, remembers meeting Maxwell at the Geneva Copyright Convention in 1974. Pankin at the time was a junior official in VAAP, the newly established state agency for authors' rights, and found much to discuss with Maxwell, both in Geneva and at the subsequent Frankfurt Book Fair. It was Pankin who helped Maxwell to set up the first Moscow Book Fair in 1977; and thanks to his own very swift rise within the hierarchy, Pankin was also able to assist Maxwell, after his stressful period at home, towards a renewal of high-level contacts with the Soviet government, including eventually Leonid Brezhnev. His successor, Yuri Andropov, remained a spectator of the process.

Maxwell's way to Brezhnev was smoothed by two men who in the political structure of the time in Moscow were on a perpetual collision course: Pankin himself, and Leonid Zamyatin, who was then the General Secretary of the news agency TASS, and at the same time, understandably, Brezhnev's press secretary. Pergamon Press had already published (in 1977) 'A Short Biography' of the Soviet leader, an unsigned work prepared by the Institute of Marxism-Leninism CPSU Central Committee. Maxwell had appended to it the entire text of the new Fundamental Law, or Constitution, of the Soviet Union, which Brezhnev had helped to draw up. 'I have thought it appropriate,' wrote Maxwell, as General Editor, 'to include in this volume the official English text.' He was doing his best. 'If this little book,' wrote Brezhnev in a Foreword (the book was 240 pages long), 'helps readers in other countries to understand better our land, to appreciate the human, creative essence of our Party's policy, to trust in the frankness and self-denial behind the noble desire of the Soviet people for peace, then I believe that the Publisher's aim in producing it in English will be achieved.'

The Publisher fully intended to follow up this exciting venture with another Brezhnev volume, based this time on interview material. 'Unfortunately it didn't work out,' says Zamyatin, 'because that sort of thing was unpopular at the time.' This sounds a poor explanation of the failure of the plan, and indeed Zamyatin himself hints at a better one when he says: 'The thing was that Brezhnev, by those days, had become the sort of man that avoided the press. Avoided the sort of meeting that would be captured on video. Brezhnev at the end of the Seventies is a different Brezhnev from the one at the start of the seventies.' Pankin, more frankly, says that Maxwell was shocked at Brezhnev's condition when they met. The Soviet leader seemed to have sustained extensive brain damage from the stroke he had suffered in 1976, and was 'incapable', so Pankin has said, of understanding what Maxwell was telling him about the publication of his book by Pergamon[1]. This meeting was perhaps set up as a kind of test for Maxwell; for Pankin points out that the visitor realised the importance of keeping his observations of Brezhnev to himself if he wanted to continue to do business with the USSR.

Maxwell continued to publish biographical material on Brezhnev, including an instalment of his memoirs, called *How It Was*, which Pergamon billed enticingly as 'The memoirs that the Soviet people are now reading'; and then *Pages From His Life*, containing an address 'To the British Reader', allegedly direct from the typewriter of the moribund Brezhnev. Maxwell had reached his man too late; but in getting to Brezhnev at all, he was already beginning to deal with the next generation which was actually running the country. Whether Yuri Andropov, the KGB Chairman who would be Brezhnev's successor, gave Maxwell the time of day is very doubtful. Stories have circulated of Maxwell's meetings with Andropov in 1968, or even earlier, but all the indications are that Andropov was the prime representative of the KGB culture that had distrusted Maxwell from the beginning. Particular reference has been made to a photograph of Maxwell and Andropov together, published in *Pravda* in 1978; but a study of the *Pravda* file for that year discloses no such photograph.

---

[1] In 1988, the Moscow press, which had already deconstructed his fictional 'war record', reported that Brezhnev had been declared clinically dead by doctors in 1976, but that he had been revived. He had never regained the competence to deal with matters of state.

(The same goes for 1979.) Not only does Maxwell's picture not appear, but it is clear that it was not the practice at that time to single out the KGB Chairman for any sort of individual attention.

Maxwell had been newly ruled out, once again, as a recruiting target. Mikhail Lyubimov, returning to Moscow to head the KGB's British section, had raised the possibility of repeating the approach to Maxwell he had made in London in the early Sixties:

> We discussed it at the top, and came to the conclusion that it will be against the grain, because you see he was very much the Central Committee man, he was very much 'up'. Imagine, he could say to Brezhnev, or to somebody subordinate to Brezhnev, 'Look, the KGB tries to recruit me, they try to use me – and this is the end.' Because at once, Brezhnev will say, he will tell Andropov, 'These fools! What a fool you have in your British department! Why are you trying to recruit my friend Robert Maxwell? What for? He's our man, he helps us without recruitment.' So that I am sure I would be demoted, you know!

The KGB, therefore, continued to lay off, while remaining fully aware that Maxwell regarded his Pergamon hagiographies as a virtually unsaleable means to a personal political end. Mikhail Lyubimov recalls receiving a report from one of his agents, '. . . who said that Maxwell brought one MP to his rooms and there were piles of Brezhnev's works over there, and he said, "Look at this rubbish! Look at all that!" you see. They both laughed. And so the report was very compromising for Maxwell.' But the KGB merely sat on it. 'Our position was very neutral.' Lyubimov concludes that Maxwell 'was not connected to the KGB at all, so simply he used his private contacts and his prestige to publish the memoirs of our leaders, for his own purposes.' Those leaders were beginning to be awkwardly numerous. With the help of Boris Pankin, Maxwell on his late Seventies visits also met Konstantin Chernenko, who was destined to succeed Andropov as General Secretary. In both their cases, the investments of effort on Maxwell's part were to bring limited returns, since Andropov and Chernenko proved to be the two shortest-serving Communist Party heads on record, at fifteen and thirteen months respectively. But what the chosen leaders could not provide by way of continuity, Robert Maxwell seemed determined to supply in his tireless attendance at the Kremlin.

*Pravda*, meanwhile, continued to publish its traditional anti-capitalist cartoons, featuring that age-old class enemy, the bow-tied capitalist fat-cat. Take away his bizarrely outdated top hat and spats, and this character looked, in all essentials, exactly like Mr Maxwell.

# CHAPTER THREE

## 'Big Politics'

'By the end of the Seventies,' says Leonid Zamyatin, 'he felt himself ready to enter the arena of "Big Politics".' Indeed, Maxwell had probably felt ready all along, but had been delayed both by the lingering death of his domestic political ambitions,[1] and by the need to re-establish his commercial viability after the damning DTI reports. His experience of the world, as he approached his sixtieth year, was enormous. Betty Maxwell records (*A Mind of My Own*) that, even by 1950, with his businesses in their earliest infancy, her husband had made more than fifty journeys abroad, including two trips to New York, and – a great rarity for those times – a visit to Japan.

Maxwell's travels would not always have as their goal the commercial advantage he claimed he was looking for. He went, as often as not, in search of contacts, and to introduce himself personally. His famous world tour of 1967, undertaken with the stated goal of selling *Chambers Encyclopaedia*, was advertised by him as a selling binge of unparalleled productivity, but he admitted in private that it had been nothing of the sort. Here and there, he had obtained some loose and non-redeemable pledges of sales, but it is scarcely to be doubted that his real purpose was to impress himself upon the minds of the political leaders whom he had arranged to meet at each location, from India, Thailand and Japan on through Oceania and into Mexico, the USA

---

[1] Maxwell's last attempt to achieve selection as a candidate, this time for elections to the European Parliament, failed in 1979.

and Canada. It was the beginning of Maxwell's ambassadorial crusade, undertaken ostensibly on behalf of his export business – for which he had just won the Queen's Award to Industry – but ultimately aimed at establishing him as a freelance emissary with a programme of his own.

His 'biographies' of national leaders (which were usually collections of essays and speeches, prefaced by some fairly terse biographical material) clearly played an important part in this programme. At home in Britain, they attracted nothing but scorn – and also bafflement, since it was evident that the printing of these works could never be justified by sales. Some observers believed that a combination of abstract power-worship and sheer toadying sufficed to explain Maxwell's efforts in this area; others felt he was clearly in the Communists' pocket, though his tactic in making it so very obvious remained difficult to explain.

As Maxwell had discovered in Moscow in the late Seventies, Leonid Brezhnev, after more than a dozen years as First Secretary, was no longer able to play more than a symbolic walk-on part in the ceremonials of the Soviet Union. While the system cranked itself up to induct a successor, who proved to be Andropov, Maxwell turned his attention elsewhere. Pergamon's 'Leaders of the World' series had not been making much progress around a world which, at that moment, did not feel particularly safe for leaders anyway: both President Reagan and the Pope had been shot and wounded in 1981, President Sadat of Egypt had been machine-gunned to death, and even in Britain, a domestic parody of these events had been played out when six blanks were fired at the Queen in the Mall. In such an atmosphere, it was wise to settle upon a leader who looked pretty well dug in, and Maxwell chose Todor Zhivkov, the Bulgarian dictator.

*Todor Zhivkov: Statesman and Builder of New Bulgaria* was first published by Pergamon late in 1981, at a time, Maxwell's Foreword said, when 'Bulgaria has been playing an increasingly important role in international politics, especially in the pursuit of peace in the Balkans; this as well as the country's domestic achievements derive largely from the President Zhivkov's leadership'. The longest-serving leader in Eastern Europe, Zhivkov was destined to resign in 1989, during the general collapse of the old regimes, at the age of seventy-eight. But in 1981, he looked unlikely to be removed by any influence short of death. The book, a standard compost of speeches and admiring biographical blurb, was for the most part the product of the regime's in-house hagiographers; and though there must have been a momentary pang for Maxwell in sentences like, 'He was born on 7 September 1911, in the village of Pravets, in the country of Botevgrad . . .' which could almost have been written about Abraham Lajbi Hoch himself, even he can hardly have gone much further with the kind of cabbage-soup prose that followed: 'A man of lively and uncommonly active nature, Comrade Zhivkov is not only the inspirer and the architect of the basic April Party line; he is also its indefatigable motive power . . .'

For Maxwell, the heart of the book was the interview that concluded it. 'Todor Zhivkov talks to Robert Maxwell', beginning opposite a cheery photograph of Zhivkov and Ceauşescu of Romania greeting each other, is a strange mixture of those near-Oriental *politesses* which were traditional in making an approach to a hard-line Communist leader, and some questioning from Maxwell which, in the context, falls not far short of impertinence. The interview gives as vivid an impression as we are likely to get of the way Maxwell operated behind the Iron Curtain, and the mixture of flattery and needling he applied to the senior figures he met. The oiliness of his introductory remarks, and the exactitude with which he replicates the standard bureaucratese of his hosts – the notorious 'correct approach' – leads one to fear the worst:

RM: Mr Zhivkov, may I express my most sincere condolences for the untimely death of your daughter, Mrs Ludmila Zhivkova, Member of the Politburo of the Central Committee of the Bulgarian Communist Party and Chairman of the Bulgarian Committee for Culture.

TZ: Thank you.

RM: The Bulgarian people grieved deeply for the loss of Mrs Ludmila Zhivkova. Hundreds of state and government leaders, leaders of Communist and workers' parties, politicians and cultural figures the world over expressed their condolences to the Bulgarian people, to the Central Committee of the Bulgarian Communist Party and personally to you for this great loss. This corroborates the great significance of the work of Mrs Ludmila Zhivkova for the development of Bulgarian culture, for its propagation and growing prestige in many countries. I would like to ask you in connection with this: How does the project of Mrs Zhivkova on 'aesthetic education' (defined as 'realisation of the vital necessity to live according to the supreme laws of truth and beauty') fit into, if I may express myself so, the more orthodox targets of the 'Communist education'?

To a British eye, this reads like a satirical sketch, with Maxwell toying with the absurdity of a search for the 'supreme laws of truth and beauty' under the kind of regime Zhivkov was running. But in reality, Maxwell was merely playing the game – and in doing so, repressing utterly his personal taste for brevity and conciseness. His towering insistence on snappy phraseology was a familiar component in Maxwell's bullying of his young sons, but he would go to the limits of totalitarian euphuism to get Zhivkov in the mood. Later in the interview, however, some straight talking was introduced.

RM: The way the Bulgarian press reported the events in Northern Ireland in hostile commentaries (in *Rabotnichesko Delo*, for instance) was offensive to Britain. Don't you agree that to speak of 'British imperialism' when Northern Ireland is part of the United Kingdom is tantamount to 'deliberate misinformation'?

Zhivkov's reply ('It is just as natural for our journalists to have the free right of a political commentary of their own on one event or another as it is for their colleagues in the capitalist countries . . .') is less interesting than the question that arises as to who briefed Maxwell on this, and other matters of detail in the same interview. Bulgarian was not one of Maxwell's languages; nor was the Northern Ireland situation one of his obsessions. His question reads like an ambassadorial protest, very lightly disguised. And in his next question, Maxwell allows his contempt for Communist economics to be glimpsed:

RM: In what way does the 'new economic approach' adopted in the Theses of the 12th Congress of the Bulgarian Communist Party differ from the previous attempts at reform, and from the 'new economic system' of August 1968 in particular?

TZ: Your question takes us to a sphere which may be regarded by many as tedious. That is why I shall do my best to be as brief as possible . . .

His answer takes up two pages. Maxwell goes on to enquire about the construction of an atomic power plant; to wonder how the Bulgarian National Assembly can be expected to play a proper role in national life when '99.96 per cent of the electors in Bulgaria voted for the unified list of the Fatherland Front'; to question the use of trade unions as 'a transmission line for the policies of the Party and the government'; to raise an International Amnesty Report citing 'a point of improper attitude' to the Muslim minority in Bulgaria; and to ask why emigration to Turkey was 'obviously stopped'. This is by no means a toothless performance on Maxwell's part. He even asks the classic embarrassing Cold War question – one to which Zhivkov could not have supplied any useful answer, and which he clearly recognised as Maxwell's attempt to make him squirm. And squirm he did.

RM: Does Bulgarian foreign policy differ from the foreign policy of the Soviet Union?

TZ: The question is not new and it does not surprise me. There is a tiny pitfall in it. If I say a simple 'No', some may interpret it as a confirmation of the allegations widely spread in the West describing Bulgaria as a 'satellite' of the Soviet Union. If I say 'Yes', I will bring grist to the mill of those who are seeking at all costs

> to detect cracks and controversies in the relations of
> Bulgaria with the Soviet Union . . .

Maxwell had to have his bit of fun in the course of producing these awful books. Perhaps in this case, he felt he had gone a little too far in goading Zhivkov; for the Second Edition of the book, published in 1985, included only 'excerpts' of the 1981 interview. The more barbed exchanges had all gone, to be replaced by a short follow-up interview with the ageing Zhivkov. Apart from a question about drugs, Maxwell did no more than pursue his semi-satirical enquiry into the progress of Communist economics ('How is the New Economic Mechanism introduced in 1982 developing?').

Some small fraction of the information gathered by Maxwell from Zhivkov during these verbal fencing matches in Sofia will have been of interest to information-gatherers of one sort or another in Britain. To learn the latest views of the man in charge of a despotic system can never be a useless proceeding and Maxwell would seem to have been quite skilled in alternating flattery with provocation in these encounters. But that very alternation suggests that Maxwell was merely satisfying the expectations of both West and East: honouring the subject of his book, as its very publication demanded, but at the same time raising a few contentious issues on behalf of the West. (If he had not done this, would Zhivkov have trusted him to produce the book at all?)

But Maxwell's purpose in flannelling these powerful men would seldom emerge in their lifetimes – certainly not in the lifetime of their power. In dealing with the Soviets years before, he had grasped the elementary truth that to secure the co-operation of the top men was automatically to qualify for the respect, and with any luck the connivance, of those in the hierarchical ranks below. In the case of Bulgaria, as elsewhere, Maxwell's first investment in the country had been himself. Later, when Zhivkov was out of the way, his mercantile design could be revealed. What Maxwell was looking for behind the Iron Curtain were contacts who knew, as he did, that the Communist way was doomed, and in the short-term rather than the long. As his Commons speech of 1968 had indicated – although it was not in his interests to repeat the point subsequently – Soviet hegemony in Eastern Europe really had only bought itself a respite. Certainly Maxwell expected the collapse within his lifetime, and he was right. What he needed to find were the people who were still going to be in place, and ready to go with Maxwell's own programme of take-over, investment and expansion, when the great change overtook the Communist bloc.

In the meantime, Maxwell must spread his contacts as widely as possible across the doomed world of the Warsaw Pact. This he continued to do throughout the Eighties. We are fortunate to have, direct from the lips of one of the leaders he approached during those years, a particularly full account of what it was like to be made the target of one of Maxwell's in-person campaigns. General Wojciech Jaruzelski had taken over as Prime Minister of Poland early in 1981, in the middle of a period of strikes, demonstrations and general unrest previously unparalleled in the nation's history under Communism. Later the same year, Jaruzelski was confirmed as Party leader, but in an attempt to absorb the reformist mood within Poland, he proposed a working alliance between the Church, the existing government, and Solidarity, the new voice of the working populace. When this failed to quiet the political turbulence, Jaruzelski imposed martial law in December 1981, and travelled three months later to Moscow, apparently in search of advice or instruction. Although he was later to lift martial law, Jaruzelski's early reputation as a (paradoxically uniformed) moderate had been for ever lost.

It was, as usual, at the moment of his greatest isolation from the West that Jaruzelski was approached by Maxwell. Not only had his official suppression of Solidarity attracted hostility, but a few months before, Father Jerzy Popieluszko, a pro-Solidarity priest, had been abducted and murdered by a small task-force of secret policemen – the individual evil that highlights the widespread horror. It was at this point that Maxwell turned up. 'I first met him,' the General says today, 'on 26 May 1985, in Warsaw. We had four further meetings after that. I had, of course, heard of Robert Maxwell before then, primarily as the head of Pergamon Press which maintained certain links with the Polish Scientific Publishing House, providing it with several scientific works in the English language, which was very advantageous for us.' Maxwell's initial offer was a familiar one. 'He approached my office in the spring of 1984 ... with the proposition of publishing a biography about me. At first I was not keen on the idea, I simply did not want such a book, I considered it premature. But as a result of my colleagues' persuasion I finally agreed and the meeting took place.' The security aspect of the exercise did not concern General Jaruzelski, who considered that '. . . anyone who had, for a book, conducted interviews with Brezhnev, Chernenko, Honecker, must have been thoroughly vetted by their respective services. So I did not have to engage our services for such a vetting.'

Maxwell had timed this advance perfectly, as is indicated by Jaruzelski's explanation of why he accepted it:

> It was a complicated time for Poland. Various restrictions, sanctions were in place, imposed by the Western states, though not by all of them. As early as 1983 we had a visit from Genscher, in 1984, Andreotti, Papandreou, visits from American senators and businessmen. England was less flexible on this score and we had not found a way of establishing certain links, and so Maxwell's offer appeared to be of interest to us. I agreed to talks with him and the publication of the book, thinking that it might contribute to an improvement in relations above all with Great Britain.

The fact that the British government was seldom in the front line of those who wished to reopen lines of communication after a political breakdown always counted in Maxwell's favour: his unofficial overtures always arrived years in advance of Britain's diplomatic unbending.

What's more, Jaruzelski says, Maxwell was able to produce indications of his potential usefulness to Poland:

> And here I'd like to say that, just a few days after our meeting, on 31 May, Maxwell went to see Mrs Margaret Thatcher with the purpose of interceding in what was for us a very

important matter, namely, thanks to British technology and credits, we had begun the construction of a large factory in Wroclawek, a city in Poland, for the production of PVC. As a result of the restrictions, supplies and credit had been suspended. Maxwell asked Mrs Thatcher that at least in this case a step forward should be made. Mrs Thatcher replied by letter, dated, I think, 13 June.[1] Maxwell sent me a copy of this letter. Unfortunately the answer was negative. Mrs Thatcher said that we were seriously behind with our repayments of existing loans and at the time, she could not envisage a solution. But for me this was an illustration that Maxwell really did have highly placed contacts – and secondly, was favourably disposed towards our Polish problems. And this decided that our relations continued to develop.

The fact that Maxwell lost absolutely nothing by making this enquiry, the result of which he almost certainly foresaw, does not seem to have discouraged the General.

On the contrary, Jaruzelski looked for ratification of his instincts about Maxwell in the history of the visitor himself, and found confirmation of his positive feelings:

I had the impression that Maxwell had two and maybe four souls. On the one hand, he had after all been a young boy from a very poor and backward part of Europe, Transcarpathian Ruthenia, from an impoverished Jewish family, who at the same time had retained a certain warmth of feeling towards Slavs – from his childhood, despite the fact that it was such a difficult one. And on the other hand, he was a man who had climbed Mount Olympus, had ascended the highest levels of business and, in some sense, of politics; he had after all twice been elected to a seat in the British Parliament. And his aim was as if to 'lock together' those things that he had retained from his childhood memories and also the things he had achieved in the course of his turbulent life. And the other two souls were manifest in the fact that, on the one hand, he was a member

---

[1] Col. Gornicki, Jaruzelski's adviser, has confirmed this date. In the letter to Maxwell, Mrs Thatcher said the release of credits 'would not be appropriate'.

of the Labour Party and constantly stressed his leftist views –
frequently, too, he would address one as 'Comrade' – and on
the other hand he would say quite rigidly, indeed brutally,
that he had made 35 per cent of his workforce redundant,
thus reducing the overmanning, and that one should not
be afraid of unemployment . . . And maybe that was why
he accepted the fact that we had to introduce martial law.
He understood it was the necessity to stand up to processes
which were ruining the economy, above all.

When you consider that this is a former East European head
of state talking about a private citizen from Britain, it becomes
clear that the personal impact registered by Maxwell was utterly
out of the ordinary. Not being a British functionary, having
no governmental line to sell, and yet demonstrating strong
political views, he attracted immediate attention; and there
was enough of the Eastern European left in him to evoke a
sense of vague familiarity in the leaders he met, and to suggest
a graspable psychology which Jaruzelski, for one, had worked
out in some detail. But Jaruzelski was also one of those who
failed to see how much of Maxwell was sheer showbusiness. As
another example of Maxwell's bona fides, the General cites the
publication party for his biography, the date of which '. . . was
not entirely accidental: 22 July 1985. 22 July is – that is, was – a
national state holiday in Poland, in its previous "edition"[1] – the
anniversary of the Manifesto of the PKWN, Polish Committee of
National Liberation. Today that date is no longer a feast day.' An
official reception was held on that day at the Polish Embassy, but
the following night, Maxwell replied with a party of his own: 'a
party on a very large scale, attended by many outstanding British
politicians, led by the former Prime Minister Wilson, whom he
treated very much as a friend, saying he had been his adviser'.
Foreign Office officials were present, '. . . and many others; and
the party was held in honour of my adviser who was then paying
a visit to the UK, a man whose status was not in fact very high,

---

[1]The translator of Jaruzelski's testimony marked this word '[sic!]', indicating that
the General really had referred to Poland as if she were a book reissued after
revisions.

Colonel Gornicki. So when I heard of this, I was reassured that Maxwell has a high standing in Britain, considerable authority, that this party given for a not particularly ranking guest was attended by people of such status.' Jaruzelski's advisers had failed to indicate to him how easy it is for a rich man to throw a well-attended party in London.

In a roundabout way, Jaruzelski was even impressed by Maxwell's bravado over the matter of language:

> Of course, he did not know Polish at all, at most five words, but when I granted him an interview he asked that we don't translate for him as he understood everything. Well, we realised he was bluffing and so we made a recording just in case, which was later transcribed. He knew a few words of Russian and so on, but he clearly had that friendly attitude.[1]
> A further instance of his emotional side lay in the fact that he had been a soldier. I too am a frontline soldier, and this in some natural way brought us together, created a common feeling.

Maxwell had evidently found ways of accentuating all possible sources of camaraderie.

Jaruzelski maintains that Maxwell was not looking towards the fall of Communism:

> The issue was to reform it, adapt it to the modern world, introduce into it certain elements from the free market system ... Today there are many 'discoverers' who claim that they had always thought it would get nowhere and the system would have to collapse. No, they are pretending, after the fact, that they were wiser, which they weren't in reality. I remember my talks with Gorbachev, with many other politicians whose views we shared and understood

---

[1]In the transcribed interview, Maxwell says this: 'Since I have a good understanding of Polish, it might save time if your replies were not translated. The way you speak your language is so splendid, so precise! I was born in Czechoslovakia, which gives me some command of the Slavic languages. Your staff will supply me with a detailed translation later on. Could you accept that, Prime Minister?' It appears from the course of the interview that Maxwell's understanding of Polish was reasonable, for he was able to respond appropriately to Jaruzelski where necessary, and advance the argument.

very well; it was Gorbachev who even in 1988 in a talk with President Weizsäcker – which was published – when Weizsäcker timidly asked about the possibility of Germany's reunification, and Gorbachev answered, 'Mr President, we'll return to this topic a hundred years from now.' And in 1989 the wall came down.

But Gorbachev was an innate conservative who had not completely understood how strong was the impetus set up by the reforms he himself had introduced. Maxwell had always been much more interested in the introduction of those 'elements from the free market system' than in the ultimate fate of governments. This is made absolutely plain in his original Jaruzelski interview, much of which masquerades as an enquiry into Poland's economic future, and is accepted by the Polish leader on that level – not without some momentary grumbling ('I am not sure your readers will expect so much on economic matters, but please go on . . .'); but it is really a business pitch by Maxwell, so blatant that one is surprised he had the gall to reprint it, even in one of his throwaway biographies.

Maxwell starts as he means to go on. His offer is on the table almost from the beginning. 'As I see it,' he assures Jaruzelski, 'this is a solid and durable government which should therefore be afforded some category of co-operation.' The idea of a large blue category with a red bow-tie forms itself already in the mind. Maxwell allows Jaruzelski to give out the expected bromides on the return of the national economy 'to the point of normalcy', and then moves in a little closer, brandishing his bona fides as he goes: 'Please remember that I was an adviser to Prime Minister Wilson on issues of science and industry, so I understand perfectly well the problems which you face. I would say more – that I am passionately interested in them. I have lectured at Harvard University, and I have also lecturered at the Soviet Akademgorok.[1] I am intensely interested in what you are attempting.'

This bull-like rush is answered by Jaruzelski with the sweeping bow of the matador: 'Yes, I have heard you are an eminent

[1] In Novosibirsk.

economic specialist, hence the humility which I feel as a self-taught man in this field.' As Jaruzelski must have been aware, nobody in the field could have been more thoroughly self-taught than Robert Maxwell.

Maxwell then asked Jaruszelski to '. . . elaborate further the lines along which your restructuring is to move. Perhaps you are thinking of using Western experience as well?' This move is countered by Jaruzelski with the introduction of the name of Maxwell's familiar rival in the East–West communication game. 'I believe you know Armand Hammer? I met him some two years ago, and we were sitting just here when I asked him: "Mr Hammer, are you not thinking of introducing the principle of [workers'] self-management in your enterprises? I mean, because it is so democratic?" "Never," he replied, "no self-management bodies! The director's hand must be strong."' Poland's approach to such matters, Jaruzelski explains, is necessarily different, because of Communism's commitment to full employment.

After a brief detour into what we now call 'rationalisation' – linking small industrial plants into large groups, for efficiency, and labour savings – Maxwell returns to the attack on the question of 'the reinstatement of balanced development' (alias a mixed economy with capitalist input). This time Maxwell brandishes one of his cheque-books – one in which posterity has taken a special interest:

> I am only asking you this, Mr Prime Minister, for a specific reason. Apart from being a journalist and politician, I also manage a pension fund to the tune of £500 million. Many leading bankers whom I meet in Europe, including those in the European Economic Community, are going to ask me what the prospects are for economic reform and what the present situation is in Poland, in terms of economy. That is why I am so interested in fully understanding what your endeavours are in this respect.

One might say that Maxwell introduces the subject of pension fund here, and gives an idea of its size, merely in order to explain why he is in contact with leading bankers right across Europe. But such an explanation was not needed. Jaruzelski will have

expected his visitor to have banking contacts, as all capitalists
necessarily do. Maxwell's real purpose is to entice Jaruzelski
with the idea of capital investment (using other people's money,
but no matter) before pressing his own proposal upon the Polish
leader later in the interview.

First, Maxwell permits himself a long, didactic interlude,
explaining his opinion that the Polish government is 'too slow
and too gentle in injecting realism into your economy'. As
the exemplar of an opposing method, Maxwell naturally cites
himself[1]:

> I employ 20,000 people in my companies and I certainly do
> not intend to create unemployment, if for no other reason
> than that my father was unemployed for most of his life. I
> no more like firing people than you like declaring companies
> bankrupt and sacking people. But an economic shock, proof
> that the government means business and is resolute, would act
> like a cold shower, and is absolutely imperative. Of course, I
> am only a foreigner . . .

And as a foreigner, Maxwell was at liberty to put an outrageous
construction upon his recent industrial record at home:

> I am saying this as someone who was invited by the banks
> three years ago to salvage the British printing industry from
> bankruptcy. This I did, as a Labour party member, in con-
> sultation with the unions. I recommended that employment
> be slashed by 35 per cent. And, three years later, the industry
> is yielding a profit . . .

Maxwell's 'consultation with the unions' had in fact been
interrupted, at moments convenient to Maxwell, by his reported
absence abroad on business (in fact, his simple refusal to

---

[1]He could also have cited János Kádár, First Secretary of the Hungarian Socialist
Workers' Party, whose 'Leaders' volume had just been assembled. 'The New
Economic Mechanism,' Maxwell had reported in his Introduction, 'has brought
about major changes in industry which even allow workers to use State factories
out of normal hours to produce goods for their own profit at privately negotiated
prices.' The likelihood of Maxwell's allowing such a system in his own places of
work cannot be considered very strong.

negotiate) and terminated in November 1983 by the direct action of a gang of management Luddites, who broke up the Park Royal presses of the *Radio Times* with sledgehammers. Perhaps these gentlemen constituted the sort of 'cold shower' he had in mind.

After this self-advertising preamble, Maxwell was almost ready to get down to business. 'My question is this: does the Polish government intend to employ foreign consultants to advise it on how to organise the large industrial groupings you mentioned? Are you going to use the services of foreign consultant companies?' The voice of the encyclopaedia salesman becomes at this point unmistakable. 'If you are not doing so already, I very sincerely suggest that you give the proposal your attention. It costs next to nothing, but brings huge benefits.' Jaruzelski, however, continued to resist, arguing forcefully that Poland enjoyed 'an unsaturated demand for blue-collar manpower' which would make Maxwell's strong-arm tactics ineffective.

Yet again, the visitor was undeterred: in fact, eager to take up his private theme even more brazenly than before. 'I want to return to the matter of consultants,' Maxwell urged:

> First, I should like you to know that I am a consultant to the Bulgarian Government in modernising their printing industry. I may add, with satisfaction, that I have also been approached by the Soviet Government Commission for Scientific and Technical Progress. Of course, I am not applying for a job in Poland . . .

Jaruzelski may inwardly have taken leave to doubt this, but he said nothing as Maxwell surged on, coming ever closer to nominating himself as the source of all capitalist wisdom:

> It is impossible to talk about genuine consultation with a manufacturer of goods. Such consultation may only end up with a proposal to order goods from his company. In the West, however, there are whole chains of companies which are not involved in production at all, and which provide independent consultation . . . The consultants whom I mentioned are in a

position to advise banks and other units to commit themselves to co-operation with such new industrial groupings ... But you should never seek the assistance of those who have a relationship with any system or pressure group.

Jaruzelski must have been glad of the psychological refuge of his habitual dark glasses as he answered, 'Thank you for that advice, which could come in useful for us and which I shall keep in mind.' But Maxwell had not finished. 'Such possibilities also exist in printing,' he confided:

The Polish printing industry is now in deplorable shape and needs reorganisation. This could be relatively easily achieved, without high costs ... I have been using the services of the Polish printing business, to a certain extent, for more than thirty years and I shall continue to do so. I would be glad to offer my own time to assist with this task.

Maxwell had been driven to admit, after all, that he was indeed applying for a job in Poland. Jaruzelski did not rule it out:

Thank you very much for your offer. It is with appreciation and respect that I welcome your interest in our printing industry. I am sure we shall revert on working terms to this matter in the near future.

What is surprising is that they did so revert. 'Maxwell proposed that he could modernise Polish typography,' Jaruzelski now reports:

We knew that he had done a lot in this field in Bulgaria, having created a very serious typographic centre there. Of course I agreed to this and we embarked on a period of protracted research into this matter. Teams were even sent to Great Britain to get acquainted with Maxwell's typographic potential. The subject was studied, the results were presented to me, concluding that the financial conditions offered by Maxwell were unacceptable to us, were disadvantageous to us. Well, by that time it was already 1988. Quite possibly Maxwell was encountering some problems, some financial difficulties, involving credits, and he no longer showed that generosity, those wider prospects that he had had. At any rate we did not take advantage of this [offer].

Maxwell also arranged for contracts to be established with 'British professionals to help reform our industry'. By then, however, Jaruzelski was no longer the Chairman of the Council of Ministers, but Chairman of the State Council, and not directly involved in economic policy. What he does recall, however, is a true bargain-basement offer of Maxwell's:

> . . . to sell to Poland 10,000 small Sinclair computers, I think they were called Spectrum. They were meant for schools, to teach the use of computers. They were even quite cheap, but our experts stated that the product was already somewhat dated, that much newer and better ones were available, and we were ourselves involved in the production of various kinds of computer software. So this deal was never made. As I later found out, Maxwell was keen to sell as many of these computers as possible since he had bought Sinclair's company, which was going through a crisis, and he had inherited an enormous surplus of these very minicomputers and he wanted to sell many of them off to Poland. But that's perfectly understandable. The laws of business.

Maxwell had actually made his offer to rescue Sinclair in 1985, just a few days after his Pergamon interview with Jaruzelski; but having advertised himself on the front page of the *Mirror* as the saviour of Sinclair's enterprise, he abandoned the computer deal later in the summer, apparently not before he had lumbered himself with some old stock. His attempt to dump it on the Poles – in the tradition of Arthur Daley rather than Jaruzelski – was perhaps the most forlorn monument to Maxwell's Polish adventure.

But he had found someone in Poland with whom he could deal at a comprehensive national level. Maxwell did not want the

reliable old soldier Jaruzelski replaced by turbulent commit-
tees of democratically elected and democratically squabbling
ex-union men after the pattern of Lech Walesa, who would
never, in Maxwell's view, be able to commit funds on the
same scale as Jaruzelski's government still might. Returning to
London, Maxwell himself took an early opportunity to make this
unpopular point of view more widely known. As guest speaker at
a lunch given by the Foreign Press Association, he announced to
the throng: 'Solidarity, as an organisation, has no future: indeed,
it could never have had a future. It was not a political party.'
Here Maxwell began to show how much of the Eastern bloc's
orthodoxies he had actually absorbed, and how attracted he
was to the power invested in individual leaders. 'Solidarity,'
he continued, 'could never have replaced the government. Its
leaders were not politicians.' Having done enough to keep
Jaruzelski sweet, he went on to pay lip service to the will of
the people. 'It was a protest movement against an oppressive
political and economic system which made Poland a country of
shortages and denies any freedom of expression.' Thunderously
straddling the fence, he concluded by thumping his fists on both
sides of it: 'Because [Solidarity] has no permanent place in the
political structure of Poland, I repeat, it is dead, or nearly so.
What cannot die in Poland, or anywhere else on this globe, is
the spirit which inspired it. It is not within the power of man,
or any political system, to destroy it.'

The *Daily Mirror*, doubtless internally compelled to report
this event, parked it in a top corner of page 7. At that point, the
paper was experiencing its nadir of ridicule as the house organ
of Maxwellism and the personal scrapbook of the proprietor
himself – who, the day before leaving to meet Jaruzelski, had
contrived to get himself photographed for the front page with the
Prince of Wales and Prince William in the garden of Kensington
Palace, nominally raising money for the Red Devils air-display
team. But Maxwell's local reputation for self-advertisement
did not trouble Warsaw, where his speech had the desired
reassuring effect.

Maxwell, says Jaruzelski today, '. . . laid himself most open
when he announced the demise, as it were, of Solidarity – that
Solidarity had really used itself up and had no further prospects.

Actually that was my opinion too, wrong as it turned out. But the very fact that he said this, publicly, proved beyond doubt that he was determined to support me, our line of limited reforms which we were carrying out within the framework of that system.'

Maxwell was now at the stage of life when he could not afford to spend much more time and energy on buttering up new regimes. He wished to advance hand in hand with the red devils he knew – especially if, like Jaruzelski, they were sincere patriots with a respectably anti-Nazi past. As old soldiers, Maxwell and Jaruzelski were almost sentimentally close. Their bonds were strengthened when the General received Maxwell:

> ... on 1 September 1989 in the Presidential palace at Belweder, and awarded him the Cross of Valour – not the 'Order of merit with some huge star on it', as he wrote in his book, but a simple iron cross of merit, that is, the Cross of Valour, which is awarded to soldiers serving on the front. I myself have two such crosses. And Maxwell came to the ceremony in a battledress, but one from the Forties when Maxwell had been as slim as you are now. In 1989, Maxwell weighed 120 kg, so that battledress was bursting at the seams on him[1], and I remember that, when I was pinning on the cross, he had tears in his eyes, he was so moved by it all. And he said that he particularly valued the fact that it was a military decoration.

At such a moment, Maxwell may have regretted leaving his first contact with Poland as late as 1959, and his approach to the nation's leader another quarter-century later still.

The changes of leadership in the Soviet Union, from Brezhnev to Andropov to Chernenko to Gorbachev, happened so fast, by political standards, that Maxwell was hard pressed to keep up with his programme of Pergamon monographs – or obituaries, as they all too soon became. Andropov was a particularly interesting case, as he had been Chairman of the KGB since

---

[1] According to Nicholas Davies (*The Unknown Maxwell*), the battledress had been made up at forty-eight hours' notice by Maxwell's tailor. It was still too tight.

1967. It has been stated more than once that Maxwell had made Andropov's acquaintance almost immediately, in 1968; but if such a meeting did take place, it is extraordinary that Maxwell failed to mention it in his Introduction to Andropov's volume in the 'Leaders' series. Maxwell was in the habit of presenting his every meeting as a high-level consultation, his every contact as a friendship. Yet in the 'Leaders' volume, no mention, for once, is made of any personal knowledge on Maxwell's part. Merely to have met Maxwell was normally a leader's guarantee that he would be presented with some warmth in Pergamon's pages; but Andropov, by contrast, is rather frostily received by the publisher on to the world stage:

> Most people on earth have recently asked themselves whether the election of Mr Yuri Andropov is a good thing for world peace and prosperity or otherwise. There is really no answer to this question until we have witnessed the results of his leadership during the next few years. Very little is known of Mr Andropov in the Western world . . .
>
> Like many people who read this volume, I do not agree with everything Mr Andropov says or writes. I hope this volume (containing a selection of Mr Andropov's speeches and writings during the past twenty years as he has worked his way to the top post in his country) will be useful for all those who need to know, understand, interpret and anticipate the broad outline of possible Soviet policies at home and abroad.

This sounds like a Maxwell who, for once, was extremely unsure of his man – and perhaps of the KGB culture from which Andropov came. Having avoided the KGB so far, Maxwell suddenly found the chief representative of its tradition hoisted right to the top of the Central Committee apparatus. A second edition of the book produced a Foreword by Andropov himself (coldly deploring the proposed deployment of medium-range US nuclear missiles in Britain); but if Maxwell sought an interview, during which to discover a softer Andropov, he was not granted one.

Altogether, the Maxwell–Andropov relationship seems to emit a faint odour of bad feeling. It is possible that they had not so much met as crossed, and that Andropov, as head of the KGB, had stepped in between the Central Committee and an over-importunate Maxwell, in order to demonstrate to the visitor where the limits of his inquisitiveness were set. But these were conspicuously bad times for East–West relations in general. The incident which most violently shook the international reputation of the Soviet Union during Andropov's tenure of office was the shooting down of Korean Airlines' flight 007. This off-course Boeing 747 had overflown the island of Sakhalin, off Siberia, and been destroyed by missile-firing Soviet fighters, with the loss of more than 250 lives.

As the shock of the event was still rolling around the world, Robert Maxwell paid a visit to Moscow. This fact was noted at the time by the KGB station in London, although its second-in-command at the time, Oleg Gordievsky, insists that the organisation did nothing to inspire or facilitate it. 'That trip had nothing to do with the KGB. It means that it was Robert Maxwell's and the Soviet Ambassador's initiative . . .' Gordievsky's belief is that the Central Committee, at Maxwell's traditional high level of contact, felt in need of advice:

I think that, in September, October and November '83, Moscow was shocked and embarrassed profoundly by the negative results in the world as a result of the accident, and they were desperately thinking about all possibilities, how to whitewash themselves and how to find additional channels of pro-Soviet propaganda . . . and that's why I think they invited Robert Maxwell, in order to consult him [on] what else could be done about the publicity, and probably also what he himself was able to do in order to help Moscow in the counter-propaganda.

This visit of Maxwell's naturally attracted the attention of British monitors at home. An enquiry directed to Lord Howe's[1] office, regarding Foreign Office contact with Maxwell in relation to the Korean airline incident, brings confirmation:

[1] As Sir Geoffrey Howe, the Foreign Secretary of the day.

> . . . that Mr Maxwell was in Moscow shortly after the shooting down of the Korean airliner on 31 August/1 September 1983. The purpose of the visit (about 10–12 September) seems to have been to sign an agreement on the second edition of Andropov's speeches, articles and interviews and also to receive an honorary doctorate from Moscow University. Mr Maxwell gave an interview to TASS [the Soviet news agency] on 10 September, in which he criticised the US for using the KAL incident to step up anti-Soviet propaganda.

Since the Soviets had admitted only as recently as 6 September that they had indeed shot down the plane, this appearance of Maxwell's in Moscow would count as an urgent response.

Correspondence from the British Embassy in Moscow in mid-September 1983, it is further confirmed, shows that Maxwell called on the Chargé d'Affaires on 11 September. 'It seems that Mr Maxwell had tried to see Andropov but had been told that the latter was unwell.' (Andropov died the following February.) 'Mr Maxwell was still hoping to see Tikhonov (the then Soviet Prime Minister) but was studiously vague about the other high-ranking personalities he implied he had already been in touch with over the Korean airliner incident.'

This remarkably frank and comprehensive response from the former Foreign Secretary's office offers the judgement that: ' . . . the overall impression was that Mr Maxwell was freelancing over KAL. The fact that he chose to share with the Embassy his perception of Soviet concerns about KAL is not, of course, evidence of "links" with the British government, still less of his performing specific tasks for them.'

Maybe not, but it is curious that Lord Spens, managing director of Ansbacher's, Maxwell's merchant bank during those years, has claimed that Maxwell 'was sent' as an unofficial conduit of the British government to discuss the crisis with Andropov. At that moment of extreme frost, the sending of any sort of official emissary would indeed have given inappropriate signals, so the usefulness of an unembarrassable traveller like Maxwell may have suggested itself. It is clear, however, that Britain derived somewhat less benefit from the visit than either the USSR or Maxwell himself. The letter from Lord Howe's office concludes by reiterating, with a sly understatement highly characteristic of the former Sir Geoffrey himself, that, 'None of this is inconsistent, of course, with the possibility that Mr Maxwell may have been freelancing in this field, in pursuit of a variety of objectives.'

On the death of Andropov, Konstantin Chernenko took over the Soviet leadership, still in an atmosphere of Cold War gloom. Chernenko himself was not a man to cause the heart to leap with sudden optimism. His age, his bearing, his very physique identified him as the archetype of the frostbitten old ex-Stalinist: four-square and white-quiffed, designed by nature as if for the very purpose of looming over Red Square in muffler and trilby, waving woodenly at a military parade. The world hoped, in fact, that Chernenko would not last, and for once was not disappointed. The best Maxwell could do, in his Introduction to *Chernenko: Speeches and Writings*, was to make a flat denial of the general opinion, which he did. 'Mr Chernenko,' he asserted, in the Second Enlarged Edition of 1984, 'is definitely not an interim leader.'

But then, Maxwell had owed Chernenko two things. One was, yet again, the comradeliness of the old soldier. 'Mr Chernenko is one of the generation of Soviet leaders who were deeply affected by Nazi Germany's unprovoked attack on the Soviet Union, a war which took the lives of twenty million Soviet citizens and wiped out a third of the then existing national wealth.' The other debt was much more personal: 'Some eight years ago, it was Mr Chernenko who introduced me to Mr Brezhnev, whose short biography became the first of the "Leaders of the World" series. From the brief exchanges I have been privileged to have with him since then, I have formed the opinion that he is a highly capable, cautious world leader who will do anything in his power to prevent the Soviet Union becoming involved in a third World War.' As Maxwell rightly intuited, this unsensational opinion was not worth expanding to a chapter's length, so no interview with Chernenko was sought for inclusion in the book.

This would seem to have been a dead time in the development of Maxwell–Moscow relations, and yet behind the scenes, a new move was being made – by no less controversial a figure than

Oleg Gordievsky. 'At that time, I was number two in the KGB station in London,' Gordievsky relates, 'and I was responsible for political reporting to the centre. One day a cable arrived from Moscow on the KGB channel, asking the KGB station to write an analytical and lengthy, detailed report about Robert Maxwell and his role in the British life.' Gordievsky sensed that this request came not from his in-house superiors but, as ever with Maxwell, from higher up. 'The text of that request suggested very strongly to me that the political leadership in Moscow – not the KGB, the Central Committee – was thinking about some extension of either its relationship with Robert Maxwell, or his role for the Central Committee in Moscow.' The KGB, in any case, had plenty of information about Maxwell, Gordievsky says, and still believed (as the Central Committee did not) that he was a British spy.

In its broad domestic essentials, the assessment was an easy one for Gordievsky to draw up:

> I produced a long report, which included positive aspects of Robert Maxwell and negative aspects. For example, I mentioned that he was not popular with the people on the extreme left wing of British politics, like in the Communist Party; that he was not popular with the Trade Unions because they regarded him as a very bad boss and a real old-fashioned capitalist, despite his background as a Labour MP, and so on.

Gordievsky refrained from mentioning the possibility that Maxwell was (as indeed Gordievsky himself had become) an asset or agent or officer of the British Intelligence Service; but this was judged a mistake by his superior officer:

> The number one was Colonel Nikitenko, acting head of the KGB station, and he was in many respects an old-fashioned man and he was also a careful man. He said, 'Now look, in the KGB, they still regard him as a spy. I don't want to be a revolutionary, destroying that KGB opinion. Let's add that, yes, he has got his good signs and bad signs [and] apart from it all he's probably still in touch with the British Intelligence

Service, and when he goes abroad, his requirement is to speak to the Soviet leaders and other East European leaders, and then to write detailed reports, sending them to the headquarters of the British Intelligence Service.

Very unwillingly, Gordievsky says, he did add such a 'fanciful paragraph – a folly really', and off the message went in the form of a telegram to Moscow. 'I didn't know how the KGB informed the Central Committee, but it was clear the Central Committee would ignore all the negative opinions recorded by the KGB because they liked Robert Maxwell and they wanted to make business together with him.'

Two editions of the Chernenko 'biography' doubtless helped in this; but Chernenko had scarcely taken a grip on power when illness began to loosen it. Oleg Gordievsky also lost track of the story hereabouts, because 'in the middle of '85, I had to leave the Soviet scene because the KGB caught me, arrested me, and then I had to flee, escaping from the Soviet Union'. His impression that some new plans for Maxwell were in the making had been confirmed, however, by activity in London: 'I know that Mr Popov, the Soviet Ambassador of that time, he backed very much the idea of Maxwell's role, writing long telegrams to the centre, telling Moscow how important Robert Maxwell was, and how influential, and that he has got some unused, unexploited possibilities. His influence on Moscow – I mean Popov's influence – was very strong.' It is imaginable that Popov's view, in its turn, was not uninfluenced by the person-to-person self-advertisement of Robert Maxwell himself.

During Chernenko's brief, but supposedly not interim, period in charge, Maxwell made what contacts he could with the next man in line. It seemed clear that, after three old and ailing leaders, Mikhail Gorbachev, at a sprightly fifty-two years of age, was much the likeliest to succeed to the General Secretaryship of the Party – the youngest man ever to do so. According to Leonid Zamyatin, 'Maxwell first met Gorbachev during his, Gorbachev's, first visit to London in December 1984.' Maxwell, newly self-appointed as Publisher of the *Daily Mirror*, naturally did not fail to present this meeting, in his organ, as 'private top-level talks with the Soviet leader' . . .

> During their discussion, Mr Gorbachev promised his support to ensure the co-operation of the Soviet authorities for a special issue of the *Daily Mirror*. This will celebrate the fortieth anniversary, next May, of the victory over Hitler by the wartime grand alliance between Britain and the Soviet Union, America and France.

As Maxwell would later discover, this nostalgic-solidarity approach worked far better with Soviet leaders of his own generation than with those, like Gorbachev, who were ten years younger and had not experienced the war in the same way. But some sort of start had been made.

> Then Gorbachev met, at Thatcher's request, a group of industrialists [Zamyatin continues]. A large dinner was arranged. Maxwell came up to me and asked to be introduced to Gorbachev. This was not that simple because there was a whole row of people in front of Gorbachev waiting to shake his hand, to talk to him – you know how it goes, when there's a new face, everybody wants to be introduced to him. But Maxwell with his persistence and stubbornness got to see Gorbachev, and they talked for about ten minutes.

It was then, Zamyatin says, that Maxwell's 'very first ambitions, that he could be useful to Gorbachev, were expressed'.

In the Soviet Union, at long last, Maxwell had every hope that the new leader would not only last long enough, but would be receptive enough to Maxwellism, to make a large investment of obsequiousness worthwhile. Gorbachev was always cautious over the matter, and has remained so. He has declined to be interviewed about his dealings with Maxwell, and his friend Jaruzelski, for one, doubts that such dealings were significant. 'At any rate, I have remained friends with Gorbachev to this day – besides, we are in touch and exchange correspondence – and I have never heard Gorbachev say that he was getting any inspiration from Maxwell[1].' But Jaruzelski, as he admits, is not infallible, and this was another of the things he was wrong about.

Naturally, some of Maxwell's ambitions concerned investment and trade possibilities, but here Gorbachev was not at first inclined to get involved. 'In those days,' Zamyatin confirms, 'Gorbachev wasn't thinking actively about the economic side of our society's development.' Political restructuring, we now know, was at the forefront of his concern, and here Maxwell was extremely keen to follow, using Ambassador Zamyatin himself as a guide: 'When we entered, in 1985, the epoch of *glasnost* and *perestroika* – that ill-fated word which is now repeated with quite different connotations – Maxwell began to get himself very actively involved in the situation. When I arrived as Ambassador in April 1986, then some of the first contacts I ever had were those with Maxwell, and they really were political discussions.'

Britain at this time was still obsessed with Maxwell's take-over of Mirror Group Newspapers, and its consequences: chiefly the featuring of the Publisher's activities in the paper itself (the 'Daily Maxwell' effect) and, behind the scenes, the drastic job-cutting programme of which he was to boast to Jaruzelski the following year. But as the columnist Keith Waterhouse rightly observed, Maxwell was playing with newspapers 'like a child with a Meccano set'. His eye was not really on these matters at all, but on political developments noticed by few others at the time. The alert Leonid Zamyatin was immediately impressed by Maxwell's perspicacious reading of his own Ambassadorial movements in London:

> He was primarily interested in why, so soon after my arrival – I arrived on the 28th of April – and on the 30th, before I had even received my credentials, I was received by Thatcher, the Prime Minister. He was very interested in what I had

---

[1]The translator of Jaruzelski's interview (conducted in Polish) marks this phrase as indistinct, but it is clear from the context that the sense of the remark is accurately rendered, whatever was the precise term used.

come with. He knew that I had not gone empty-handed to Thatcher. That was just before the start of the Big Seven summit in Tokyo where Thatcher was headed and I arrived with specific instructions from Gorbachev, and therefore insisted on this meeting. Thatcher realised it was necessary to leave diplomatic formalities aside.

Having so recently proclaimed Gorbachev to be a person with whom she could 'do business' (a formulation Maxwell surely approved, and may even have inspired), Thatcher could hardly insist that Zamyatin wait to be formally inducted before passing on his message.

It is normal in such cases for a newly arrived emissary to outline his position to the Foreign Office, so that it may be passed on to the Prime Minister; and the fact that things had been done differently this time attracted Maxwell's attention. He was quick to pursue the matter privately with Zamyatin: 'At the reception on the 1st of May, he approached me and said that he would like to speak to me at his place. I was at his place afterwards and retold him the rough outline of the discussions. Here he had already started his political activities. Though only through the Ambassador, naturally.'

Nevertheless, this is a remarkable pattern of events: a private citizen asks the Soviet Ambassador for the gist of the urgent and unscheduled discussions he has just held with Britain's Prime Minister, and is obliged with a résumé of the exchanges. On the face of it, Robert Maxwell had no more right to this information than you or I. He was greatly favoured.

Indeed, it is almost as if Zamyatin had been provided as a compatible workmate for Maxwell – or so one might deduce from Oleg Gordievsky's reading of their relationship:

It's important to remember that, during the late Seventies, in the early Eighties, the head of the foreign propaganda department in the Central Committee was Mr Leonid Zamyatin; so the person who was particularly interested in the publications by Robert Maxwell, who was organising it on behalf of Soviet leaders like Brezhnev, Andropov and so on, it was Leonid Zamyatin. In 1986, Leonid Zamyatin is appointed Ambassador to Great Britain, so here he is now in personal direct touch with Robert Maxwell. So I connect the tremendous and sudden extension of Robert Maxwell's role in his relationship with the Central Committee [with] Leonid Zamyatin emerging in Britain as Ambassador of the Soviet Union.

And it was not only at the London end of his dealings that Maxwell was marked out for special treatment. The changing political climate in Moscow – the 'new thinking' – gradually allowed for much freer discussion of controversial aliens such as himself; and while this brought Maxwell a gratifying degree of notoriety, it left his reputation open to some questioning. As this possibility grew, those watching over Maxwell decided to afford him some extra protection, according to Oleg Gordievsky: 'I happened to read a text of a KGB telegram from a period when I wasn't in the KGB any longer, but I believe that it was an authentic telegram. And from that telegram I gather that the KGB was asked by the political leadership, by the Central Committee, to protect Robert Maxwell from attacks on him, from unpleasant or negative publications in the Soviet Press and so on.'

For Gordievsky, this means that Maxwell had begun to play a yet more important role on the Central Committee's behalf. 'But why exactly, I don't know.'

Which is to say, you find out.

# CHAPTER FOUR

## 'No head of state I meet escapes me on that issue'

That 'place' of Maxwell's, where Zamyatin spilt the beans about his early introduction to the Iron Lady, was his new tenth-floor penthouse at the *Daily Mirror*. Furnished with accoutrements dismayingly reminiscent of one of the international hotel styles (possibly 'Memories of Casablanca: Plush Version'), it saw very little activity that *Mirror* readers would have recognised as overlapping with their concerns. Maxwell himself, as his regime was to prove, did not understand those concerns anyway. He had never been inside the working-class British culture – some of his private remarks about its homelands are unprintable – and he did not realise that what he took to be its simple-minded idiom was really the echo of demagogic voices like his own.

Not all his newspaper ideas were bad. The *European* survived him, and deserved to. It is the purest expression that he left behind of the genuine internationalism he could scarcely have avoided feeling. Maxwell knew more about Europe than the British customarily wanted to know. All his children had been born in France. Becoming British had been a matter of accident, first, and secondly necessity. He had made his way to this country at a time when Britain was the only nation still waging effective war against Nazi Germany: in that sense, he was offered no choice as to his destination in 1940. Half a century later, he did not feel Britain had treated him very well. Britain was anti-achievement: its 'scribblers' and its 'Establishment', often the same people in Maxwell's lexicon, were always trying to drag him down. He sensed anti-Semitism in both.

He had even had cause to re-evaluate the British anti-Nazi effort in which he had participated. There remained in his mind a blame attached to Britain over its submission to Hitler's ambitions at the time of the Munich meetings, in 1938. In his confabulations with Eastern bloc leaders, he brought this matter up several times. There was a point of agreement here between these men and Maxwell: namely that the efforts and sacrifices of the Soviet Union, and not Britain or America, had been ultimately responsible for the crushing of Hitler – and thereby the saving of the Jews, who had been undergoing the Nazi extermination programme since 1942. In his otherwise dull account of Gustáv Husák, President of Czechoslovakia, in the 'Leaders of the World' series, Maxwell achieved one moment of urgency in his Introduction when he explained:

> The razing to the ground of Lidice in June 1942 symbolises to the Czech and Slovak peoples all that was to be feared in German hegemony. Husák, lawyer, journalist, writer, but above all fierce nationalist and fighter for his country, believed, like Benes and all other post-war Czechoslovakian leaders, that Czechoslovakia had no alternative, after Munich, other than to turn to the Soviet Union as guarantor of its independence.

The same point was more feelingly made to Maxwell by General Jaruzelski, during their 1985 interview. 'Did the military actions of the Allies on the Western Front,' the General wanted to know, 'force the Germans to withdraw one single tank from the battlefields in Poland? We were fighting heroically, but we were desperately, hopelessly, alone. My generation will never forget this. You cannot imagine the feelings of a man belonging to a nation doomed to extinction.' Maxwell's reply was short, but dramatic. 'I certainly can,' he said.

To which nation was Maxwell referring? Hardly Britain, which even in 1940 did not for a moment consider itself doomed to extinction. The only nation to which Maxwell 'belonged' which had faced such a threat was the Jewish nation of Israel – from his first visit to which Maxwell was returning even at that moment. He was now 62 years old. It is odd that a man of his resources should have waited so long before even witnessing what his fellow Jews had made of their nationhood. True, he had denied his Jewishness publicly for many years, in a continuing effort to be more British than the British. The 'Buy British' campaign, the red-white-and-blue costume, the football clubs, bingo and *Daily Mirror* all blazed with a low-grade pop-culture Blightyism.

But as his wife, Dr Betty Maxwell, was at pains to point out in her book *A Mind of My Own*, the man's most private dreams concerned the fate of a nation he had not even seen. He had articulated his own political ambitions for Israel as early as 1957, in a letter to her which included the following passage:

As for my thoughts, I am dreaming about the help which I would like to give the State of Israel to enable it to become one of the world leaders and a paradise on earth. My dreams very often revolve on this one line. This evening they were brought about by the big opening headline in the American journal, reading in red letters ISRAEL DESTINED TO LEAD MIDDLE EAST IN 10 YEARS, followed by a dispatch from the paper on Hearst, who is there on a visit justifying the headline.

Why did Maxwell wait almost thirty years more, before seeing for himself the possibilities of this potential 'paradise on earth'? The answer must be that he feared to do so. He was able to contemplate Israel's future from afar, but the story of its citizens' immediate past was more than he could bear to absorb. No visitor to Israel could avoid feeling the weight of recent history – some of it the history of Maxwell's own family – and this he had never been able to face. In fact, it was one part of himself that he had managed, rarity of rarities, to delegate, or as psychiatrists would say, displace: for the burden of Jewish suffering in the twentieth century was borne for him by his wife. It was Betty Maxwell who studied the Holocaust, and traced its consequences upon the conscience of Western man. Maxwell stood aloof, except when evidences of the past caught him unawares. Then he wept.

Had Maxwell already done the Israeli state some service? Too much should not be read into the wording of a single letter; but his musings of 1957 do perhaps suggest that the giving of help to Israel was a project that lay entirely in Maxwell's future. Not every commentator on his life has thought so. In 1994, John Loftus and Mark Aarons devoted a chapter of their book *The Secret War Against the Jews* to an alleged early exploit of Maxwell's, under the heading 'Robert Maxwell's Czech Guns'. This twenty-page narrative gave Maxwell credit for a very significant service indeed: that of providing the Czech government with information so important that he was able to demand, as a quid pro quo, the supplying of Czech arms to the nascent Israeli nation.

Their story ran like this. The Zionists battling to establish Israel were severely underarmed. The British mandate in Palestine had not yet expired, and the Zionists were regarded as a terrorist organisation – especially after the notorious explosion of 1946 at the King David Hotel in Jerusalem (where Maxwell in his late years would always stay). A tight arms embargo was operated by the British, the Americans and their allies. Across Europe, in the meantime, the nation-state of Czechoslovakia was also struggling for survival. Alone in an Eastern bloc otherwise dominated by Stalin, Czechoslovakia still enjoyed a form of social democratic government. One might have expected the Western allies to encourage this, and yet – the Loftus–Aarons thesis states – the West was persuaded to turn against Czechoslovakia on the advice of the Balkan expert of M.I.6, one Kim Philby. Mr Philby, naturally, was under orders from Moscow to see democratic government in Czechoslovakia undermined and dismantled.

Philby supposedly advised M.I.6 that Stalin had the current Czech government secretly under his thumb, and that its leaders should therefore be replaced. The replacement chosen was Ferdinand Durčansky, leader of the Slovakian Liberation Movement, 'a Fascist and an opportunist', who was financed with money routed through the Vatican. Robert Maxwell, however, had allegedly come to hear about the plot against the legitimate Czech government. He contacted Vladimir Clementis, a Czech Communist leader whose acquaintance he had made a few years earlier, when both men were detained in a British camp after their arrival from France with the escaping Czech legion. Once the Durčansky plot had been made known, through Maxwell's intervention, the Communists came to power – apparently completing a full-house for Stalinism in the Eastern bloc, although in Loftus–Aarons' view, holding up Stalin's plans by three years, during which Czechoslovakia remained an independent socialist state.

'In return for saving his native country from Durčansky's civil war,' these authors say, 'Maxwell begged the Czechs for weapons for his adopted country, Israel.' His strategy over Czechoslovakia, they add, had probably been co-ordinated all along by the Zionist leader Ben-Gurion, and his 'secret double agent inside Soviet intelligence'. Israel, at any rate, received the Czech arms, and by one of those grotesque ironies of war, Jewish airmen found themselves battling for independence in Czech-built Messerschmitt fighters, against the Spitfires of the Arab world. 'Maxwell's Czech guns', and, more especially, planes, held off an Egyptian onslaught long enough for Israel to recover, and with the war still continuing, the existence of Israel was officially proclaimed at the expiry of the British Mandate, in May 1948. All this was traced back to the action of a single individual, Robert Maxwell. 'Whatever else can be said of the man,' write Loftus and Aarons, 'he saved a nation,' and his burial amid national honours on the Mount of Olives becomes easy to explain.

All important parts of the testimony upon which this theory relies are drawn from 'confidential interviews' with former intelligence personnel and members of diplomatic corps. It asks us to take for granted that Maxwell was both willing and able, while still in uniform, to risk throwing away all that he had accumulated in credit on the Allied side since his adoption by the British army. We are required to believe that 'by 1946, Maxwell had learned that M.I.6 was moving against the post-war government of Czechoslovakia.' It is difficult to see how Maxwell, tied to his duties with the British occupation army in Berlin, could have known such a thing – or how, if he had somehow got wind of it, he could have made himself believed. Even if we accept that he passed on the details of Philby's destabilisation plan to the Czech government (and this is some months before the late 1947 meeting when M.I.6 eased Maxwell into the import-export information business), it is a very large step from there to the conclusion that the Czech supply of arms was granted out of gratitude to the hero, Maxwell. 'The official Israeli version,' say Loftus–Aarons, 'is that the Czechs were keen on the deal because the Zionists paid for the arms in US dollars.' This is an inadequate explanation, but it carries more weight of authenticity than their intricate version.

Moreover, it is expecting too much of Maxwell's personal self-control to imagine that, having played a role in the founding of Israel somewhat analogous to Paul Revere's in the establishment of American Independence, he could have refrained from deriving some early advantage, commercial or otherwise, from Israeli gratitude. As David Kimche, a former Deputy Chief of the Israeli intelligence service, the Mossad, remarks, 'Maxwell was the sort of man that, if he had done it, a lot of people would have known about it.' Kimche also claims: 'I knew the person who had organised that arms deal, a man by the name of Edward Abriel, and I'd heard from him in very detailed ways how that deal was made, and he never mentioned the name Maxwell.' Nor does the Loftus–Aarons account mention the name of Abriel.

A Maxwell who had played such a role in a nation's founding, and then failed to present himself at the scene of his triumph, would not be the Maxwell we know. And yet, the Maxwell who waited forty years to visit Israel at all is also difficult to account for. We know that, once contact had been made, Maxwell began openly re-attaching himself to his Jewish roots, anxious to undo the effects of many years of denial of his religious and racial affiliation. Through Joe Haines's authorised biography, Maxwell made it known in 1988 that: 'Politically, he was intervening in Zionist meetings in Solotvino when he was only twelve. He joined the Betar, a religious movement but also a para-military organisation which went on training exercises and made preparations for going to Israel.' This is not a message he would have been keen to put across some twenty years before. During his Parliamentary years, his standard reply to enquiries about his religious affiliation had been the formula: 'Can a Jew read the lesson in church?' His wife, Betty, was a French Protestant, and Maxwell's claim seemed to be that he had followed her lead. On 30 October 1964, the *Jewish Chronicle*, reporting on the new intake of Jewish MPs, printed the following message at the foot of page 12: 'Captain I.R. Maxwell, the new Labour MP for Buckingham, has informed the *Jewish Chronicle* that he is now a member of the Church of England.'[1]

Now, in 1986, with the experience of Israel fresh in his mind, he assured the same newspaper that his family had been observant Jews and that he had received a traditional Jewish education. Though he had ceased to be a practising Jew when he left home (he had cut off the identifying ringlets of the orthodox Jew while in Budapest, the more freely to operate as a delivery boy and bartering trader), he claimed to be still faithful to the moral precepts of Judaism. 'I certainly do consider myself Jewish. I was born Jewish and I shall die Jewish.' This sort of breast-baring had come as a shock to many observers, some of them Jews and visiting Israelis.

In 1985, Chaim Herzog, at that time President of Israel, made a semi-official visit to Britain, the first he had undertaken in that capacity.

> The Jewish community in Britain, or the British Isles [Herzog says today] arranged a huge dinner at the Hilton in London, with about a thousand participants. And I can still recall one of the important Jewish leaders coming into the ante-room where we were waiting and saying, 'Believe it or not, Maxwell has come.' This was the first time, apparently, he'd turned up at a Jewish affair.

It had not, in fact, been quite unknown for him to do so

---

[1] This information came by way of a postscript to brief profiles of Dr David Kerr (Wandsworth Central) and Mr Jack Dunnett (Nottingham Central). Both were Labour MPs, and their election brought the number of Jewish MPs in the House, the paper said, to thirty-five.

previously – but always before his career as a Labour Party candidate. The veteran writer Chaim Bermant recalled, in a *Jewish Chronicle* piece shortly after Maxwell's death, that he:

> ... first came across him in 1956 at a dinner in aid of the Jewish Secondary Schools Movement, the then head of which was Rabbi Solomon Schonfeld. They sat together at the top table ... But one did not in those days associate Captain Maxwell with Jewish religious education, or indeed with Judaism at all ... In the country at large, however, he was never thought of as anything else.

This latter thought must have weighed heavily with Maxwell by 1985. He had fought for Britain, received one of the nation's highest military honours, acted for its secret services, contributed to, and campaigned for a revival of, its commercial life, employed some of its people, represented others in its Parliament; but he had still not been accepted. The reaction to his take-over of the Mirror Group was now indicating all over again that private opinions of him among the British were no more positive than they had been in 1968, when Maxwell's attempt to take over the *News of the World* had been repulsed by its editor, Stafford Somerfield, with a volley of xenophobic rant:

> Why do I not think it would be a good thing for Mr Maxwell, formely Jan Ludwig Hoch, to gain control of this newspaper which, I know, has your respect, loyalty and affection – a newspaper which I know is as British as roast beef and Yorkshire pudding? ... This is a British paper, run by British people. Let's keep it that way.

This editorial, undoubtedly actionable under today's codes of practice, might not have been so hurtful to Maxwell if the subsequent manoeuvrings of the City had not appeared to confirm its tendency by working so obviously in favour of the rival bidder, Rupert Murdoch – and if the bank acting on behalf of Sir William Carr, the *News of the World* Chairman, had not been Hambro's. At a crucial stage in Maxwell's attempted take-over, Hambro's stepped in to bolster the Carr family's resistance with an input of £750,000. If Maxwell had maintained any sentimental attachments to the old M.I.6 days of Butterworth-Springer, then he must have abandoned them at that moment.

After his political and commercial decline, and subsequent renaissance, Maxwell adopted an international outlook that took no great account of British interests in general. Even at the moment of his take-over of the *Daily Mirror* in 1984, a certain detachment is observable in his announcement of his intentions, as reported by the *Mirror* itself. 'I certainly would hope to make a small contribution,' he ventured, 'to halt the retreat of Great Britain, which has gone on for so long that the natives have forgotten they are going backwards.' In years gone by, it would not have occurred to Captain Robert Maxwell MC to call the British 'the natives'. Now some of the colour had drained from his adoptive jingoism, to be replaced by a slightly chilly objectivity.

But his sympathies could not be directly identified with any particular foreign power until his involvement with Israel began in 1985. An early visit there is described by Betty Maxwell in her book *A Mind of My Own*. She had been engaged in reconstructing the Hoch family tree, partly in a gestural attempt to halt the growing estrangement between herself and her husband. 'On a trip to meet relatives in Israel,' she writes, 'Bob came with us; he was attending a meeting in Jerusalem of the editorial board of Pergamon's *Holocaust and Genocide Studies* and wanted us to be present to take the minutes.' *Holocaust and Genocide Studies*, published in association with the US Holocaust Memorial Council, and Yad Vashem, the Holocaust Martyrs' and Heroes' Remembrance Authority in Jerusalem, was first published in 1986. Though Maxwell appeared on its editorial advisory board, he made none of his characteristic irruptions into its content, apart from a 'Publisher's Announcement' congratulating Elie Wiesel on receiving the 1986 Nobel Peace Prize.

It would seem that, at this point, Maxwell had decided to admit the memory of the Holocaust to his mind; and that the decision at last opened the way for him to discover Israel. No sudden onrush of maturity or self-control accompanied this advance on Maxwell's part. Indeed, the trip was desperately unsuccessful in bringing the couple together again, because, as Elisabeth Maxwell interprets the matter, 'Bob had not managed to reconcile himself with his grief or overcome his guilt complex at having married a Christian. Confronted by Israeli Jews, most of them survivors, and dealing with the subject of the Holocaust, he took his distress out on me.'

But if Maxwell commonly disguised mourning and guilt with odious displays of contemptuous arrogance, there were also witnesses to Maxwell's private grief in Israel, one of whom testified in a German television programme on the Maxwell case, *Mann Über Bord*, broadcast in September 1994. Ido Dissentchik was editor of *Ma'ariv*, the Israeli newspaper in which Maxwell bought a large interest in 1988. Dissentchik recalled sitting in Maxwell's room at the King David Hotel in Jerusalem: 'And he looked out of the window and began to cry. I asked him why he was crying. He said, "At last, I am home." I asked him, "Where is your home?" and he replied, "Here in Jerusalem, here in the Holocaust Museum." He added that, for him, everything of any importance was wiped out in the Second World War.'

This is a glimpse, and only a glimpse, of a vulnerable Maxwell; but in the sense it gives of an old pain finally acknowledged, it is entirely convincing. The incident found a public echo at the international congress called 'Remembering for the Future', held in England in July 1988, and sponsored by Pergamon Press. During his inaugural address at Oxford Town Hall, Maxwell was again overcome by tears – or as the *Jewish Chronicle* reported:

A public eruption of private grief ... His anguish over-whelmed him as he struggled to recite the words of Professor Elie Wiesel: 'They knew they would survive, and most of them did not. But they wanted to be remembered. They wanted the tale to be told.' Mr Maxwell's wife, Elisabeth, a French-born Protestant and the inspiration for the conference, which drew 650 delegates from twenty-four countries, had to finish the quotation for him.

Such was the suspicion in which Maxwell was now held in Britain that a small controversy over his platform appearance even broke out within the *Jewish Chronicle's* own pages, when the columnist Chaim Bermant mentioned cynics who had suggested '. . . that he was putting it on for the benefit of the cameras; but the one thing Maxwell is not is an actor. The breakdown may have been out of character, but he is rarely less than his irrepressible, insufferable, unpredictable self.' The following week, an indignant reader, Gershon Ellenbogen, wrote in to protest that, 'having listened to his address from a few yards' distance', he would describe such cynics, rather, as 'malevolent imbeciles'.

The cynical construction put upon Maxwell's demeanour at the Holocaust conference arose directly from the well-remembered court case of November 1986 in which Maxwell had sued *Private Eye* for libel over allegations that he had sought to buy honours by contributing to Labour Party funds. The infamous name of Adolf Eichmann, one of the chief organisers of the Nazi extermination programme against Jews, had arisen during the proceedings, and Maxwell once again had cried, protesting that Eichmann had destroyed his family. This spectacle was received with private derision by the *Private Eye* satirists, who, characterising it in their public-school style as 'blubbing', sought to suggest that Maxwell was parading a contrived emotion. The tears, indeed, had done Maxwell's cause no harm in the courtroom; yet the likelihood is that they were involuntary tears, of rage as much as grief. His complaint was upheld by British justice, but it probably accelerated his inner estrangement from Britain.

Maxwell's 'discovery' of Israel in 1985 could not have been more propitiously timed for a man seeking to extend his influence. An election the previous year had removed the Likud majority in Israel, and replaced it with a novel power-sharing scheme in which first Shimon Peres of the Labour Party would serve as Prime Minister, whereafter he would hand over power, halfway through the allotted term, to Yitzhak Shamir of Likud. When out of the leadership, each man would serve as the other's Foreign Minister. Any outsider who got to know both men had the chance to play one off against the other. It was a whole new arena for Maxwell, though he was well aware of the difficulties Israel faced.

At that moment, the nation stood at a low point in international esteem. Over the previous half-decade, it had shown itself to be dangerously volatile in adopting punitive military measures against the Palestine Liberation Organisation. Attacks on the Lebanon had caused the Americans, under Reagan, to withhold delivery of fighter-planes. The 1982 massacres in the West Beirut refugee camps of Sabra and Chatila had clearly been countenanced, if not positively facilitated, by Israeli forces. International opinion had been shocked by the willingness of Israel – of all nations – to associate itself with the kind of atrocities that had been visited upon its own people, only half a lifetime before.

It was in this climate of international censure that Maxwell introduced himself to Israel: his usual well-timed approach to the outcast. Within five years, he became the largest foreign investor in the Israeli economy. So acquisitive did he prove that, as Dr Saul Zadka, the Israeli investigative journalist, remembers, the Maxwell campaign of buying became a kind of national joke – especially when stickers were printed to encourage the new arrival: 'Everybody could find it on the back of his car – "Maxwell! Buy Me!" Many people in the morning, when they would confront their mirror before shaving, would say, "What's going on, what's wrong with me? Maxwell hasn't bought me yet!"' Robert Maxwell had turned himself almost instantly into a brand-name for international commerce, and indeed almost the only brand-name in that line at the time: for this was, as Zadka says, '. . . a time when Maxwell was regarded as one of the few Jewish businessmen all over the world who did not turn his back to Israel during the *intifada*, the Palestinian uprising in the occupied territories. Of course, later on it turned out that he made plenty of fortunes out of this.'

But as ever, the buying, and even the fortunes, were often secondary to the political programme Maxwell had chosen to pursue. He had come to Israel with two goals in view. One was to bring Palestinian resistance under control without encouraging Israel further to blot its reputation with cross-border strikes, raids and local oppression. The second, in the words of ex-President Chaim Herzog, was 'to get the Jews out of Russia where they were more or less in a jail'. This latter aim could not be broached until Maxwell's lines of influence with yet another new regime in Russia had been reconnected. In February 1985, the expected change had taken place in Moscow, and Mikhail Gorbachev had succeeded Konstantin Chernenko. But Gorbachev's attitude to Maxwell, so far, had been a cagey one. The new General Secretary, for all that he was incubating some 'New Thinking' about the innards of Soviet society, was nevertheless an Andropov man by training and tradition; so Gorbachev had inherited not the Central Committee's intrigued and even tolerant attitude to 'Comrade' Maxwell, but a wariness heavily tinged with the suspicions long harboured by the KGB.

For the first time, too, a generational difference had entered Maxwell's dealings with the USSR. 'Although he is the eighth leader of the Soviet Union,' he wrote of Gorbachev in his 'Leaders of the World' Introduction, 'he is the first not to have fought in the Great Patriotic War (1941–45) . . . His personal experience equips him to look forward to the future, instead of backwards to the devastating losses suffered by the Soviet Union at the hands of Nazi Germany.' Maxwell was able to present this new-age outlook of Gorbachev as a refreshing change, but he was really not sure what to expect of it. Gorbachev, for his part, could have been forgiven for seeing Maxwell as a left-over Cold War profiteer, a back number who was unhelpfully tainted with contacts reaching well back into Stalin's time.

Maxwell's campaign to get close to Gorbachev had already begun, of course, in London, in December of 1984. But there was a lot of work still left in it. The Palestinian problem, meanwhile, remained urgent, and Maxwell already had most of the contacts necessary to make some impact upon it. It was not Israel's policy so much as 'the world's policy' that needed changing. Maxwell naturally said nothing of this, publicly, at the time. But in his famous *Playboy* interview, recorded in the spring of 1991 – possibly the most fateful interview ever printed in that strange magazine – Maxwell was asked what he saw happening in the post-war Middle East. 'The world's policy,' he replied, 'has been to blame everything on Israel, to help the PLO and keep down democracy at the same time. That's gone.' And Maxwell had done his part in banishing it. It was to the abolition of that 'world's policy' that he had bent his efforts in the mid-Eighties.

The rights and wrongs of current Israeli strategy entered only marginally into the process. It was Maxwell's belated response to the Hitlerian genocide that was being enacted here. He seemed almost to reserve a special tone of voice for dealing with the subject. In all the recorded interviews and transcripts he left behind, it is notable that he answers enquiries about it in a clipped speech that reins in an almost palpable emotion. Tears, this time, were not shed, but Maxwell's normal confident flow of speech is choked. Perhaps for that very reason, one senses that this is a subject on which Maxwell can be believed. Thus:

*Playboy*: And your parents were killed in the Holocaust.
Maxwell: Yes. I cannot ever forget it. I can't forgive it. To me, the big mystery is why my parents went to their death without a complaint. I remember everything about that. My mother was a great influence on me. I was her favourite.
*Playboy*: The experience shaped much of your political and social involvement.
Maxwell: I do a lot to make sure people don't forget, yes. It is behind my Zionism. No head of state I meet escapes me on that issue.

These are feeling words, but again they betray a kind of infantile rage. What complaint could Maxwell have expected his parents, or any other Holocaust victim, to register, in the face of the Nazis' military–industrial programme of homicide? And if they had complained, how could their voice have reached their son? His remark, to be sure, is a cry of pain at the whole event, and the apparently gentle submission of entire Jewish populations to the German horror; but it emerges in the uncomprehending voice of the spoilt, 'favourite' son. And in the words 'my Zionism' is a proprietorial hint that reminds one how much Maxwell owed his wife for appointing herself the curator of his Judaic-historical heritage, and putting in work on it, during years when Maxwell simply could not face this theme at all. His emotions were uncontrollable on the subject of the Holocaust; and as Elisabeth Maxwell's book makes clear, he treated his wife, during their last years together, uncontrollably badly. Both sets of behaviour, as she knew, had the same psychological root.

With politicians and policy Maxwell was able to deal, however, and there is evidence that few heads of state did, indeed, 'escape' him, at least on the issue of Middle Eastern peace. General Jaruzelski was the first leader he met after introducing himself to Israel. Maxwell immediately made use of the experience. 'He spoke to me,' Jaruzelski says, 'of his meeting with Shimon Peres during his stay in Israel. He mentioned, very tactfully, I must say, that it would be a good thing to establish contacts with Israel.' But Jaruzelski's point of view on such matters was not, in those days, altogether independent. 'At that time we were functioning within the framework of the [Eastern] bloc, of a jointly agreed policy in relation to Israel and the Arab nations, and, well, Poland could not depart too much from that line.' (As for older history, Maxwell will not have needed reminding of Poland's lamentable history of anti-Semitism.)

Maxwell, Jaruzelski says, did not present himself as a representative of the Israeli government: 'We treated this less as his having the power to act on behalf of Israel, and more as his personal attitude to the matter, of a man of Jewish descent who wished to see the normalisation of relations between Jews and Poles. As a friend of Poland, he wanted the time to mature, to come about, when relations could be normalised.' Once more, one has to remind onself that Jaruzelski speaks here of a visiting British businessman, not an ambassador or an elected representative.

The particular reasons why Poland could make no sudden moves on the Arab–Israeli question were familiar to Maxwell. As Jaruzelski now expresses it:

The politics had to be conducted very carefully in order not to provoke any perturbations in relations with Arab countries, which, incidentally, were important customers of our armaments industry, very profitable arms exports, especially to Libya. Poland exported a lot of arms, including tanks, anti-air defence systems, we were involved in the construction of a variety of military projects – in Syria, yes. And so, given our economic difficulties, we could not allow ourselves to go too far at that time in relation to Israel, otherwise that side of our co-operation would have collapsed. Economics was an important factor in our operations.

Poland, Jaruzelski insists, 'categorically' dissociated itself from international terrorism. 'Our counter-intelligence noted the occasional arrival in Poland of representatives of various terrorist organisations, such as Abu Nidal's – the Americans even informed us of their presence – and as soon as we knew, we would expel them from Poland.' But the Eastern bloc was also committed to sustaining the PLO on what Jaruzelski calls an 'official and legal' basis. And indeed there were PLO embassies in all the Communist countries of Europe. But Poland's contribution here was small, according to Jaruzelski: 'Poland was undergoing very serious economic difficulties and therefore our services to such movements as the PLO or other liberation–insurgency movements, whether in South America or Africa, were supported by us only to a very small degree. We simply did not have the means, nor, quite honestly, the desire.'

So in Poland, at least, Maxwell found himself pushing at the half-open door of what was presented to him as a virtually empty arsenal. There was no point in trying to dissuade the Poles from doing something they claimed they were scarcely able to do in the first place. This kind of pressure would have been better applied to the East Germans:

Generally speaking [Jaruzelski confirms] the GDR was in the front line of co-operation with all these nationalist and insurgency movements. I think that the Soviet Union even did this partly through the GDR as intermediaries. And for the GDR this was important because, after all, they were fighting for their place, their position in relation to such a powerful neighbour as the other half of Germany, the Federal Republic. And so, just as they did in sports, they wanted to achieve dominance and raise their prestige by this means.

It is not easy to discover how aggressively Maxwell carried the pro-Israeli argument into the camp of Erich Honecker, the East German head of state. Honecker had been easily flattered into making an early appearance in the 'Leaders of the World' series – his *From My Life* came third in line, after Brezhnev and Morarji Desai of India – but in the published Maxwell–Honecker interview ('A dialogue on current political issues'), no mention of Middle Eastern affairs was made. The date of the interview was 1981, some four years before Maxwell's open involvement in Israeli affairs. The two men remained in touch right up to the fall of the Berlin Wall (which Honecker had caused to be built); but there is no sign that Maxwell made very much impact on GDR sponsorship of militant Palestinians.

To attack Arab aspirations directly was not Maxwell's way. Vladimir Kryuchkov, Chairman of the KGB in the last years of the Soviet regime, says this made Maxwell, 'as one would say in Soviet jargon, a "Jew-Internationalist", since he never spoke ill of the Arabs. He understood the difference between the Arab and Jewish worlds and saw the need to find a common language.' Maxwell's interest was thus attracted by any nation which managed to retain working contacts with both Israel and the Arab nations. Romania, curiously, was one of these, though Maxwell got little change out of Nicolae Ceauşescu ('Builder of Modern Romania and International Statesman') when he brought the matter up in 1983, still before his own internal dealings in Israel began:

Maxwell: The situation in the Middle East is still a long way from being satisfactory. You, Mr President, have had an important role in the effort of ironing out the problems plaguing this region, given the good relations you have with both the Arab world and Israel. What do you think about the peace initiatives concerning the Middle East and the claim laid by some that the PLO should have to accept the idea of a homeland? Or do you consider that a *sine qua non* now for a settlement to the problem is Palestinian statehood?

Ceauşescu: Romania has always spoken out for a real solution of the Palestinian question based on the right to self-determination and to independent Palestinian statehood.

This, however, was merely the conversation, or that part of a conversation, that was approved for publication. In all such meetings between Maxwell and the leaders he targeted, there came a moment when aides were banished, and only the two principals remained, along with a translator, where required. Peter Jay, Maxwell's 'Chief of Staff' during much of the *Mirror* period, sometimes travelled with his boss and was among those banished on such occasions: 'Rather like the Communist traditional way of doing things, there'd be the kind of everybody-sits-on-sofas [or] grinning at each other on either side of the table, exchanging boiler-plate bits of gibberish about the wonderful nature of their system and other things; and then, well, those people, including myself, would disappear and he would then talk alone.'

There would scarcely have been much point in Maxwell's insisting on a private dimension to these talks if he had not had a different register of communication, a more serious level of negotiation, to broach in their tête-à-tête sessions. But Peter Jay, the former Ambassador to Washington, finds it difficult to imagine that important business was being done behind the closed doors, if by business one means the kind of confidential dealing that would have been of interest to intelligence services, on either side of the Iron Curtain:

I just can't imagine it. I can imagine the blarney, but I just can't imagine him being an effective operator in any of those ways. Nor can I imagine any service which called itself a secret service or a security service wishing to repose any reliance whatever in such a loose cannon on the deck, unguided missile, whatever metaphor you want to use. The last thing you want in your organisation – if it's that kind of organisation – is somebody like that, who's completely indiscreet, completely uncontrollable, completely impulsive, completely undisciplined. Why on earth would you want such a person? Unless it was for some very limited, special, narrow role.

Such a verdict is understandable, coming as it does from a highly intelligent man who suffered continually from Maxwell's in-house caprices and diktats. But it underestimates Maxwell's capacity to lead several lives at once. Jay and his colleagues were preoccupied with the chaos at hand, the day-to-day shambles Maxwell was leaving them to clean up. But other aims he was pursuing by himself.

# CHAPTER FIVE

# Any Other Business?

Maxwell by now was no longer 'controlled' by anything but his own grandiose vision of himself. He had a past record which showed that world leaders would take him seriously – and the photographs to prove it. His 'limited, special, narrow role', completely self-defined, was to be the head of a global communications empire he had pledged to build to a revenue of three to five billion pounds by the end of the Eighties. The size of this undertaking, in Maxwell's mind, justified his thinking of it in terms of statehood, nationhood. It sounded like a game, but Maxwell had begun to mean it. Within his organisation, he preferred governmental to business jargon. Not only was Jay his 'Chief of Staff', a term borrowed from the White House, but Sir John Morgan, the diplomat and linguist, was for a time his 'Foreign Minister' (officially 'Head of International Affairs'); and the little knot of aides who accompanied him on his more ostentatious sallies into Europe were called 'the Politburo'. Appropriately enough, Maxwell borrowed from everywhere in matching a nomenclature to his 'regime'. According to Nicholas Davies (whose own role was 'a sort of equerry'), Chairman Maxwell would even refer to his travelling *Mirror* snapper, Mike Maloney, as 'my Royal photographer'.

Maxwell had also begun to travel independently of other people's timetables. In 1986 he had bought a company called Music Agency Management Aviation, whose engineering department he then sold on to Mohammed Al Fayed. He retained for his own use a Gulfstream 2 executive jet, at that time the largest and most advanced in its category. Its call-sign was GO-VIP. In 1988 he replaced it with the next generation model, the Gulfstream 3, and gave the Gulfstream 2 over to his Macmillan executives in New York. The new plane's identification number was VR-BOB. These planes were destined to transport not only Maxwell and his corporate guests, but political figures ranging from Henry Kissinger to Yitzhak Shamir and Shimon Peres. Thanks to one of his captains, who left Maxwell's employ, like so many, in acrimonious circumstances, we have a fullish record of his flights between 1986 and the end of 1989 – though as this particular captain preferred not to fly to the Soviet Union, Bulgaria or the GDR, those destinations are under-represented in, though not excluded from, the log.

Nicholas Davies participated in some of the foreign visits. His description of the 'boiler-plate gibberish' stage of discussions tallies very much with Jay's:

> I was sitting with him in his meetings with Honecker and Jaruzelski and Zhivkov, for example. We sat, you know, and the Presidents or the General Secretaries [were] across the table, with only two of their men, and there'd be Maxwell and perhaps Sir John Morgan and myself on our side of the table, and generally speaking Maxwell was always trying to put together deals, he was always giving messages. For example, he would say, 'General Secretary Gorbachev sends you his best wishes, I was with him only the other week.' Now whether in fact he sent good wishes or not, I don't know, but it brought smiles from the other end of the table.

On occasion, Davies seems to have penetrated beyond diplomatic niceties to the core of a discussion. He was particularly impressed by Maxwell's demeanour in Moscow:

> He would hector them, he'd say, 'Israel is now a very important country in the Middle East, you have to start dealing with it, maybe in the past you took the Arab side but now things are changing, the Arabs and Israelis are getting closer, you've got to do deals with Israel, it's going to benefit

both of you, you've got many Russian *émigrés* now in Israel . . .' They would take this from him, remarkably. I mean, sometimes he would actually bang the table at them, which he loved doing, and it would make them sit up a bit. And I took my hat off to him doing that. You know, it took some guts to do that.

A central figure with whom Maxwell dealt throughout the Eighties was Dr Valentin Falin, then Chief of the International Department of the Central Committee of the CPSU. Among Falin's responsibilities were the funding of overseas pro-Communist and terrorist organisations, and the organisation of counter-espionage; but with Maxwell, Falin liaised, he says, on a range of issues from publishing to Soviet–Israeli relations. Falin's intervention became unnecessary after 1989, when Maxwell began to have access to Gorbachev himself, to Prime Minister Pavlov, and to Vladimir Kryuchkov, the Chairman of the KGB. If the KGB was no longer shunning Maxwell, it was because the KGB, according to Mikhail Lyubimov, was no longer shunning anybody: 'The main new policy of Mr Kryuchkov, sort of a continuation of Andropov's policy, is to enlarge the functions of the KGB, to make the KGB seem everywhere, in the Foreign Office, in the publishing business, and so on. So more and more KGB people appeared in different state organisations, and the KGB actually played a more powerful part than it played before, just by its presence.' This very swelling of the ranks is interpreted by Lyubimov as a symptom of decay. 'You get bigger, bigger, bigger – and then bang! This is the end, you see.'

Vladimir Kryuchkov today says that he first met Maxwell at the latter's initiative. 'I was told that he had led a very interesting life, was very hardworking, capable in both business and politics, or rather more in politics than in business. Although these are not equivalent terms, yet I would place them in that order.' It would seem that the KGB's mid-Eighties profile of Maxwell, prepared by Gordievsky, had been updated to include his latter-day impersonation of a State Supremo. Maxwell had not sought out the KGB before; but the manner of his entrance into Kryuchkov's office does much to explain why he had judged it advantageous to do so now. He had discovered a personal detail about the Chairman upon which he could base a special relationship.

> The door to my office opened [recalls Kryuchkov] and in tumbled a very large, energetic, smiling man. Suddenly, I heard my second native tongue, Hungarian. I knew that he spoke Hungarian. I believe he spoke everyday Hungarian well, but was weaker in '*hoch*'[1] Hungarian. So we conversed in Hungarian and had therefore little need of interpreters, which annoyed them greatly as they would have liked to know what we were talking about. I also did not wish to miss out on this opportunity, because it's not one you get every day.[2]

And so the visiting bow-tied capitalist and the head of the Soviet State Security Committee sat and chatted in a language they both enjoyed. 'Obviously the Chairman of the KGB presented an opportunity to get an access to delicate insider information. I appreciated his interest and therefore tried to satisfy him,' says Kryuchkov, with a straight face. Maxwell, for his part, evidently managed to attune his remarks to the conservatism of the head of a security service. At all events, Kryuchkov gives it as his opinion that: 'After contemplating the issue at hand, he would reach the correct conclusions . . . Maxwell was one of those foreigners who realised that there was something amiss in the USSR and that things weren't going the way our friends would have liked. And I believe that he really was a friend to the USSR.' Maxwell was also looking to the future of his Soviet business amid the remarkable social changes within the Republics. 'He was concerned by the very first rises in crime, in fact I often think that if he saw the rises of crime now, he would be amazed.'

---

[1] High or standard Hungarian – an interesting way for Maxwell's original surname to resurface.

[2] A tape reportedly exists of a conversation in Hungarian between Maxwell and Kryuchkov, possibly recorded on this occasion. Its owner, Valery Rudnev, states that the conversation predominantly concerned Israel, after which 'business issues' were discussed, and then the fate of Raoul Wallenberg, the Swedish diplomat responsible for the escape of hundreds of Jewish refugees from Nazism. Kryuchkov independently confirms that Maxwell raised the issue of Wallenberg's disappearance. (He was seized by the Russians, and his subsequent fate remains unknown.)

Some of Maxwell's suggestions corresponded pretty well exactly to those he had put before Jaruzelski in Poland, four years earlier. Kryuchkov says that Maxwell 'came up with' the idea of a business school to educate Soviet businessmen, and offered to give a series of lectures there. Under Prime Minister Pavlov, some progress was indeed made towards the foundation of such an establishment. But by now, these cross-cultural and commercial projects, few of which ever became bricks and mortar, had become ritualised gestures with Maxwell, exchanges of paper promises which put an imprint of co-operation on his meetings with men of influence. It was to the political themes that Maxwell continued to return in his meetings with Kryuchkov, the one recurrent topic being Israel and the Russian Jews. The KGB Chairman, having defined Maxwell as a 'Jew-Internationalist', accepted that two allegiances were being played out simultaneously: 'He was a loyal British subject and patriot. He was indisputably a patriot of his country and never allowed any insults against her. Sometimes he would disagree with certain political decisions, but this was quite different. He was also a big patriot of Israel, he loved this country and always wanted to help it. I didn't see anything wrong with it.' Jewish students of Kryuchkov's career may be permitted a discreet guffaw here at this vision of twinkling benignity.

Even the Chairman of the KGB may from time to time be disarmed by honesty, and such was the case, Kryuchkov claims, with Maxwell and his Israeli connection: 'The questions that he asked concerning Soviet–Israeli relations were posed in, so to say, very honest, unofficial and direct terms. For example, he wanted the process for the emigration of Soviet Jews to Israel to be facilitated. He wanted them to have the right to go directly to Tel Aviv or to any other country that they wanted to go to.'

Maxwell also told Kryuchkov, and this formulation does have a very convincing Maxwellian ring about it, 'that he did and would continue to make the life of the Israeli state as easy as possible'. The notion of his own supra-nationhood had conferred upon Maxwell a godlike perspective. If he was not exactly dispensing international justice, he was watching over the world's progress towards some such ideal.

'He never said if Tel Aviv had asked him to ask certain

questions,' Kryuchkov says. 'But he certainly kept the politics of Tel Aviv in mind. What also impressed me was that he not only discussed the emigration rights of Jews in the USSR, but also talked of improving trade, technical, cultural and economic links between the two countries.' Maxwell knew that his message would be more acceptable if he wrapped it up in the expected cocoon of trade-seeking – which might bring him eventual profit anyway. Otherwise, his dialogue with Kryuchkov (parts of which were conducted in English, when Hungarian palled) was maintained on as personal a basis as Maxwell could contrive: 'If he received an unsatisfactory answer to, say, Jewish emigration, he would grow very concerned, not because he had failed in executing an order, but because his personal desire had not been fulfilled and because we were not in agreement with each other. Then he would say, "Let us return to the question on my next visit, perhaps by then you will have changed your mind and will have a more favourable outlook for Tel Aviv." These sorts of things would take place, and his politeness was most pleasing.' It was no good pounding the table with the Chairman of the KGB.

There is no doubt that Maxwell would have preferred to be talking with Mikhail Gorbachev himself; he was the star of world politics, an astonishing arrival, the limits of whose innovatory vision had not yet been exposed. But Gorbachev had remained elusive for several years. 'Gorbachev made him wait,' says Nicholas Davies. 'Gorbachev would not do anything for Maxwell until Maxwell produced.' There would come a time when he did 'produce', but at no stage could Gorbachev be relied upon to make himself readily available to Maxwell. He was in fact one of the few figures by whom Maxwell was prepared to be snubbed – though such instances seemingly arose as much from Maxwell's own extreme presumptuousness and over-expectation as from the Soviet leader's desire to keep him in his place.

An account by Roy Greenslade, *Daily Mirror* editor from February 1990, has Maxwell travelling by private plane to Moscow with an entourage including Greenslade's wife, the journalist Noreen Taylor, who was to conduct an interview with

Raisa Gorbachev. On the way, Maxwell revealed that, while this pleasant discussion between the ladies was taking place, he was going to be elsewhere, buttonholing Mikhail. On arrival, the Maxwell party received all the exceptionally favourable treatment its leader had come to expect – its passports, for example, were checked on the plane – but neither an interview with Mrs Gorbachev, nor an improvised chinwag with her husband, actually ensued. The planeload returned home with only an early Christmas message from the General Secretary to show for its journey.

Maxwell must have felt puzzled by this. After a promising start, his relations with Gorbachev had not developed. Flattery had only got him so far. The trusted biography-publishing gambit, for once, seemed to have purchased little long-term credit, in spite of the fact that the Mikhail S. Gorbachev contribution to the groaning shelf of 'Leaders of the World' was a two-volume job, generously basting the General Secretary with the kind of compliment which, as usual, served simultaneously as a puff for the book – 'which should indeed,' the Publisher wrote, 'be required and exciting reading for every student of contemporary affairs, indeed for every thinking person'.

Having no interview of his own to include, Maxwell made do with one drawn from the pages of *l'Unità*, the Italian Communist newspaper. One reply of Gorbachev's will certainly have been of interest to him. 'You ask about Soviet–Israeli relations,' Gorbachev had said to the Italian journalists. 'As far as diplomatic relations are concerned, I have already explained our position in a recent speech. These relations can be restored provided there is real progress in a Mid-East settlement. We have no reason (with the exception of one – Israel's aggressive policy with regard to the Arabs) to regard Israel differently from any other state.' Here at least was something to work on, if only Maxwell could re-establish decent contact with Gorbachev himself.

It had always been Maxwell's habit, when stuck for an opening of this kind, to use his publishing and cultural base to invent some new 'McGuffin', or fictive aim, through which to tempt the target back into his orbit. Luring Raisa Gorbachev on to the editorial board of *Our Heritage*, an equivalent of

America's several glossy magazines on the theme of Living History, proved relatively easy. But bigger promises were required to get her husband on the same podium with Captain Maxwell.

Eventually, Maxwell would come up with a scheme which became known as the 'Gorbachev–Maxwell Institute'. Bizarrely sited in the state of Minnesota, with the co-operation of star-struck Governor Rudy Perpich, the Institute was supposed to provide an international forum for scientists, in the best traditions of Pyotr Kapitsa and Pergamon; but once it had brought Gorbachev and Maxwell together for a grand inaugural ceremony, its job, in Maxwell's eyes, was done.

Worse, its job no longer needed doing, for he had finally acquired the ear of Gorbachev without artificial persuasions, in 1989. Naturally, Maxwell never paid over his share of the start-up money, and the Institute is scarcely a memory, even in Minnesota. So many of Maxwell's announced international schemes came to nothing that one wonders how many of them he ever believed to be capable of reaching completion. Maxwell was like the randy bachelor who propositions every female he corners, in the belief that one in twenty will take him on. Such a policy requires the unembarrassable temperament which accepts that a slap in the face is statistically the most likely outcome. Maxwell possessed it.

But in the early years of Gorbachev's regime, his traditional contribution to Anglo-Soviet exchange was not, for the moment, required. Margaret Thatcher's relations with Gorbachev were extraordinarily good, and she maintained her own lines of communication with the Kremlin. It would have been under-standable if Maxwell had turned his attention elsewhere – and even more understandable if he had been invited to do so. It was in the mid-Eighties that his activities acquired a new and deeper international background, brilliantly camouflaged by the furore in his own back yard. At the time, the British public, always concerned first for the fate of its own institutions, tended to look no further for a Maxwell story than the Mirror Group take-over. The new proprietor played up to his role like an all-in wrestler ballyhooing a bout. 'An *enormous* sum of money,' he assured us, in announcing his bid of £80–100 million. It was the Maxwell we all expected to see, presenting himself to us in giant close-up, like a huge cardboard cut-out.

But a more formidable Maxwell was in the making during the mid-Eighties. The KGB, as we now know, was checking him out for what its London bureau felt could only be a new and expanded role, to be played on behalf of the Central Committee. The following year, Maxwell made his grand entry into Israeli life. It would not take a seriously overheated conspiracy theorist to see a connection between the two events. A lachrymose Maxwell, all along, had needed persuading to identify himself with Israel. Was it the Soviets who applied the persuasion? Why would they need him at such a moment?

It is in the nature neither of retired KGB personnel nor veteran Israeli politicians to make a present of such information to the external enquirer. One is driven to examine the political situations in the USSR and Israel at the time – which might be characterised as 'unusually fluid' and 'chaotic' respectively – and draw conclusions. In all the mass of detail, there is only one new circumstance that would seem to call for Maxwell's intervention, and it comes from a much disputed source: the book *The Samson Option*, by Seymour Hersh, a history of the development of Israel's nuclear capability. The Hersh book, as its Pulitzer-prizewinning author would probably admit, was not his finest hour, depending as it did on the evidence of one of history's flakier eye-witnesses, Ari Ben-Menashe. At the time of his death, Maxwell, in his traditional style, had brought the weight of the libel laws to bear against Hersh (and others) on this score. Liberated by the litigant's demise to say what they liked about him, Hersh and his publisher jumped too soon at the chance, and fell for a 'corroborating witness' who was nothing more than one of Fleet Street's hoaxers-for-fun-and-profit. This all left Hersh looking a sorrier figure than he was used to being taken for, especially when, the following year, his informant Ari Ben-Menashe came up with a wild-eyed book of his own (*Profits of War*), some parts of which were demonstrably off the clock.

Ben-Menashe is an Iraqi Jew, born in Tehran, who emigrated to Israel in 1966. In the Seventies, he served in signals intelligence in the Israeli Defence Forces, and later became a civilian employee (some say this means no more than a dogsbody) in the External Relations Department of Military Intelligence. Like Maxwell, he was linguistically versatile (his languages included Arabic and Farsi), and thus became increasingly useful to Israel, he claims, in the ebb and flow of the Middle East crisis. 'From 1987 to 1989,' states his biographical blurb, 'he was a special intelligence adviser to Prime Minister Yitzhak Shamir.' Since he became a figure of international notoriety in 1990, however, he has been unable to return to Israel. When he contracted to write his book *Profits of War* for Allen & Unwin in Australia, so he says, a close colleague of Shamir's offered to secure him Australian citizenship, and a quiet life, if he let the project drop. He didn't.

That Shamir should have been especially interested in discouraging Ben-Menashe is believable. Some of the most startling pages in Seymour Hersh's book, using Ben-Menashe as one of his sources, concerned Shamir's tactics as caretaker Prime Minister in 1984. At that time, Menachem Begin had recently resigned from the post, victim of an implosion of morale after a cruel concatenation of personal and political setbacks, ranging from the assassination of his fellow Peace Prize Nobelist, Anwar Sadat, through the Sabra-Chatila massacres, to the death of his wife. Yitzhak Shamir emerged as his successor at the beginning of September 1983.

One of the problems he inherited, according to Ben-Menashe's testimony, was the continuing receipt of a generous outflow, indeed a glut, of leaked intelligence information from the United States, courtesy of Jonathan Pollard, a disaffected Jewish operative born in South Bend, Indiana. Pollard was sending an embarrassment of material; but a useful fraction of it was of real importance. The eventual discovery of this channel of information proved, of course, a matter of extreme embarrassment to Israel in its relations with the United States, and the occasion of a life sentence for Pollard. But in the meantime, Shamir was in possession of a large amount of sensitive military information for which he saw, according to Ben-Menashe, more than one use.

Acting upon what Hersh-Menashe variously describe as a 'visceral dislike' of the United States, and a need to 'balance, or offset, Israel's traditional reliance' on American support, Shamir allegedly entered upon the bold experiment of authorising the passing of some of Pollard's revelations to the Soviet Union. In early 1984, while still acting Prime Minister, he is said to have 'authorised the exchange of intelligence with the Soviets on US weapon systems'. The material, as might be imagined, was somewhat abridged, censored, and re-presented, but it was still a version of something entirely new. The shock to the intelligence community was reportedly considerable. As described by Ben-Menashe, it generated a directive to the representatives of the Mossad to initiate similar trial exchanges within Romania; an invitation to Israel to participate in an intelligence conference in India, where the state of the Pakistani nuclear capability was discussed; and a job for Ben-Menashe himself, who claims to have travelled to Warsaw to negotiate with Jaruzelski's people the sale of sundry weapons for transfer to Iran. Hershe states that the gist of all this was corroborated independently by another Israeli source, whom he cannot name, but who supplied a psychological sidelight on Shamir. The Israeli leader, he said, 'has always been fascinated with authority and strong regimes.' The words Maxwell spoke to a *Playboy* interviewer in 1991 – 'Mr Shamir and I have an identical policy' – seem to re-echo here.

Maxwell, huge and bloated, and the tiny, desiccated Shamir do not look like a natural, matching pair, and in fact relations were never easy between them. Israeli leaders lived then, as now, in an entirely different climate of politics from those in Maxwell's home ground of Eastern Europe. Their political idiom is different, and because they are both more urgently pragmatic and less grimly subordinated to the demands of a system, personality differences count for more. Maxwell was not Shamir's type. David Kimche, who was present at some of their meetings, recalls that: 'Yitzhak Shamir was very attentive to what Maxwell was saying, but Maxwell had the habit of, let's say, bragging a little bit. He wasn't modest, and he had a very dominating personality. And Shamir, being Shamir, being the sort of person he was, he preferred modest people, he preferred people low-key. He didn't quite know how to react to a person of such a high profile as Maxwell, and he wasn't quite sure whether it was for real, let's put it that way. He wasn't quite sure if this was what we needed in Moscow.'

(It seems Maxwell's blustering approach had at least convinced the Israelis that his offer was to represent Tel Aviv to Moscow, and not Moscow to Tel Aviv.)

David Kimche remembers no instance of Maxwell's having talked of attempting to detach the Eastern bloc leaders from their Palestinian affiliations; but then Kimche, by his own account, did not come into contact with Maxwell until 1988, so he did not witness Maxwell's first approaches to the Israeli government. Yitzhak Shamir himself is extravagantly vague on the date of his first meeting with Maxwell ('I think it was between '87 and '92!'); but he is clear that 'it was his initiative always'. No political figure, since Maxwell's death and disgrace, is anxious to be seen as having actively sought his company. Shamir, however, does remember a time when Maxwell was advertising himself as an adept in Eastern bloc politics as a whole. 'You know,' Shamir confides, 'all this sphere of Eastern Europe was unknown, quite unknown to all of us, and in a short time he became an expert on that, and it was very interesting to talk with him about it and to listen to his descriptions of the situations there – and, well, I remember that he talked about Bulgaria, about Poland and others, and we learnt from it.'

It is not necessary wholeheartedly to accept Shamir's picture of Israel as helpless naïfs in Mitteleuropean politics in order to believe that Maxwell had useful information to contribute on this theme. But when asked whether Maxwell had tried to dilute, say, Erich Honecker's support for the PLO, Shamir, an old Mossad hand himself, becomes Reaganesquely forgetful: 'Well, Honecker was a very strong personality in Germany at this time, and I can understand him to do something in this direction, but I didn't know about it . . . I don't remember that he told me sometimes about it, I don't remember.'

If any sort of United States intelligence material did begin to reach the Soviet Union via Israel in 1984 – and some of it is said to have gone directly to Yevgeni Primakov, the Foreign Department specialist in Middle Eastern affairs (later the post-Soviet head of Russian intelligence) – then the reaction at first must have been one of perplexity and suspicion, rather than pure delight.

Early 1984 was the beginning of the brief Chernenko interlude. Gorbachev had not been heard from; the USSR had given no signal, made no overture that might invite or provoke such a gesture from Israel. It needed explaining. But there were no diplomatic channels through which to begin an exploration of what it might all mean. And we learn that it was at this point, in 'the second half of 1984', that the KGB was belatedly let loose on Maxwell's case, to examine his credentials and ripeness for future development. Early in 1985, his journeys to Israel begin. Maxwell the Travel Agent is in business again.

It might reasonably be objected that the Central Committee in 1984 could merely have been looking to ask for Maxwell's help in exploring the *détente* with Israel which so many former Kremlin insiders now claim they had in mind all along. (Vladimir Kryuchkov, for example, would like it to be known that 'Maxwell had fertile ground to work with, due to the fact that I had, for a number of years, campaigned for the complete re-establishment of Soviet–Israeli relations. I acted in the interests of "big politics" and I acted pragmatically.' A small round of applause seems to be called for.) But such a timetable does not accord very well with the one set out by Valentin Falin, Maxwell's usual International Committee contact throughout the Eighties. Falin says he had a meeting with Shimon Peres in 1987, and explained to him that the restoration of relations at some point in the future was not in question, but that the timing of the initiative was still an issue. Falin was determined, he says, that a *rapprochement* with Israel should not be achieved at the expense of the Soviet Union's existing influence with the Arab states of the Middle East (which was Gorbachev's stated line).

It was soon after this 1987 meeting with Peres, Falin points out, that Maxwell came to him offering his services as an intermediary in negotiations with Israel. He told him that he was known and trusted by both Peres and Shamir (which by then he was, within the limits of those gentlemen's capacity to trust a conspicuous and bumptious foreigner) and would thus be able to assist all parties in resolving their differences. Falin was still mulling this offer over when a directive came through informing him that Israel was a matter on which Maxwell would now liaise directly with Gorbachev and Kryuchkov, and cutting

Falin himself out of the line of communication. He was not the last of Maxwell's contacts to find that his function had been usurped by his bosses. Maxwell was still 'very much up'.

So was Maxwell requested (and helped) by the Soviets to make himself an insider within Israel? Were there odd things coming out of Israel that needed explaining? Ex-Soviet officials naturally do not confirm that any sort of unusual or surprising information, let alone detail about United States weapons systems, was emerging from Israel at that time. Nor will Vladimir Kryuchkov say whether he knew exactly what Maxwell was taking back to Shamir, although his answer to the question ('I think we are entering spheres of operative diplomacy which cannot be of interest to you ... even though ... no, I cannot') indicates that the withheld answer is an interesting one. Ex-Soviets prefer to emphasise that a desire to initiate a new relationship with Israel had been brewing ever since the disappearance of the Andropov-Chernenko generation. Leonid Zamyatin says: 'Gorbachev's policy in the area of internal affairs in the Middle East was, from the very beginning, to overcome the protests of the Arab nations and to establish, first of all, Consulatory relations with Israel, and later full relations. This was not an easy step to take. Therefore here a mediator was required.'

Zamyatin is certain that Maxwell's role was important here: 'He was in contact with Russians who were dealing with this issue at its highest levels: not only with Gorbachev, but also, let's say, Kryuchkov, the Chairman of the KGB; with Boldin, special aide on questions of national security; Alexander Nikolevich Yakovlev, the second most important man in Russia's government at the time; and Maxwell began to meet often with these people.' In Soviet eyes, the great advantage of using Maxwell in this area was that his presence, relatively covert to begin with (in that he was now travelling in his own executive jet) and overlaid at all points with the business motive, would not arouse the suspicions of the Arab countries, a development much feared by both Gorbachev and Kryuchkov.

Zamyatin himself, in his Ambassadorial role in London, participated for a while in the process: 'I often met, in his flat with a special lift serving it, people from Israel. People of important stature, ministers, members of the opposition which is now in power. I could feel that there, behind other closed doors, heated negotiations were taking place.' Zamyatin felt his presence on the tenth floor provided Maxwell with extra information; but in his normal Embassy life, he had no dealings with Israelis at all: 'I had no direct contact with these people – only through Maxwell. There were discussions about the normalisation of relations, questions concerning the countries neighbouring Israel. There also took place discussions concerning the potential construction of a special aeroplane using combined Soviet and Israeli engineering and technical resources.'

This remarkable project was co-sponsored by Maxwell and the Israeli industrialist Shoul Eisenberg. Two other participants in the prospective deal were the Canadian developer Albert Reichmann, and, from the US, none other than Armand Hammer – a rare instance of open co-operation between Hammer and Maxwell, the two veteran straddlers of the Iron Curtain. David Kimche, the ex-Mossad executive, was by now working for Eisenberg: he appears in Maxwell's personal telephone directory of the time as 'International Relations Director, Group Eisenberg'. Shoul Eisenberg had wanted to do business with Maxwell in Russia, Kimche says, so the two Israelis flew to London and met Maxwell for the first time: 'There was an idea to create a new plane, a passenger plane,' Kimche continues, 'using the fuselage of a Russian passenger plane and wedding it to Western engines and Western electronics. Because the fuselages of Russian planes are very, very good – they are as good as any Western.' The engines were to be American, and the navigational equipment provided by the Israelis. Maxwell liked the idea, immediately 'came in on it', and before long he and Kimche were flying together to Moscow.

What happened there was 'typical Maxwell', Kimche says. On the Maxwell agenda was a meeting with the Deputy Minister of Education on another matter entirely:

... a project dealing with scientific publications, which he told me about. He spoke to me for about five minutes on it. And then just before that meeting was supposed to take place, he was suddenly called to something else. So he said to me, 'I've told you about it – you lead. You conduct the talks with the Deputy Minister of Education. And there were about thirty Russians – it was still the Soviet Union at that time, of course – there were about thirty Russians on their side, and there was I with a very, very vague idea of what the whole thing was about. And I had to conduct the negotiations.

One may deduce from this that publishing matters had now sunk low on Maxwell's list of errands.

Kimche was further astonished by the way Maxwell was received in Moscow: 'He stayed in the guest house of the Central Committee of the Communist Party, which was a very, very closed place; and he wanted me to come and see him there. One of the leading Israeli Communists was staying at the time, and he just couldn't believe his eyes when he saw that I was there as well.' It was, indeed, not a place where former bureau chiefs of the Mossad were expected to turn up. Among others who were surprised were representatives of the PLO, in whose large dossier on Maxwell are surveillance photographs taken of him in Moscow, in company with Kimche and other senior Israeli figures.

The airliner project, which might have given the Americans, in particular, an interesting commercial challenge, became a natural casualty of change and decay: Armand Hammer died in December 1990, and in the following year, two major contributors, the Soviet airline Aeroflot and Robert Maxwell himself, came to grief. But this was, in any case, only an example of a cross-border economic deal, the primary, commercial level of Maxwell's activity. Beneath that surface came his political involvement, which included agitation on behalf of a Soviet–Israeli *rapprochement*, and the kind of secret meetings Leonid Zamyatin describes as having taken place in Maxwell's London penthouse.

The ultimate goal of a restoration of Israeli–Soviet reciprocity at the full diplomatic level was preceded, unusually perhaps, by progress towards a more practical and humanitarian aim,

described by Vladimir Kryuchkov as 'more conducive emigration procedures' for Soviet Jews wishing to leave for Israel. Even
here, though, there was a risk of provoking Arab alarm. Saul
Zadka, in Israel, remembers that the PLO Chairman, Yasser
Arafat, '. . . went mad in trying to persuade the Soviet authorities
not to let the Soviet Jews leave their country and go to Israel.
His reason for such a protest was that they would eventually
go to the Occupied Territories and settle there, creating a new
demographical fact in the Occupied Territories. Of course, we
are talking about the time when the Cold War was not over yet,
and Israel did not have any agreement with the PLO.' Maxwell
himself was hawkish on these questions: populating the Occupied Territories with Russian arrivals was fine by him, and the
PLO, he believed, should apply to Jordan for their homeland.

In spite of all misgivings, the emigration of Soviet Jews began
in earnest in 1987. Individuals had been allowed to leave before
that time, if there was some compelling medical or family reason
to expedite their case. But by mid-1987, several hundred Jews
were emigrating every month, while the Western press kept
a regular tally of their numbers. Demonstrations continued
within the Soviet Union in favour of a faster rate of release, and
against the refusal of emigration rights to certain Jewish figures
who were judged to be in possession of sensitive information.
But the process, in general terms, was under way.

Since that time, according to ex-President Chaim Herzog, the
'demographical facts' of the influx into Israel have not taken
the shape that Arafat feared: 'I don't believe there's any area
of preponderant settlement of Soviets, they're just all over the
country. They've disappeared – in other words, they've become
completely absorbed. At one stage, you heard mainly Russian on
the streets; today you don't hear it at all, and I think in the final
analysis it'll be a great success story.' The only cultural overload
that Herzog reports is a superfluity of medical personnel: 'We
were the leaders in the world with three doctors to one thousand
population. We now have approximately twenty doctors to a
thousand population. We just don't have the facilities or the
work for them, so they have to move to some other subject.'

A new readership of native Russian-speakers naturally

attracted the attention of Publisher Maxwell, who catered to their needs through the foundation of a new Israeli newspaper, *Vremia*. 'We now have half a million Russian Jews who have arrived here,' Herzog reports, 'and they have a very thriving press, multiplying all the time, a radio station, special news on TV and so forth. And in many of these things, he was involved.' Amid the ruins of Maxwell's commercial empire, this settlement now appears to have been the great success story of his life. He was naturally not solely responsible for it – as Kryuchkov darkly warns, 'If you believe that Maxwell was the only channel of communication between the USSR and Israel, you are wrong' – but any tendency to minimise Maxwell's role was driven from President Herzog's mind when, in mid-June 1992, Mikhail Gorbachev visited Israel:

> We gave him a state dinner when he came. He said to me, 'Despite everything that happened, Maxwell was one of the most impressive people I've ever met in my life. You have every reason to thank him for what he did, because if there was one single element that really was active in helping to get the Jews out of Russia, it was him, and he was successful.' He said that he understood our attitude to Maxwell, and there was every justification for it. This Gorbachev said to me.

This resounding testimonial gives Maxwell the credit he certainly deserves for his persistence in restoring Soviet–Israeli relations, and ultimately facilitating the whole Middle East peace process; though it does not fully explain Herzog's funeral oration for Maxwell, in which he lamented 'the tragic and untimely passing of a mighty man, a man of courage and vision, and daring enterprise, a man cast in a heroic mould'. This outspoken tribute caused surprise at the time. When Herzog went on to assert that 'Robert Maxwell was a figure of almost mythological stature', onlookers began seriously to ask themselves whether they had got the measure of Maxwell's contribution to the Israeli cause. In time, they were going to have to sort through some very grubby evidence.

# CHAPTER SIX

## 'I give advice'

Ambassador Leonid Zamyatin was comfortable in his dealings with Robert Maxwell in London, unorthodox though they were. The two men had enjoyed an unusually productive relationship, both at the official, recorded level, and in their very unofficial exchanges in Maxwell's tenth-floor apartment. They were roughly of an age – Zamyatin the older by a year – and had much in common. After representing the USSR briefly at the International Atomic Energy Agency, Zamyatin had turned his attention to information management, becoming successively Head of the Press Department at the Ministry of Foreign Affairs, Director-General of the Soviet News Agency, TASS, and Chief of the Central Committee's Department of International Information. They had plenty to talk about.

So Zamyatin was a little miffed to discover that claims were being made on Maxwell by the Soviet Union at a third level of involvement, in which he, as Ambassador, was not allowed to engage: 'When Maxwell began to visit Moscow more often and began meeting people at the level of the Chairman of the KGB,' Zamyatin says, 'there were questions raised that went beyond the boundary of affairs that could be handled between an Ambassador and someone like Maxwell.' He remembers the circumstances of the discovery, because they offended his professional pride as a diplomat. The first symptom he detected came in an order he received from Moscow, a communication belonging to a specially coded category: 'They were not signed by the Chairman of the KGB, but the secret here is simple:

if under the telegram was written the common Russian name "Ivanov", then the information had been, so to speak, approved by those in charge. And I was told – this was just after a visit of Maxwell's to Moscow – that one of the aides at the Embassy, who belonged to the KGB, had to be brought into contact with Maxwell.'

What irked Zamyatin was that he had to facilitate this under cover of his own Ambassadorial presence: 'After all, the Ambassador's the Ambassador, and an aide is an aide. I fulfilled the order. I drove this man to Maxwell's flat, but when it became clear that my presence was supplementary, I told both Maxwell and this man that, next time, I would not come as cover. "Cover yourselves as you want to, but not thanks to my presence, nor to my car with its flag."'

Zamyatin did not take part in ensuing meetings: '. . . but I know that this man continued to meet Maxwell. He was the head of our network in London, but what they talked about I cannot tell you.'

Special invitations for Maxwell's visits to Moscow came through this same channel, Zamyatin said. By this time, Maxwell was proud of his contacts with the KGB: 'Sometimes on his returns he would show me photos of him with Kryuchkov. I had one of these photos. Once I jokingly commented that, after what happened in Moscow, I would probably have been able to receive lots of money for such a photograph, but unfortunately I never kept it.'

Invited to speculate on what the theme of these extra-private discussions had been, Zamyatin nominates the question of Germany, '. . . as the preparation for unification was a key issue at that moment. Maxwell had very good unofficial contacts with Germany and together with the official contacts we already had, these were very helpful.' It is true that not many contacts of Soviet Russia's were simultaneously on speaking terms with Erich Honecker of the GDR, and the West German Foreign Minister, Hans-Dietrich Genscher. But German reunification, while a sensitive matter, did not lie outside Maxwell's normal range of discussion with Zamyatin himself. By the Ambassador's own account, he did discuss it with Maxwell:

. . . and I asked him how, in his opinion, such a process would be executed. He said, 'Wait a moment, Ambassador, we'll just find out.' He picked up the telephone, talked briefly with his secretary, and asked her to connect him with Genscher. Indeed, in a little while he was talking with Genscher, in my presence, highlighting that Ambassador Zamyatin was in his office; and he would start asking him various questions. I would say that their conversation was by no means purely political [but] even friendly, showing his warm association with this man.

It would seem that, towards the end of his life, Maxwell relied on Genscher to be the most available of his telephone contacts; Genscher's, at least, is the celebrity name most often mentioned when conversations with Maxwell are interrupted by telephone messages (in the *Playboy* interview, for example, where Maxwell's New York Secretary Carolyn Barwell breaks in on the journalist's interrogation of Maxwell to say, 'Mr Genscher has called back.'[1]

Such grandstanding tactics belong to Maxwell's first and second agendas: his communications tycoonery, and the involvement in back-door diplomacy of which, at the end of his life, he was unwisely beginning to boast. But the existence of a third agenda for Maxwell is traceable right through his final years. It necessitated the removal from Maxwell's case not just of Zamyatin in London, but of Valentin Falin in Moscow. Maxwell had become too big, and his tasks too sensitive, to be handled by anyone but Gorbachev and Kryuchkov themselves.

---

[1]It must have occurred to many of Maxwell's occasional visitors that he was making and accepting bogus calls for sheer effect. Dr Saul Zadka: 'He used to impress [visitors at the King David Hotel] when during routine meetings with them he would tell his secretary, "Oh, please get me the Prime Minister of Bulgaria on the phone, please get me the Prime Minister of Canada." And people at the beginning suspected him, that he really is doing it only for the show-off, that indeed there is nobody else on the other end of the line. But apparently these people were very close to him. He was maybe one of the only people who did not lead a country who was capable to have direct access to anybody.' See also the *Playboy* interview:
*Maxwell Associate:* The Prime Minister wants to speak to you.
*Maxwell:* Which one?
*Maxwell Associate:* The Honourable Brian Mulroney [of Canada].
A sceptical view of this unnecessarily stilted exchange might be that (a) Mulroney was indeed on the line, but (b) Maxwell's staff had been trained to communicate the fact laboriously, so that its effect would not be lost.

The 'promotion' of Maxwell coincides with the beginnings of what the former KGB general Oleg Kalugin has described as an extensive KGB money-laundering operation. It was conducted, he says, at the behest of the Central Committee, which issued a directive to the KGB on the subject early in 1990. Kalugin believes that this directive came directly from Gorbachev. The political situation within the Soviet Union was at that moment extremely disturbed, with the republic of Lithuania openly preparing for secession from the Union, and Gorbachev responding with the draft of a law designed to make such a manoeuvre legal, if not, according to the Lithuanians, definitive or irrevocable. A turbulent spring culminated in a bizarre new version of the May Day parade in Red Square, where the traditional ranks of hardware representing the military might of the USSR were replaced by an uncoordinated rabble of protest, some of it emanating from nationalists and libertarians, and some from disgusted hard-liners bearing the old insignia of Communism. It would not have been surprising if, in such an atmosphere of dissolution, realists within the Moscow hierarchy, seeing the end approaching, had sought to lodge some assets overseas.

It is simply unimaginable that Maxwell, knowing of this process, did not offer himself as its facilitator. The mechanisms for the transfer of money had all been in place since the early Pergamon days; and indeed, it has been confirmed that, at the time of Maxwell's death, the Moscow office of Pergamon, though no longer his property, was owed half a million roubles, or a similar number of pounds when calculated at the conventional rate (the rouble being a non-tradable currency internationally). The trading arrangements for the English-language books Maxwell generated in Moscow had always been a mystery, even to those instructed to run the business. For his Pergamon science journals, there was an eager market throughout the world, if not a vastly profitable one. But such ventures as the 'Leaders of the World' – interesting though they are now as tiny pimples giving a diagnostic clue to the general infection that was Maxwellism – were clearly loss-makers all along. Richard Newnham, a Maxwell assistant of the late Seventies, is reported to have told Maxwell to his face that the books were commercially 'valueless', since they brought only translation and printing costs, and scarcely any sales. Maxwell's reply ('Stop showing me negative reports. Just do it') is transparently the Chairman's paraphrase for 'Don't ask questions.'[1]

It looks very much as if the books acted from time to time as an excuse for the shifting of currency in and out of the Soviet Union, and perhaps more especially out. Oleg Gordievsky has no particular knowledge of Maxwell's life as a publisher, but as an observer he remarks: 'I'm sure that Robert Maxwell profited very much from publicising those works of the Communist leaders. He would publish several thousand copies of the very expensive and very beautiful book – who would buy it in Britain? Nobody, apart from some few libraries. It meant that the whole edition, 90 per cent of the copies, would be bought for generous money by the Soviet Union, by Bulgaria, by East Germany and so on.'

So books for which, by rights, Maxwell should have been paying money to his East European 'authors' and hosts were, in fact, finding their way back to the Eastern bloc in return for hard currency. It makes no business sense – no wonder the publishing executives were baffled – but as a way of feeding out money to Maxwell in the West, it would have worked well. The receipt by Maxwell of decently large sums would have meant that the interest alone could have financed Pergamon's production of a small print-run of the books, and still leave a large personal cut for the Chairman himself. That Pergamon was classified by the Soviet regime as a 'friendly firm' is commonly explained by the publication of the biographies and Maxwell's general willingness to put Moscow's point of view, but a role as a hard-currency conduit renders explanation unnecessary. The reception centre for the outflow of moneys is believed to have been Pergamon's Paris branch.

Knowing what they know now about the hall of mirrors that was his accounting system, survivors of the last days of the Soviet Union are not keen to admit that they were once in awe of Maxwell's wealth and capitalist expertise. Vladimir Kryuchkov, wise after many events, chiefly those of 1991, now talks of:

[1] Tom Bower, *Maxwell: The Outsider* (Aurum Press, 1988).

... the myth surrounding his wealth. In my opinion, he wasn't as rich as some people made him out to be. There were people who thought that he could arrive in a country bringing with him billions of dollars, to provide credits at low interest rates to invest in that country, to benefact someone. I believe there was more myth in this than truth. I do not think that he had massive amounts of dollars to spare. When some of our comrades were attempting to negotiate receiving large amounts of credits from Mr Maxwell, I told them all along that nothing serious would come of it.

Nothing did, but this is all easy to say half a decade after the fact. Though the KGB had certainly investigated Maxwell's financial background and detected weaknesses, he remained one of the best money-technicians known to the Soviet Union, and certainly the most available. His advice was actively sought on the matter of credit policies and the foreign debt – and also, deeply ironic though it now seems, on the tracing of foreign aid that had gone missing within the Soviet Union. It was these chores that brought him close to Gorbachev at last, at the end of the Eighties. Pressed to recall some details, even Kryuchkov can almost dredge them from his memory: 'There was talk of the Soviet Union receiving, I can't quite recall, I think some five or six billion dollars of credits through Maxwell.' Nicholas Davies, who was travelling with Maxwell at the time, remembers the sum as four billion dollars: '. . . a four-billion-dollar secret loan for Gorbachev, which in fact never came about. But he got the Germans involved and he got the Americans involved, and he was involved. This is of course at the time when the collapse of the Soviet Union was happening and Gorbachev was desperately short of money, and the fear was that they'd be starving on the streets.'

Maxwell's notable intimacy with Hans-Dietrich Genscher, and also Karl Pöhl, President of the Bundesbank, dates from the period of the loan's negotiation, some details of which were noted by Davies as they passed through Maxwell's office: 'I saw faxes relating to it. And when he had put that together, then Gorbachev would see him and greet him and be friendly.' The Maxwell-Hammer-Eisenberg aeroplane project was part of the same economic rescue effort: all the Soviet input would be made at home, and financed in roubles, but the profits would come in hard currency.

Speculation in currency had long been one of Maxwell's international games, and one which he had often played with conspicuous success. Through the Eighties, his thoughts had turned increasingly to the international money markets, and the possibility of turning himself into an itinerant Financial District, available for the processing of any financial transaction from which a percentage rake-off could be claimed. But Maxwell was conscious that he lacked the prime tool of the fiscal engineer: a bank of his own. As he knew from painful experience, experiments in this line needed to be conducted as far from the City of London as possible; so once again, he turned to a nation which, as one of the temporary outcasts of the world, was likely to receive his overtures with gratitude. In a particularly bold departure from his usual beat, he chose Argentina: his flight records show the Gulfstream arriving in Buenos Aires in October 1989. An audience with President Menem was naturally on the schedule, and Maxwell took the opportunity to propose himself as a prospective proprietor of, or partner in, an Argentine bank. More grandiosely yet, he offered Menem his services as a processor of Argentina's entire foreign debt, which he undertook to take under the wing of his international organisation. Neither offer appealed to the President, but both these ambitions of Maxwell's remained alive.

He was indeed pursuing them simultaneously in Bulgaria. His earliest links with this nation are difficult to trace. It seems hardly likely that the publication of Zhivkov's biography, and a small contribution to the cultural foundation of his daughter, the late Ludmila Zhivkova, would have been enough to win for Maxwell the award of the Order of Stara Planina, First Class – the highest honour in Bulgaria – which he received as early as 1983. But he had, at all events, remained in touch with the unlovely Zhivkov throughout the decade, until finally, in 1989, a coalition of pseudo-reformed Communists, campaigning under the banner of Socialism, removed the old tyrant from office. (Zhivkov, like Al Capone, was nailed for 'economic crimes' only, and subsequently jailed for seven years.)

Instead of shunning Maxwell as a crony of the deposed dictator, the new-ish regime welcomed him as their pet capitalist, as he knew they would. Andrei Lukanov, the new Prime Minister, made himself available, and Maxwell went into the same spiel he had tried out on Carlos Menem. He wanted his own bank (initially postulated as the 'Maxwell Bank of Bulgaria', no less), a partnership in an existing bank, and the opportunity to redistribute Bulgaria's enormous international debt, at the advantageous rates of interest he claimed to be renowned for.

Lukanov had been a close aide of Zhivkov's. Maxwell had courted him assiduously during the last years of the old regime, even inviting the Bulgarian to his home-cum-headquarters at Headington Hill Hall in Oxford. Lukanov's name appears in Maxwell's personal telephone directory. The assumption was that Lukanov would take over after Zhivkov's removal, which came to pass; and though Lukanov actually lasted only nine months in office, there is evidence that a good deal of economic manoeuvring went on during that period. Dimitar Popov, Prime Minister in an interim Bulgarian government that took over in December 1991, just after Maxwell's death, has repeatedly asserted that two billion dollars of foreign reserves vanished during Lukanov's tenure. Another of Maxwell's telephone contacts in Bulgaria, Milko Balev, was sentenced to two years' imprisonment for violating foreign currency restrictions.

Both Dimitar Popov and Belcho Antonov Belchev, who was Trade Minister under both Communism and the purported 'Socialist' government of Lukanov, have given their versions of Maxwell's involvement in these complicated times. Belchev was specifically brought in to discuss financial plans for Bulgaria with Maxwell. Their first meeting occurred late in 1989, under Mladenov's Presidency. Maxwell showed off photographs of meetings with George Bush and Gorbachev, and announced that he was travelling on to Israel. Rather than objecting to the crassness of this approach, the Bulgarians seem to have accepted it as Maxwell's shorthand version of letters of credit. He saw Bulgaria, he explained, as a future bridge between East and West, and indeed between the Christian tradition and Islam. (As such, Bulgaria became a giant projection of himself, serving both sides, learning from both, and earning from both.)

Among his practical proposals was a business school which had been on his agenda since well back into Zhivkov's time. Another business-academy building project was an updating of an old scheme generated by the Culture Committee of Ludmila Zhivkova. 'Realisation of the vital necessity to live according to the supreme laws of truth and beauty' had turned into a forcing-house for Maxwellian business ethics. Printing, as usual, had been targeted as a buy-up: Maxwell had his eye on the new state printing-house, which he saw as a possible centre for all printing in Eastern Europe, including Greece. How much money Maxwell actually did introduce into the Bulgarian economy has yet to be established. Belchev says that Maxwell invested $5 million 'in agricultural production'. The same source says that Maxwell, pending the establishment of the Maxwell Bank, or the European Bank of Bulgaria, as it more seductively became, tried to take a 20 per cent interest in the Bank of Agricultural Credit, but his money was returned. Nicholas Davies records that a Bulgarian antibiotics company was bought by Maxwell on behalf of Scitex, an Israeli concern in which Maxwell had bought an interest in mid-January 1989.[1] A report in the Bulgarian newspaper *Trud* has confirmed that as much as $5.2 million was invested 'through the Business Bank in the Combinate for Antibiotics in the town of Razgrad'. (The same report suggests Maxwell had ambitions to acquire further pharmaceutical plants in Sofia and Stanke Dimitrov, and that these acquisitions were serving a co-ordinated, secret agenda connected with military applications of Scitex's products.) But this time, Maxwell's fellow directors at Scitex blew the whistle, and again, the money was returned to the bidder. His bold propositional technique was meeting with the standard quota of rebuffs.

Belchev reports – it is scarcely a surprise – that Maxwell wanted to manage Bulgaria's foreign debt. In Belchev's opinion, Maxwell knew that 'as an adviser he would be able to control the politics.' This is a pretty accurate interpretation of Maxwell's

---

[1] Just over a month later, an MGN press release announced, 'Scitex returns to profit'. Maxwell disposed of the company as part of his general sell-off of 1991: the deal went unrecorded in his press releases, even though he had made a profit of some 800 per cent on the deal.

use of the term 'adviser'. As Maxwell told *Playboy*, 'It is not my business to run governments. I let it be known how I feel. I give advice.' But in Bulgaria, Maxwell expected his advice to tally with the way the government was run. It was the closest he ever came to enjoying the sensation of real political power. His advice to Lukanov during 1990 included a programme of co-operation with the opposition parties; but Bulgarians like Lukanov were watching developments in the Soviet Union, and wondering whether a weakening of centralised power would serve their short-term interests, particularly in economic matters.

Maxwell must have taken this point, because in the free elections of June 1990, which were monitored closely by representatives of the democratic West, the Communists actually won – with the support of Robert Maxwell. While nominally supplying both sides with material and know-how, in the name of democratic choice, he had sent out two of his staff to advise the Communists on their election strategy. As with Solidarity and Jaruzelski almost a decade before, Maxwell preferred the central despot, with whom he could deal comprehensively on all issues, to the amorphous and sluggish people's democracy, which could give him neither quick decisions nor guarantees of their permanence.

Maxwell already enjoyed messianic status in Sofia – and enjoyed enjoying it. Three days after the June election, his birthday came round. At his party in Oxford, Nicholas Davies reports, he was given a mock coronation as 'King of Bulgaria', and wore a T-shirt bearing that legend. His 'subjects', meanwhile, were about to endure some extremely tense months, culminating in a general strike, and the withdrawal of Lukanov. The United Democratic Front finally overcame the Communists in a second election. Dimitar Popov (one of several prominent Bulgarian figures bearing that name) took over the leadership. Maxwell arrived, Popov says, 'with his ideas and a very strong will'. They talked for a whole night. Popov was aware that Maxwell had already played a role in Bulgaria's economic development. The nation had received $12 billion in credits during the Eighties, according to Popov, and Maxwell had been an intermediary in this arrangement. He did this 'in the shade, so to speak'. The outcome, in the former Prime

Minister's view, has merely been the deepened dependence of Bulgaria on the West.

All features of Maxwell's well-known agenda resurfaced in Bulgaria, including his relatively blameless agitation on behalf of Jews emigrating to Israel. The logistics of the process had proved difficult, in that the Arab nations had threatened to apply oil boycotts to countries aiding the passage of the Soviet Jews. Bulgaria was vulnerable in this regard; but the Jewish lobby, with Maxwell as its most persistent representative, did persuade Popov to make one airport, and the port of Varna, available for their purpose. No money changed hands here: it was a humanitarian effort. Popov, who as head of state enjoyed the advantage of seeing Bulgaria's collected intelligence reports on the British visitor, believes that Maxwell had favoured Bulgaria all along because he himself had been born in a Slavonic country, and because Bulgaria 'had always been good to the Jews'.

Maxwell's economic clout remained to be demonstrated to the new generation of Bulgarian politicians. He did manage to satisfy them, though the evidence he produced, as ever, took the form not of ledgers and certificates, but of sheer personal influence. Nobody believed more fervently than Maxwell in what has become known as 'networking' – the improvised abutting of contacts. In the early weeks of 1991, Maxwell put Bulgaria back in touch with Moscow. A large consignment of Bulgarian exports had not been admitted to the Soviet Union. Popov credits Maxwell with arranging the meeting between himself and Gorbachev which set aside the problem. Both Maxwell and Popov then attended the World Economic Forum in Davos, Switzerland, in February 1991. Hans-Dietrich Genscher gave a lecture on new developments in European policy. Within half an hour, Popov says, the Bulgarian delegation had an appointment with Genscher, arranged through Maxwell. In forty-seven minutes, the former Bulgarian Prime Minister relates, they 'talked away forty-seven years. It was a very important psychological moment'. It must also have provided Maxwell with a moment of supreme satisfaction. Davos was a kind of political heaven, where no unimportant people were visible.

an Robert Maxwell, publisher and traveller: a 1952 studio portrait
by Baron.

ir Charles Hambro in 1953, at the
Bishopsgate bank from which he
unded Maxwell.

Robert Maxwell MP, dressed
for travel, leaves his Pergamon
Press office in 1968.

Inside Maxwell House: the bedroom and dining-room of the global
communications emperor.

Peter Jay, shortly before he joined the Mirror Group as Maxwell's Chief of Staff.

Mikhail Lyubimov,
who tried to recruit
Maxwell for the
KGB in London.

Leonid Zamyatin,
former Ambassador
to London, and a
frequent visitor to
the Maxwell
penthouse.

Vladimir Kryuchkov, head of the KGB, with whom Maxwell
conversed in Hungarian.

Working on Gorbachev's problem of debt and missing aid, Maxwell finally has access to the Soviet leader.

Playing the Saviour: Maxwell displays the regenerated *Daily News* in Manhattan, spring 1991.

The MV *Lady Ghislaine*, named after Maxwell's youngest daughter, and now sailing under another name.

The stateroom of the *Lady Ghislaine*: Maxwell's last resting-place in life.

The Maxwell tomb on the Mount of Olives.

There was more of the same to come. Genscher, during the meeting, had advised the Bulgarians that they should consult Karl Pöhl of the Bundesbank. They withdrew to the lobby, where Maxwell was, and told him their news. It was then that Maxwell demonstrated the usefulness of the freelance contact man, for at that moment, Pöhl himself happened to appear, coming down the stairs in his skiing clothes. Maxwell persuaded him to postpone the skiing, and Pöhl talked to the Bulgarians for two hours instead. Popov comments that, 'Maxwell was the man who put his foot in the door and let in the Bulgarians.' Even the humblest citizen of Sofia was aware of Maxwell, for his name appeared on the shirts of the local football team, Slavia, which he had sponsored with a six-figure sum. Here as at home, football offered Maxwell a way of talking to the people in what he considered to be their language.

But his main concern was to plug Bulgaria into the Western economic circuit, and this he did tirelessly, establishing the country in the world community, former Prime Minister Popov says, in a matter of twelve months. Maxwell initiated talks on his government's behalf (Popov's government, that is, although some confusion is understandable) with the International Monetary Fund, the World Bank, and Jacques Delors, the European Commissioner. Through Maxwell, Bulgaria was also enabled to make its first visit to NATO, and to engage in a four-hour meeting with its Secretary-General, Manfred Wörner. Maxwell remained in the background once such discussions were under way.

But some of his activities belonged to another, darker background. His closest Bulgarian contact was not a post-Zhivkov government member at all, but Zhivkov's own official deputy, Ognian Doynov. Preferment came early to Doynov, who was appointed Deputy Prime Minister for the first time in 1974, before his fortieth birthday, and took the job again in 1986; but then Doynov was Zhivkov's nephew. He was also a skilled freelance operator, with a seeming preference for working outside the confines of Bulgaria itself. So close to Maxwell was Doynov that in 1990 he went to work for him. Belcho Belchev remembers taking the telephone call from Maxwell in which he asked permission for Doynov, who had latterly been Bulgarian Ambassador to Norway and Denmark, to be appointed his economic adviser on African affairs. Zhivkov was still in place at that time, and both he and Petur Mladenov, the Foreign Minister, were consulted about the appointment.

Maxwell's keenness to line up Doynov as a general Bulgarian fixer would be understandable, but the nomination of Africa is curious. Maxwell was normally scornful of black Africa and its possibilities, and made only one publicly visible gesture in its direction, when in 1988 he agreed to meet President Daniel Arap Moi of Kenya to discuss the building there of the biggest skyscraper in Africa. According to Nicholas Davies, however, an anonymous call came through – to Davies – to relay information 'from the Israelis' that the KGB planned to assassinate Maxwell on the Kenya trip. The upshot of this incident was that Davies made the trip alone, knowing even less about the project in hand than David Kimche had known about Maxwell's publishing matters in Moscow. It goes without saying that the African skies remained unscraped, though a former *Mirror* employee does suggest that some laundered money was washed in the direction of Kenya at that time.

So much for Maxwell's personal experience of Africa. No official activities of his are listed for Mozambique or Angola. But Ognian Doynov, certainly, had an expertise in those areas, having been the head of a Bulgarian commission distributing economic and other aid to Communist-inclined countries in the Third World. Indeed, Doynov's talents for processing funds appear to have been almost limitless, if Bulgarian press speculation is to be believed. After Maxwell's death, while Doynov was in Vienna, resisting extradition to his homeland on charges of various economic crimes against the state, his compatriots were engaged on the still uncompleted task of tracing his involvement in the disappearance of Bulgarian funds. One piece of documentary evidence cited[1] was a secret document between Zhivkov and Maxwell 'for the formation of joint ventures on the territory of England and Western Europe'.

[1] By Grigor Lillov, in a three-part article called 'The War for the Secret Safety Vaults': *Trud*, February 1–3, 1994.

Dated January 1987, the document is said to carry the word 'Agree', written on it by Todor Zhivkov. Thus approval was given for the buying of second-hand machines and equipment for the creation of what might be called Maxwello-Bulgarian industrial plants in the West.

Another document, which is said to exist in triplicate, marked 'Top Secret', instructs the Bulgarian secret services 'to co-ordinate and control the movement of money abroad'. Specifically, the dollar incomes from the newly created secret firms were to be placed in bank accounts in the West, controlled by the Bulgarian Ministry of the Interior. These agreements are said to have been drawn up by three men: the Minister for Foreign Trade, the Chairman of the State Committee for Research and Technology – and the Chairman of the Economic Council, Deputy Prime Minister Ognian Doynov, whose expertise in bankrolling Bulgarian projects in the Communist Third World will obviously have served him well in the implementation of these plans. What they amounted to was an excuse for moving money. Within a few simple pages, Zhivkov's men had created a perfect conduit for the exportation of currency held within Bulgaria itself.

The new schemes were put into practice at once. The Party-State Commission for Scientific-Technical Policy reportedly passed a resolution on 19 January 1987, approving a start-up fund of $100 million. Exactly a month later, another government decision, signed this time by Lukanov, set up a Special Business Directory at the Ministry of Foreign Trade. It was during the following year, 1988, that Robert Maxwell's interest in Bulgaria was suddenly seen to blossom. The new state mechanisms began working for him immediately. According to Bulgarian research, 'Resolution No. 63 of the Council of Ministers', dated 27 April 1988, provided for the investment of $2 million from Bulgaria's foreign currency reserve in European stocks and shares. The enabling British company was London and Bishopsgate International Investment.

This was a newly expanded version of a Robert Maxwell private company formerly known as Headington Investments. According to the Bulgarian Foreign Trade Bank, the $2 million payment came in the form of a loan, which was repaid after two years; but Bulgarian insiders say that the dates cited by the bank for the transaction are holidays on which it could scarcely have been accomplished. London and Bishopsgate International Investment, incidentally, grew hugely. According to Tom Bower, there was initially $20 million in its 1988 fund. By Maxwell's death three years later, it was managing almost £500 million, and was the instrument through which Maxwell had abstracted a sum not much less than that from his employees' pension funds.

It would appear, therefore, that Ognian Doynov was engaged by Maxwell for his expertise in moving money. Certainly within Bulgaria itself, Doynov today is regarded as responsible for the export of the so-called 'Red Money' amassed in Zhivkov's time. But the idea that Maxwell wanted Doynov for his African connections may not have been a complete fiction. Bulgaria has taken a particular interest in Mozambique and Angola, and has been an important supplier of arms in both areas of Southern Africa. The demand for *matériel* had been considerable: by the time a peace treaty was signed in 1992, the war in Mozambique had been going on for seventeen years. Naturally, the Bulgarian weaponry went to the Marxist movements in these struggles, as part of colossal Soviet inputs of military aid ($2 billion worth into Angola in 1985 alone). In these transactions, the Bulgarian government ran its own supply-lines, so that there would have been no need for Maxwell's intervention.

But there is evidence that Bulgarian-made armaments were also supplied to South African-backed movements on the other side. A Bulgarian career diplomat who must remain anonymous claims that such arms did turn up in South Africa during the Eighties, and that Maxwell was involved. It was again a question of 'networking': Maxwell had put the Special Defence Department in the Secretariat of Bulgaria's Central Committee (and through them the state import-export agency, Kintex) in touch with his own contacts in South Africa. There had been no direct profit in it for Maxwell himself, though the favour was returned in terms of unspecified business deals. If discovered, the diplomat adds, this contribution to the South African effort would of course have been regarded as extremely scandalous.

The same informant states that there were arms talks with Israel, most actively 'in the late Eighties and early Nineties'. According to his recollection they concerned armoured cars and Kalashnikov rifles, up-to-date models of which were manufactured by Bulgaria under licence from the Soviet Union. Oddly enough, however, the modernisation of the Bulgarian armaments industry in the later Eighties took place not under the Soviet aegis, but through Western co-operation, notably via consignments of machinery from Japan, the United States, and Britain. Dimitar Popov specifically alludes to these heavy engineering supplies, and identifies Maxwell as one of the intermediaries arranging the necessary credits.

The Bulgarian diplomat recalls the arms negotiations with Israel as difficult. The Bulgarians wanted nothing but a profitable transaction, but the Israelis wanted to draw political conclusions from the fact that a deal had been done. 'The profit,' comments the diplomat, 'does not pay for the politics.' Among the political matters to which Israel doubtless wished to draw attention was Bulgaria's profitable habit of supplying arms to the PLO. The Israelis may also have sought to make future business conditional upon Bulgaria's toning down its involvement in the international drugs trade, a principal activity of Kintex, all of whose import-export business was operated by the Bulgarian Security Service, the KDS.

So notorious had Bulgaria become as an international supplier both of drugs and of processing equipment that Robert Maxwell had been obliged to raise the matter with Todor Zhivkov, during an update of his 'Leaders of the World' interview in 1985. 'We in Britain,' intoned Maxwell, 'are very troubled about the availability of heroin. It is believed the illegal heroin in smuggled through Bulgaria. What step is the Government taking to stop this traffic?' Zhivkov replied that 'the Bulgarian connection' had lately become a favourite theme of Western propaganda. 'I'm beginning to think,' he smoothed, 'that, apart from the campaign's political motives, the bosses responsible for drug smuggling via other routes are deliberately distracting the attention of the authorities and public opinion of the Western countries.' It is not difficult to read into this reply Zhivkov's threat to make some embarrassing disclosures about 'other routes', if he and his white-powder black market were not left alone. Eventually, Zhivkov did cosmetically dismantle the Kintex operation, only to replace it with another KDS-run agency called Globus (coincidentally an appellation not unknown as a surname in Israel).

The Israeli arms connection in Bulgaria runs oddly parallel to what became known, in the West, as the Irangate scandal. The war between Iran and Iraq had continued, at different pitches of intensity, throughout the Eighties. Some observers in both East and West saw it as a not unwelcome conflict, as long as it could be contained. The military dictatorship in Iraq and the religious tyranny in Iran might well fight each other to a standstill, if provided with appropriate supplies of weaponry. International embargoes on such supplies were in force, but they merely drove up the price of *matériel*, increased the risks of dealing in it, and swelled the profit-margins of the dealer. As became clear at the end of 1986, the United States had been selling arms to Iran, via Israel, as part of a deal for the release of American hostages in Tehran. Profits received from the deal were covertly passed on by Colonel Oliver North to the Contras in Nicaragua, whose official funding had been withdrawn by the US Congress. The scheme was first exposed in a Beirut magazine. President Reagan at various times denied it, regretted it, and found he had forgotten about it.

Whether Israel's approach to the Bulgarian arms manufacturers was an attempt to replace the American supply-line is difficult to determine. Bulgaria, after all, had her own arrangements with Iran. But Prime Minister Shamir's perennial desire to distance Israel from the overpowering influence of the USA had been ill-served by the Irangate approach, which brought his country first into conspiratorial collusion, and then international opprobrium, with American partners. If he had some new customer for arms, it is not surprising that he sought the product of Bulgaria, as part of his East–West balancing policy. (Shamir had some small personal inclination towards Bulgaria, since his wife was Bulgarian-born, and made an unpublicised visit to the country in 1986.) Belcho Belchev confirms that arms customers would have been welcome in the mid-Eighties, because 'the market in arms was quite low' at that point. As for Maxwell, he never mentioned the arms industry in Belchev's hearing: but Belchev regards the possibility of arms sales to Israel as 'not fantastical, in fact, quite likely'.

Progress was certainly made in other areas, for Israel and Bulgaria signed a trade co-operation agreement in 1988, and exchanged Parliamentary delegations as an earnest of goodwill. That was the year when Maxwell's interest in Bulgaria suddenly increased – and also the time when, according to our Bulgarian diplomatic source, the arms talks with Israel reached their 'most active' level. The holder of the Order of Stara Planina, First Class, had done his best for both countries. In helping to squirrel away 'Red Money', Maxwell was taking his cut. Israel and Bulgaria were doing business again.

Moreover, Maxwell and arms had never been mentioned in the same breath in Sofia. But he was not to be so lucky back at home.

# CHAPTER SEVEN

# Kalashnikovs for Christmas

No reliable estimate can be made of the amount spent around the world in a given year on armaments; but it is a fair bet that the trade divides fairly evenly between the official and the unrecorded deals. There are probably more ambitious incompetents and fiction-fed poseurs in this line of business – or claiming to be in it – than in any other. It is an adolescent playground in which some of the players are serious. 'Big deals, as far as I've ever understood,' says Nicholas Davies, 'are always done government to government.' It depends, of course, what you mean by big.

'I, as I said at the time,' Davies declares, 'have never been involved and I have never bought or sold a single plane or bullet or ever been involved in anything like that.' There is of course no need for Davies ever to have bought anything – what use does any individual have for a fighter-plane, or a consignment of assault rifles? The art of arms dealing is to do it without ever being 'in it'. I have before me a photocopy of a letter in which a Trust registered in Guernsey presents a pro-forma invoice for 50,000 M16A1 rifles. The signatory assures the addressee (a Mr Nicholas Davies) that his organisation 'acts in this matter only in a fiduciary capacity. It has not sought, nor will it seek the above-named products and hereby disclaims knowledge of said products.' This is the way to do it. Effectively the message is that, 'if the objects exist for which we present this invoice, we have never heard of them.' The mask of innocence is transparent, but it is there.

The case of Maxwell, Davies and their common interest in Israel presents difficulties curiously reminiscent of those obtaining at 10 Rillington Place in the early Fifties, where the murderer Christie pursued his grotesque career. Verdicts of murder had already been brought in against his lodger, Timothy Evans, so that when Christie was later convicted, we were required to believe that two murderers had been operating independently in the same household. Some people still think that was the truth of the matter, in spite of the posthumous pardon accorded to Evans. In the case of Maxwell House, we have a Publisher and his travelling equerry, both connected in one way or another with Israel, though with different motives for wishing to profit from the connection. Can we convince ourselves that each operated in happy ignorance of the other's activities? It is easiest to look backwards from the end of the affair, when Maxwell and Davies were – almost – conjoined in their efforts to clear their names.

At the time of Maxwell's death, the law firm of Biddle & Co. was preparing to resist libel suits brought by Maxwell under the aegis of Mirror Group Newspapers, and, by Davies individually, against the American writer Seymour Hersh. In his book, *The Samson Option*, Hersh had stated that:

> Nicholas Davies, one of publisher Robert Maxwell's senior editors on the London *Daily Mirror*, had been involved with Israel in the mid-Eighties in the selling of arms to the Iranian government of Ayatollah Ruhollah Khomeini.

(This is Hersh's own précis of the matter, given in an Afterword to the paperback edition of his book.) Of the evidence that would have been brought to court, David Hooper of Biddle & Co. now says this: 'There were discussions of sales worth millions of dollars relating to F-104 fighter aircraft, C-130s, AK-47s, TOW missiles and Stingers.' The Lockheed C-130, incidentally, is the transport plane more familiarly known to Britons as the Hercules, and the AK-47 is the familiar Russian assault rifle (now superseded by the AK-74) commonly called the Kalashnikov, after its inventor. 'What seems to have been the position,' Hooper continues, 'was that Maxwell was involved with the Israelis, and that a lot of this equipment was going towards the Iraq–Iran War. And the money being spent on arms was absolutely massive, you had armies of a million on each side. Seven years of war, and Maxwell wanted to get his snout in the trough.'

With a delicacy he did not display at the dinner table, however, Maxwell withheld the organ from direct contact with the receptacle; but he remained a very interested party in the background.

Amid the brouhaha of Maxwell's demise, Nicholas Davies did not pursue his personal interest against Hersh and his book. 'At the time,' he says today, 'I just thought, well, it's my fifteen seconds[1], and it'll all go away, and it all did.' But while any part of Robert Maxwell's extraordinary life remains mysterious, it is doubtful whether Nicholas Davies's very curious behaviour during the Eighties will be allowed to stand unchallenged.

> When all these allegations were made [he insists] not one iota of proof ever emerged of anything actually happening or taking place at all, not since the day the allegations were first laid in the Hersh book. And I must say to you that I cannot remember Maxwell ever being involved in any deals like that, that I ever heard about or read about in any faxes – and I would see his faxes whenever we were overseas. You know, one would rip them off the machine and take them over to Bob, and have a quick look as to what was going on in life.

Presumably not every fax Maxwell received came in English, however. Even 'Sneaky' Davies (his office nickname) could have been linguistically bypassed – though as we know, Maxwell was always a 'telephone terrorist' at heart.

In resisting the world's investigations, Davies enjoys one lasting advantage: the most voluble witness against him is, at best, a compulsive embroiderer of the truth. Ari Ben-Menashe's book *Profits of War* has yet to be taken on by a British publisher. Every latter-day article on him reports that he took a lie-detector test in

---

[1]Meaning 'my fifteen minutes of fame', as per Andy Warhol's dictum.

America and registered a spectacularly calamitous failure. And yet his novelistic tendencies are interwoven with a worldwide skein of provable fact. The testimony of obviously innocent third parties corroborates a good deal of what he has said about Davies, and there is documentary evidence to support it, too. Typically, some of the documentary evidences supplied by Ben-Menashe himself, and printed in facsimile at the back of his book, are among the more unsatisfactory items on the record.

Ben-Menashe's contention is that Nicholas Davies 'had been recruited by Mossad in the Seventies'. The connection had allegedly been a former SAS officer who had specialised in recruiting mercenaries from a base in Lafayette, Louisiana.[1] As Foreign Editor, Davies was known as a traveller, a payer of alimony to his first wife, and as something of a sybarite, whose pleasures tended towards the expensive. Israeli intelligence targeted him, says Ben-Menashe in effect, as a man with both motive and opportunity to serve their cause. Davies, in his own book, *The Unknown Maxwell*, does not even give Ben-Menashe credit for making a competent approach: 'Because it transpired Menashe was not looking for me but for a namesake of mine . . .' But the admission that Menashe was actively looking for somebody is interesting in itself.

Ben-Menashe says he met Davies in 1983, which was one cause of Maxwell's extreme wrath when Hersh's allegations were made public. Maxwell took over the Mirror Group in the summer of 1984. 'My name was dragged in quite improperly,' Maxwell told the BBC, 'because I happen to be a well-known figure across the world . . . It brings my name in for a period of time when I wasn't there.' True, Ben-Menashe offers no evidence for his claim that Davies, even then, was 'close to Robert Maxwell, who at that time did not yet own the *Daily Mirror*.' But Davies's book saves us all the trouble of agonising over this. He relates that there was a series of inconclusive meetings with his new Israeli contact, during which Ben-Menashe supplied enough Israeli information to ingratiate himself with Davies;

[1] It is known to the author, from another source, that Lafayette was a centre for such recruitment.

but that 'after a year or so he told me that there was an arms dealer in London, who, he understood, was providing arms to the IRA'. Menashe arranged a meeting with these people 'in the summer of 1984': the very time of Maxwell's Mirror Group take-over. So the Davies–Menashe conversations did not turn to hardware until Maxwell was, indeed, 'on the watch', as he put it to the BBC, at the *Daily Mirror*.

Davies, at all events, went to work for the Israelis, Ben-Menashe states, using his mobility as a foreign correspondent. He contacted such dealers and suppliers of arms as the Israelis deemed suitable for each order received from Iran. The company name Davies used was Ora, the name of a woman Ben-Menashe had known since 1979 and would marry in 1988. Examples of notepaper show 'Ora Ltd' in 1984, and 'Ora Group' in 1989. But that is not all they show. In an Appendix to his book, Ben-Menashe reprints a letter dated 29 December 1984, and sent to Mr Ran Yegnes (an addressee not identified in the body of the book) at Montefiory [sic] St., Petah-Tivka, in Israel. The letter, in five single-sentence, numbered paragraphs, is a request for a quotation for AK-47 ammunition-magazines. It is identified by Ben-Menashe's caption as: 'Letter from Nicholas Davies (note that he signs the letter "Davis"). . .' It was brazen of Ben-Menashe to draw attention to this, especially when he fails simultaneously to note that the full 'signature' (which is typed) reads 'Nicolas Davis'.

This must be one of the very few letters in preservation where the sender makes two mistakes in the spelling of his own name.[1] In paragraph 1, moreover, the brand-names 'Bakelite' and 'Kalashnikov' are also misspelt. Over the page is another, rather faintly and patchily reproduced document ('also signed "Davis"', Menashe's caption eagerly points out) which confirms the ability and willingness of the sender to supply to a recipient in Tel Aviv some 5,000 rifles, five million rounds of regular 7.62 39 mm ammunition, 200 mortars, 1,000 anti-personnel mines, and so on. Again there are spelling mistakes Davies would not have made ('transferrable', 'bill of laiding') and Americanisms

---

[1] And as the present author can testify, if there is one name a Davies is unlikely to sign, it is 'Davis'.

likewise ('favor'). This time, the typed signature reads 'Nicholas Davis, UK Consultant' – a partially corrected version.

Unless a double-bluff of surprising sophistication is being carried out here, Ben-Menashe is merely impersonating Davies in these particular documents. However, he is also using Davies's known home address of the time, in Becmead Avenue, Streatham, together with its telephone number, as the commercial address of Ora Ltd, at least on the earlier document. A later letter signed by Ben-Menashe himself, and directed to the President of Sri Lanka, similarly uses Davies's next London home as the accommodation address of what has now become Ora Group. Although there are no spelling mistakes here, the text of the letter comes in Ben-Menashe's rather approximate English. He spells his own name correctly. Again the notepaper is interesting: the back-to-front way the address is set out along its bottom margin ('london, 1 trafalgar avenue, tel: 01–231xxxx', with the numbers all run together, and no postal district) strongly suggests that this was a styling devised by Ben-Menashe and not Davies. In his book, Davies is only too pleased to agree: 'Without permission, Menashe had seemingly had a letterhead printed and continued to use my new address.'

But if he did, people will have written to him there; and Davies claims he found out about Menashe's usurpation of his domicile only when Seymour Hersh's book *The Samson Option* appeared in 1991. How does one use an address for outgoing letters only? Had no incoming mail at all appeared for Ari Ben-Menashe, then, at 'his' boldly displayed Trafalgar Avenue address? That, and Davies's ignorance of the whole manoeuvre, takes some believing. Besides, a copy exists of a letter addressed to a correctly spelt Davies at Trafalgar Avenue, and naming both him and Menashe as parties in the same venture. The sender, a gentleman in Tucson, Arizona, writes to insist upon an agreed payment of $250,000 which, he says, was to have been supplied to him 'by you and Mr Ari Ben-Menashe' for the setting up of a communications company 'serving clients of your indication'.

There was an independent witness to Davies's relationship with Ben-Menashe – at least, she made herself independent as soon as she discovered what was going on. Janet Fielding had become Nicholas Davies's second wife in 1982. He was forty-five at the time, and she twenty-nine. She had come to England from Australia in 1978, working as an actress in a troupe whose work highlighted the culture, and political sufferings, of the Aboriginal Australian people. It was not long before she met Davies, whose views on South Africa seemed pleasingly compatible, although Ms Fielding became worried about his finances. His divorce had depleted his assets severely; he was paying for the education of two daughters; and he had lost money when he split with a business partner over their joint management of Viscon Oceanics, a company that manufactured underwater lighting and television equipment for North Sea oil-rigs (and, it is believed, for the Ministry of Defence). In spite of these difficulties, Davies was a pony-owning polo player, and ran a Porsche which he said had belonged to the racing driver James Hunt. At the bank near his family home in the Midlands, he was of course heavily overdrawn. It was when Davies promised to give up polo in 1982 that Ms Fielding agreed to marry him.

In an awakening property market, they were able to take on larger premises, moving house twice shortly after the marriage, and arriving at Becmead Avenue in 1984. Ms Fielding's career was thriving: for three years, she starred as one of Dr Who's best-remembered 'assistants' in the BBC's science-fiction serial. Her husband's *Daily Mirror* career, however, continued to run in counterpoint to a series of failed private schemes, ranging from the publishing of a magazine specifically devised to sell to the ticket-queues at Wimbledon to an extremely grandiose scheme which involved the buying up of ship-building yards. Janet Fielding, during this period, was coming into contact with some people she did not like. One she has independently named is Tony Pearson, whom Davies said he had met in the Middle East: he had done, Davies said, 'bits and pieces in British Intelligence.'

Pearson, interestingly, is named by Ari Ben-Menashe in his book *Profits of War*. In fact Pearson is the recruiter of mercenaries, the ex-SAS man named by Menashe as having formed the 'connection' between Davies and Mossad. Janet Fielding was told that Pearson was just somebody Davies was helping through a bad patch. She found this difficult to square with her impression that, in Pearson's presence, Davies seemed nervous. Pearson died in 1984 of a series of strokes, a manner of death which struck Davies's former wife as unusual for a man in his middle years.

It was in the summer of 1984 that the subject of Ari Ben-Menashe came up at Becmead Avenue. Davies told his wife that he had met an ex-army officer from Jordan, and that Ben-Menashe had also been present. Ben-Menashe claimed the Jordanian was a compulsive and unlucky gambler, a trait which the Israelis had reportedly exploited to make him dependent on them. A few weeks later, Davies took his wife and a couple of friends to a London casino, where they watched the process in action: the Jordanian quickly lost a three-figure sum at blackjack. Ben-Menashe, in his book, names the Jordanian officer – who in return, it should be said, is currently suing him in the United States. Ben-Menashe's version is that the first tripartite meeting, with himself, Davies and the Jordanian present, had happened in 1983. This may well be right; it is quite possible that the meeting Davies described to his wife had indeed happened the previous year. The reason why Davies was belatedly bringing up the subject of Ben-Menashe now (and demonstrating the truth of one of his stories by offering the spectacle of the gambling Jordanian) was that the Israeli was about to make a severe impact on the Davies household.

Davies's announcement that he and Ben-Menashe were embarking on arms deals together came as a particularly nasty shock to Janet Fielding, since she held the arms trade in particular contempt. Davies offered some sweetening excuses – that arms would be provided to the suffering Tamils, for example, and that he and Ben-Menashe had come to the understanding that the PLO and the IRA were out of bounds. In a rather loathsome but professionally interesting comment, Ben-Menashe remarks of Davies, in *Profits of War*, that 'He seemed anxious to please Janet, and I got the impression he was afraid of losing her. From a purely mercenary point of view this was good; it made him vulnerable.' As for payment, Davies's wife recalls that the commission would be subject to a five-way split. Apart from the two principals in London, a South American arms manufacturer, a Jewish banker in New York, and an Israeli government figure were also to benefit. In his book, Ben-Menashe alleges that

Davies received, in total, a seven-figure sum from Israel 'over the years'. He mentions three offshore banking destinations where the money was supposedly lodged. These allegations were investigated by the Inland Revenue and no action was taken.

Ben-Menashe's impressions of the Davies marriage were formed, he says, over lunch at Becmead Avenue. The occasion is recalled with particular displeasure by Janet Fielding, whose provision of kosher food went unappreciated. She felt an immediate aversion to the visitor, by whom she sensed her husband was dominated. Even Nicholas Davies himself, in his own very sparse account of these events, admits that 'she took an instant dislike to him'. What Davies does not explain is why, in view of this, the friendship with Ben-Menashe continued at all. He does not claim that he himself had any special fondness for the Israeli visitor, or enjoyed his company, though he seems to have sympathised with, and even admired, his desire to make money. Davies gives no indication of what else was in the relationship for him – apart from the half-hearted suggestion that Menashe might bring him an arms-dealing scoop for the *Daily Mirror*. Davies does describe one meeting at which he was introduced to some arms dealers supposedly in contact with the IRA, but they were so obvious as to be incapable of involvement with anything so deadly. Ben-Menashe haggled with these individuals briefly about 20,000 AK-47 rifles, Davies reports, and that was that. The incident, he comments, 'put a question-mark over Ben-Menashe's credibility'.

Showing considerable patience, however, Davies continued to deal with the man. In his excitement he would tell his wife about deals he and Menashe were assembling, little though she wanted to hear. Lodged in Janet Fielding's memory is a mention of another AK-47 deal, allegedly for the American Christmas market – the incompatibility of the Kalashnikov with the season of goodwill stuck in her mind. She found herself taking telephone calls from America and Germany, and having to make it clear that she had no part in the arms discussions.

Early in 1985, Janet Fielding was rehearsing for an Alan Ayckbourn play that was to be taken to Stockholm. It was during those rehearsals, she recalls, that Davies revealed that his and Ben-Menashe's latest scheme was to try to sell eighty second-hand Israeli jet fighters to Iran. Such a plan could not claim the excuse of aiding an oppressed minority; but Davies allegedly remarked that Iraq was winning the war against Iran too easily, which was 'no good for anybody'. The charge of embargo-breaking was rebutted by Davies with the assertion that the deal would be going through the CIA in Paris. This was all too much for Janet Fielding. She departed for her eight-week season in Stockholm, and returned to leave what Davies calls a 'Dear John' letter. They never lived together again, and a decree absolute followed in 1988.

It is a curiosity of the case that Davies has written that a 'wily old decorator' suggested he change the front-door locks on the house at this point, and he agreed. If this is true, the back-door locks must have remained unchanged, because Janet Fielding was certainly able to re-enter the house several times in order to remove belongings, taking along a witness-companion in each case. On one of these visits, some luggage bearing El Al tags was found in a bedroom, while downstairs a folder full of papers proved to have the arms-dealing connection as its theme. Ms Fielding had never seen such documentary evidence before. She and her companion extracted a couple of specimen letters from the file, hurriedly photocopied them at a nearby library, and returned them to the folder. In a later statement, Davies was to deny that this process could have been undertaken, because of his changing of the locks; but since a number of different witnesses accompanied Ms Fielding to the house, and saw her use her own keys and customary burglar-alarm code, this seems a forlorn claim. If anything, what is suspicious about the whole story is that the papers were left so conspicuously lying about, as though in expectation of a visit. Davies is known to be a neater man that this – though there is nothing neat about Ari Ben-Menashe.

One of the photocopied letters (both of which happened to originate at addresses in Ohio) was destined to catch Davies out when, five years later, Seymour Hersh's *The Samson Option* was published, and the MPs Rupert Allason and George Galloway asked in the House for the connections between Maxwell, Davies and Mossad to be investigated. The more famous Ohio letter, dated 31 May 1985, still remains to be explained by Davies.

In 1991, when the story broke, he was in Harare, Rhodesia, reporting a Commonwealth Conference. The *Mirror*, Davies has written, faxed him the Ohio letter and asked for his explanation of it; but the letterhead 'CUSTOM CAMO', at the top of the single-sheet communication, was missed off, he explains, in the transmission. This caused his failure to recognise the document, and led to his issuing an immediate denial that he had ever been to Ohio (or to the USA at all in the year of 1985).

This explanation displays a number of faults. For example, if the top of the document was misaligned in the fax machine, in such a way that 'CUSTOM CAMO' did not appear at the top, it is all the more likely that a legend running along the *bottom* of the page, in extremely bold type, would have appeared. This legend reads: 'Specialising in POLICE and SWAT Equipment'[sic]. (The abbreviation 'SWAT' stands for 'Special Weapons and Tactics'.) Apparently neither this, nor the rest of Custom Camo's address (in Hutton Road, Smithfield, Ohio) jolted Davies's memory, and nor did the signature on the letter. It is in fact signed in three ways: 'BEN' (typed in capitals), 'CB Kaufman' (a signature) and 'Ben' again, written in ink. The letter, what's more ('Dear Nick'), suggests that there had already been communication between Mr Kaufman and Davies before, since Kaufman begins by saying that it was 'really great meeting you in person', a form of words used only by those who have been in touch before. The business content of this very short letter – only nine lines long – concerns an F-104 fighter-plane, the well-known Lockheed Starfighter. Clarence Ben Kaufman says that his 'two friends' have received 'two calls from Nigeria about the F-104' and are 'on there way over' [sic] to try and do a deal. 'Looks like a possible sale,' enthuses Mr Kaufman.

One weak line of defence briefly assayed by Davies in *The Unknown Maxwell* is that 'I never saw those letters from Ohio' – meaning presumably that, after Janet Fielding's departure, Ari Ben-Menashe was the one who opened the mail at Becmead Avenue. There is certainly no possibility that the 'Nick' addressed is Ben-Menashe adopting Davies's identity, since Kaufman usefully distinguishes between the two in his second and last paragraph, when he says he is 'looking forward to seeing Ari again soon'. Davies, sure enough, has subsequently admitted that it was Menashe who suggested that he called on the Kaufmans (Davies spells the name 'Kaufmann') while he was in the States. The reason for his trip, undertaken in the aftermath of his wife's escape from the marriage, was to 'study the Amish people', Davies states. One accepts that the Amish Mennonites, with their beards, buttonless dress and strict, luxury-free living may have 'fascinated' Davies; but not that, under the spell of the Amish, 'the Kaufmanns were forgotten'.

Why Davies denied meeting the Kaufmans – even going so far as to claim, rashly, that he had never been to Ohio, which was practically an invitation to investigative journalists to find a hole in his story – is admitted to be baffling even by those former colleagues of his who do not otherwise accept the likelihood of his participation in arms dealing. In *Maxwell's Fall*, Roy Greenslade, the former *Mirror* editor, has written of Davies:

> He never gave me a satisfactory answer, claiming he had been confused and hinting that his own paper had not dealt intelligently with him once the story broke ... I cannot understand why Davies lied, since he could have openly admitted meeting arms dealers and knowing Ben-Menashe very well without there being any proof of being an arms dealer himself.

Indeed, Davies could reasonably have clung throughout the controversy to the notion that he had been pursuing a story, in the belief that an international scoop was somewhere in the offing; but his energy in maintaining such a defence seems to have run out long ago.

Rupert Allason, one of the Members of Parliament who raised the Davies-Maxwell-Israel matter in the House, also talked directly to Davies. 'He was able to deny certain parts of evidence that had been produced by Ari Ben-Menashe on points of detail,' Allason reports, 'but the overall picture he made very little effort to deny, and really seemed to confirm quite a part of it.' Since then, Davies appears to have recovered a certain robustness. He now says: 'Why they should want to say it, I don't know. To be fair, maybe they have their reasons, they've got two people here whose names they can put in the frame because they want the other people who are really involved to remain in the background. I can't think of any other reason, because there was no truth in it.' (If this pattern of defence is familiar, it is because Todor Zhivkov had recourse to it when Maxwell fed him the question about Bulgaria's drug connections.)

More evidence linking Davies with efforts to trade in weapons has become available. He registers incomprehension when the names of Colonel O'Toole, or a company called FXC, are mentioned ('I'm afraid I have to plead ignorance') but they do remember him. Colonel Joseph O'Toole, according to his 'Armed Forces of the United States Report of Transfer or Discharge', entered the United States Air Force in January 1953, and left it in February 1972, his 'Character of Service' officially recorded as 'Honourable'. Documents emanating from FXC, a company located in Santa Ana, California, identify it as a four-part company: FXC Corporation, FXC International, FXC Europe, and Guardian Parachute. Joseph W. O'Toole is named as Managing Director of the Aircraft Sales Division of FXC International. He is also the individual identified by Seymour Hersh as the 'retired US Air Force Colonel who had done operational work for the CIA while on active duty.'

His CIA connection makes the frankness of O'Toole's testimony startling, but it is entirely consistent within itself. Both in the aftermath of Maxwell's death, and upon renewal of enquiries in 1995, Col. O'Toole has relayed testimony about his contacts with Davies and Ben-Menashe. These went on 'from 1987 through 1989'. The subject of all the interchanges was the sale, shipment and inspection of military hardware, and the banking arrangements such deals might require. There were occasions, Col. O'Toole has said, when both Davies and Ben-Menashe were on the phone at the same time. The aircraft and weapons offered for sale by Ben-Menashe were 'generally owned by the Israeli government'. Particular effort was expended upon a sale of C-130s (Hercules) from Israel to Iran in 1988–1989. Before that, the sale of AK-47s from the old USSR to 'several different countries' was negotiated. A consignment of Stinger missiles from Israel was also discussed. Ora Ltd was used as an 'offering company' on a number of projects.

FXC representatives met Ben-Menashe in person in a wide variety of locations, including Israel and South America. O'Toole says he never met Davies, but spoke to him on a number of occasions, both at his office and at his home. He also spoke to a woman he assumed to be Davies's wife, but could not remember her name (it is apparent from the dates that this was not Janet Fielding, who was in no sort of communication with Davies by 1987, or thereafter). Davies himself was vouched for, in the first instance, not only by Ben-Menashe, but by an associate of his, described by O'Toole as a 'former US agent presently living in France'. This individual is identified by Ben-Menashe in *Profits of War* as another needy but available candidate whom he 'picked up' to serve the Israeli arms business, and who did so, under an agreed alias.

A theme which runs through both Ben-Menashe's erratic book and the available documentation is the availability of C-130 (Hercules) transport planes. Menashe's claim is that they were leftovers from the Vietnam War, and that he personally travelled to Ho Chi Minh City and arranged to buy eighty-five of them. They were dismantled and shipped to various destinations for repair and refurbishment. Two of the destinations were Northwest Industries, of Canada, and the state of Israel – both of which are represented in documents relating to Ben-Menashe's subsequent attempts to dispose of the planes.

Joseph O'Toole provides a letter written, in November of 1988, to a senior figure in the Israeli Defence hierarchy. O'Toole's letter notifies its addressee that FXC is in receipt of official solicitations from Korea for eight Hercules, and from Canada for a further eight (cargo and tanker models). O'Toole declares that Northwest Industries, he himself, and the wonderfully named Mr Floyd Maybee are prepared to form an inspection team to visit the planes in Tel Aviv, as required by Canada. 'We await the data sheets promised by Mr Ari Ben-Menashe,' he adds. A communication to Ben-Menashe himself, two days later, fixes a scale of commissions which differ as to the model of plane, and the client country. In another paragraph, headed 'Cargo for K[orea] and C[anada]', O'Toole adds, 'This has to be very political and to protect your friend at home, we must send him some of their correspondence.' The suggestion is that this part of the C-130 distribution scheme was a freelance operation at the Israeli end.

As for Iran, a copy of the telex[1] is available which shows Ben-Menashe presenting Davies as a bona fide representative of Ora Group. Menashe (signing himself 'ABM' on the cable) states that Davies will have the authority to sign contracts in Iran, and gives passport details: these are not totally accurate – Davies's birth date is postponed by two years – but a passport of Davies's bearing this false date is recalled by Janet Fielding as having been in his possession in 1979, not long after she first met him. The passport to which Ben-Menashe refers is a brand-new one (issued just a week before, on 18 February 1987) but Davies's personal details, though faulty, naturally remain unchanged. Ben-Menashe's telex goes on to say, in its second, numbered paragraph, that two attempts have been made to present a cheque for $50,000 to the Iranian Embassy in Vienna, but that acceptance was denied 'due to their lack of information about the subject'. Menashe proposes that it be discussed 'while Mr Davies is in your country'.

Another telex, dated two days previously, suggests what this was all about. Signed 'ABM' and directed for the attention of His Excellency President of the Republic Representative of Imam Khomeini, Ayatollah Ali Akbar Rafsanjani' (whom Ben-Menashe says he first met in 1983), it confirms Ben-Menashe's ability to supply '4,000 Units CIF at a Price of . . . 13,800 US Dollars each.' (The 'CIF' here stands for 'cost, insurance and freight'.) This accords with a passage in *Profits of War* in which Menashe records a deal struck with an Iranian representative for 4,000 TOWs at $13,000 each: after which his Iranian contact asked for $800 to be added to the price of each missile. This premium was to be paid into a special account in Europe, as 'a special fund for the revolution, whatever that meant.' According to Ben-Menashe, three batches of 4,000 missiles were eventually sent off to Iran: '12,000 TOWs in all up to

---

[1] This telex, and others detailing Iranian contacts, are reproduced as Appendices to *Profits of War*, Ari Ben-Menashe's book, but were supplied independently for the present purposes.

1987'. This documentation would therefore refer to the last of these three batches.

Nicholas Davies has written (*The Unknown Maxwell*) 'that no arms dealing had ever taken place, though there was some circumstantial evidence'. A small fraction of this evidence did emerge just before the death of Robert Maxwell, when Seymour Hersh's book *The Samson Option* was published, and the MPs Allason and Galloway raised the matter in the House. Maxwell's first instinct was to defend Davies, though only to the extent that Davies's activities had been linked to his own. When asked by a BBC interviewer whether he was concerned that Davies, his Foreign Editor at the *Mirror*, had apparently allowed his house to be used by an alleged Israeli agent, Maxwell answered, 'That's a matter that you must ask Mr Davies: it's an event that took place when I was not on the watch at the *Daily Mirror*, I only took it over in the summer of '84.' This is of course a disingenuous reply, since Ben-Menashe demonstrably operated out of Davies's premises in years following 1984; and as we have seen, Davies's conversations with Ben-Menashe turned to the subject of arms – on his own admission – precisely at the moment of Maxwell's *Mirror* take-over.

'Furthermore,' Maxwell continued, with a more confident air, 'I support Mr Davies in his denial, simply because, when the matter came up some two years or so [ago][1], the American government made some enquiries of us, and in the end they took no action against Mr Davies, and from that I read and accept that he was innocent of whatever the allegations are.'

It would have been difficult for the American government to take action against Davies without revealing their own tacit approval of some murky deals. But in fact, the Americans did not abandon their enquiries: they pursued them to the extent of requesting John Pole, Maxwell's personal security man, and latterly the mastermind of his in-house bugging operation, to investigate Davies's extra-curricular activities. Davies was monitored by an assistant of Pole's, on behalf

---

[1]Maxwell simply says 'some two years or so.' Under the strain of the interview (by Martin Dawes, on 23 October 1991), his normally idiomatic English shows signs of strain throughout.

of the US Embassy Legal Department, and his contacts with Ben-Menashe and others were noted. Their report was submitted more than once to Maxwell, but he ignored it.

Only one incident brings Davies, Ben-Menashe and Maxwell into one room at the same time. Davies himself puts the date at May 1989. Ben-Menashe had come to him with a proposal for a book about the Irangate scandal, in which George Bush's involvement, and Israel's activity as a conduit for US arms to Iran throughout that period, would be demonstrated. Davies says he took Ben-Menashe to Maxwell's private offices, where the Israeli successfully outlined the book's thesis, but asked for a ridiculously huge advance. Maxwell told the pair to put together a summary which he would forward to Macmillan, his new publishing conglomerate. Davies, very reasonably, doubts whether he ever did. Maxwell's negative answer came back a fortnight later. (As *Profits of War*, Ben-Menashe's book did appear in the United States in 1992, published by the Sheridan Square Press of New York.)

Six months after that meeting, in November 1989, Ben-Menashe was arrested in California. The charge was one of conspiracy to sell three C-130s to Iran in contravention of the US arms embargo. The ostensible destination of the planes, according to the indictment, had been Brazil, and fraudulent 'end-user' certificates had allegedly been prepared to indicate this. (The five-sided deal which Janet Fielding remembered had included a Brazilian dealer.) Ben-Menashe records his impression at the time that he had been set up by none other than Colonel Joseph O'Toole, with his American government connections; but it emerged that O'Toole himself was also facing charges. In his attempts to get help, Ben-Menashe relates, he phoned Maxwell and Davies from jail, and was rebuffed by both. He claims that Davies said, 'I'm only a journalist.'

Davies's own version of this is that Menashe had said, on his arrest, that he was researching a book to be published by Robert Maxwell, and that a lawyer in the case had phoned Maxwell, Macmillan and Davies himself to obtain verification of this. 'Of course it was totally untrue,' Davies remarks. That Davies dropped Menashe so heavily at this point may explain a lot about the Israelis' subsequent eagerness to implicate Davies.

Menashe also wrought a revenge on O'Toole, who was charged with trying to sell Stinger missiles from Israel to an unnamed nation. Ben-Menashe says that friends in the Israeli government helped set O'Toole up. As O'Toole now puts it: 'He and I ended up with some major disagreements with the US government. His problem was resolved in New York at some expense, and mine finally was cancelled at the request of the US government when a Federal judge found US government employees lying while under oath.' The US government finally apologised to O'Toole for their actions. Ben-Menashe was acquitted by a jury in New York.

Back in England, the Hersh-Menashe case had caused Davies and Maxwell to put their heads together. Davies gave his boss 'a brief outline' of what he knew about Menashe. Expecting a thunderous rebuke, Davies was surprised by Maxwell's 'earnest' admonition, which he gives as follows: 'You should have told me everything you knew about this man before you allowed me to meet him. You should have warned me about him. You should never have let him meet me.' This interesting reaction, if authentically reproduced, gives almost the sense that Maxwell felt contaminated by Menashe's visit, which had risked sending the wrong signals to some watching third party. Davies gives no indication that Maxwell felt Ben-Menashe was an inadvisable playmate for Davies himself; it was simply that he was an inappropriate presence in Maxwell's office.

Yet he had been there before, according to Seymour Hersh (fed on this topic, of course, by Ben-Menashe again). In the course of the Mordechai Vanunu affair in 1986, Davies supposedly secured an interview for Ben-Menashe with Maxwell. Vanunu, a former technician at the then secret Israeli nuclear installation at Dimona, had gone walkabout in the Far East, taking with him photographs of the Dimona plant and a desire to blow the gaff. A flaky intermediary of Vanunu's, Oscar Guerrero, had shown up in London bearing some of the pictures and offering a world exclusive on Israel's unadmitted nuclear programme. Israel was aware that this was about to happen, which accounted for Ben-Menashe's presence in Maxwell's office. The interview was brief, however, since Maxwell did not need to be brought up to speed on the subject. 'I know what has to happen,' Hersh/Menashe record him as saying. 'I have already spoken to your bosses.' If this is an invention, it captures Maxwell's natural idiom remarkably well.

Yet Ben-Menashe, given the freedom of his own book to comment on these events, does not mention this meeting with Maxwell at all, but concentrates instead on getting Davies into the Vanunu story at every possible point: as the primary recipient of Guerrero's approach, as the deviser of the 'framework' of the *Sunday Mirror*'s disinformation story, and the discoverer or betrayer of Vanunu's whereabouts in London – as a result of which betrayal, the isolated and vulnerable Vanunu was lured to Rome by a Mossad siren, kidnapped, crated up, and returned to Israel for trial. He was sentenced to eighteen years in jail. Davies recently denied involvement 'in those conversations at all, which I think took place on a Friday and a Saturday.' These would be conversations about what the *Sunday Mirror* should publish to head off the *Sunday Times* scoop; and indeed, it has come to be accepted that responsibility for inserting a noisy 'spoiler' in the Sunday paper was taken by the editor, Mike Molloy.

'The Strange Case of Israel and the Nuclear Conman' was the heading of the *Sunday Mirror*'s advance rubbishing of the Vanunu story. The Dimona photographs, some of which had been passed to the *Mirror* by Guerrero in the belief that he was being excluded from the prior 'exclusive' deal with the *Sunday Times*, were ridiculed as looking 'like an egg factory' – a phrase redolent of Maxwell's style of abuse.[1] Rupert Allason, who has examined the case, says:

> The nuclear scientist, for example, who was interviewed, really gave quite a different overview and analysis of the photographs . . . and yet the words that were attributed to him were that, far from being a production line for plutonium or evidence of nuclear weaponry, the photographs could almost be an egg-factory or a car-wash – well, that's actually not

---

[1] Dr John Baruch, a research fellow at Leeds University, was quoted as believing that 'a reasonably well-informed hoax had been perpetrated'. 'It could be a car-wash,' he had said, 'or even a food sterilisation plant!' The 'egg-factory' contribution would seem to have come from elsewhere.

really what he said. And similarly, and I think in the most compelling way, the RAF officer who examined the same photographs was interviewed by the same journalists and came to a very positive conclusion about their authenticity – he was completely ignored, and his evidence cut out of the article completely.

*Sunday Mirror* readers were not allowed properly to judge for themselves, because the only pictures published were of a dome-shaped building, indistinguishable from an observatory, and a piece of metalwork topped off by some sort of analogue dial, like a pressure-gauge. The more interesting items among Vanunu's evidence (there were thirty-seven pictures in all) had been handed in at the Israeli Embassy, on Maxwell's orders. From journalists' accounts, it would appear that Maxwell, having characterised the pictures as ridiculous fakes, insisted they be checked out by the Israelis, just in case. As he well knew, and his journalists must likewise have known, the photographs, once handed over, were unlikely to emerge again from the Embassy.

Maxwell had done what he took to be his best for Israel here; but as with any piece of journalism in which he took a direct hand, it was a clumsy effort. Much effort was expended on discrediting the middleman Guerrero, whose personal integrity was irrelevant to the story. A postscript on the Dimona plant admitted that it 'was for many years described as a textile factory, until its real purpose was revealed by an American U-2 spy plane in 1962.' This final paragraph, designed to show that the *Sunday Mirror* were not complete innocents in this area, swept away the thin cobwebs of doubt distributed by the foregoing article, which, in sum, only served as an appetiser for the story which the *Sunday Times* went on to provide a week later – and which honourable journalists on the *Mirror* had also wished to explore, before orders from the Publisher brought them up short. On any scale of priorities where Maxwell's international power-play was involved, the journalistic instincts of his employees registered nowhere at all.

How closely co-ordinated were the actions of Davies and Maxwell at any point is still difficult to establish. There are those who, like Rupert Allason, say of Davies that: '– it was inconceivable that somebody with no substantial assets behind him, no background, very few international contacts, not regarded particularly highly in British journalism, should be dealing with these huge sums and very large contracts on an international basis when he was also spending so much time travelling the world with Robert Maxwell, and it occurred to me that he was simply fronting for Maxwell.'

Many of the large sums itemised by the documents, however, were either notional or otherwise not forthcoming, and, generally speaking, Davies was not having to produce them himself. Brokerage, in itself, is not necessarily a vastly expensive business.

It is hard to imagine Maxwell himself dealing with the kind of hardware exchanges with which Ari Ben-Menashe routinely corresponded, with or without Davies's assistance. But he could certainly have been of use in securing the co-operation of foreign governments when it came to routing illicit cargoes through to their unadvertised and outlawed destinations. Here, as ever, Maxwell's contacts will have been established at a high level. It was not until the very end of his life that he was asked a direct question about involvement with the Mossad, and when it happened, he reacted in the insulted tone of a man who had just been slapped in the face with a very old fish. 'Have you ever had any dealings with Mossad?' the interviewer[1] enquired. A pause. 'With *who*?' (Maxwell gives a satisfactory impression of having just heard this organisation's name for the first time in his life.) 'Have you ever had any dealings with the Israeli intelligence service?' 'Certainly not!' The tone is shocked, and Maxwell is temporarily reduced to babbling: 'What kind of – ah – you know – it's, it's, it's *outrageous* that you should use this – I will hang up and stop this interview unless you stop spreading these . . . eh . . . libels. Why, why don't I ask you, have you no connection with American intelligence? Or the M.I.5? It's a ridiculous statement.'

This childish anger of Maxwell's, in so many other instances the prelude to the dispatch of libel writs, reliably indicates the

[1] Martin Dawes, *The World At One*, Radio 4, 23.10.91.

touching of a nerve. At the same time, Maxwell probably did feel genuinely insulted that he should be thought capable of operating on the same level as a common spy or agent. As Nicholas Davies says, 'He was on first-name terms with the Prime Ministers of Israel . . . I mean, did he really need to talk to the engine room when he could pick up a phone and speak to the bridge?' In other words, the same system applied as in the Soviet Union: Maxwell had gone over the heads of the expected bridge-builders, and addressed the architects of policy directly. Men with dirty hands, such as Ari Ben-Menashe (who in any case was due to be unpersoned by Maxwell's friend Shamir), were not welcome in the ninth-floor office.

The whole picture is complicated yet again by a particularly vicious intertwining of office politics and *la politique d'amour*. Maxwell's staff, if they could agree on no other point, would still be united in observing that Maxwell was completely besotted with his private assistant, Andrea Martin, whom he made sure to promote to a position of such responsibility that she was obliged to accompany him on most of his journeys. Ms Martin, however, nourished a preference for Nicholas Davies, whose wife she has subsequently become. Maxwell's own wife has written that 'in the end, the infatuation of an ageing man for a young girl appeared to take precedence over his duties as the chairman of a vast empire'; and it is true that Maxwell did seem to devote a dangerous amount of his tactical energy to the management of this three-cornered struggle.

Sometimes his attitudes to Davies were distorted or disguised by his continuing wish to have Andrea Martin close to him, so that his motives have been misconstrued. Roy Greenslade, for example, has explained that he forbore to ask Nick Davies 'about being in league with Maxwell, since I viewed this as beyond probability, having in mind the lengths to which Maxwell went in trying to get me to sack Davies back in March 1990, hardly the act of a spy sharing a dark secret with another spy'. But as can easily be imagined, and Davies's book confirms, Maxwell's motive here was to get Davies off the premises so that his own bulky pursuit of Andrea Martin could continue unobstructed. And Davies was not so easy to fire: first, he might disclose something of what he knew about Maxwell, and secondly, a summary dismissal might involve the resignation of Andrea Martin, in sympathy.

It was a bad time for an unrequited affair of the heart to be afflicting Maxwell, now in his later sixties. Exasperation and infatuation ruled him alternately, sometimes within the space of a single utterance. Subjected to a mixture of tenderness and terrifying rage at work, Ms Martin eventually went into a cycle of resignations and returns, culminating in the irrevocable walk-out that took her finally out of all of Maxwell's orbits, save that of 'telephone terrorism'. Davies says that Maxwell continued to call Andrea Martin persistently, 'until a couple of days before his death.'

By that time, Davies, too, had left Maxwell's employ, fired at last. The Seymour Hersh allegations had brought a measure of support from Maxwell, albeit in a fuddled form: 'The allegation that he betrayed Sununu is a lie,' he assured the BBC[1], a week before his death. Sounding a touch 'tired', in the euphemistic sense favoured by Fleet Street jokers, Maxwell had confused Mordechai Vanunu with John Sununu, the Havana-born former Governor of New Hampshire and White House Chief of Staff (1989–91).[2] But Davies's inability to defend his denial that he had ever spent time in Ohio was so glaring that, if he had made a case for excusing it, the Publisher would have attracted even more hostile and inquisitive publicity than he was already getting. 'Unfortunately he lied to the editor,' Maxwell explained to the radio audience, as if it went without saying that such a nadir of journalistic mendacity is seldom reached. 'But if Mr Davies lied over the meeting in Ohio,' the interviewer persisted, 'might he not also have lied about his links with Mossad?' 'No, because his links with Mossad – he was being accused of having denounced Sununu [sic] to Mossad – has [sic] been totally disproved as a lie and fabrication. The *Sunday Times* themselves, in this week's edition, confirm that.' The Vanunu accusation, as Maxwell knew, was easily the weakest of the

---

[1] *The World At One*, Radio 4, interviewer Norman Smith, 29 October 1991.
[2] Maxwell rediscovered the correct name of Vanunu towards the end of the interview.

purported links between Davies and Israel. On that point, he himself was the more vulnerable party.

The *Mirror* itself made a ceremonious job of parting with Davies, putting the story on the front page, and then devoting a full-page editorial sermon to it (featuring easily the biggest colour portrait of Davies ever published by the paper) under the title 'A Question of Trust'. The piece is something of a classic of journalistic sanctimony. 'The truth,' it sobbed, 'is our only currency. We cannot duck and dive around it, play fast and loose with it, or regard it as an occasional companion.' It is a shame the Mirrormen did not stand up to Maxwell on these principles when he was attempting to discredit Vanunu.

The Publisher was dead within a week, and speculation about Davies soon disappeared under heaps of Maxwelliana. Freed by history to say what he likes about his old boss, Davies today tells the story of running into someone at a party who 'worked for one of our agencies', meaning M.I.5 or 6. Davies was researching his Maxwell book, and eager to discuss the subject. 'We started to talk about Maxwell, because he knew who I was, and he said – very telling words – he said, "You have never realised what an evil man Maxwell really was."' Picking him up on the use of the word 'evil', Davies asked whether he was speaking personally or on behalf of the people he worked with. 'We all believed he was an evil man,' was the reply.

> I then of course tried to draw him out [Davies goes on] saying, well, come on, you know, you can't just make a statement like that without backing it up with some proof or telling me what on earth you're on about. 'I can't tell you anything,' he said, 'but he was an evil man, you have no idea.' That's a very strong statement to make about anyone. I never saw any evil in Bob – I mean, there are many things he did wrong in his life, and we know now what happened at the end, leaving the poor pensioners without any money and that sort of disgraceful, appalling behaviour, you could describe that as evil. But this man wasn't meaning that. He was meaning something of far greater substance.

This reported speech sounds like the obtrusion of one of those little filaments of anti-Semitism that run through Britain's security services. Then again, coming from this source, it could be nothing at all.

Nicholas Davies is a tease. He is also very much less encumbered by the strangenesses of his past, and his non-explanation of them, than he would appear to have a right to be. His chief accuser, Ari Ben-Menashe, he disdains as '. . . a mental case . . . it all went on in his head. I mean he's mad, unfortunately for him.' In 1992, Ben-Menashe went so far as to allege, with every appearance of satisfaction, that 'Scotland Yard, M.I.5, the Serious Fraud Squad and the Inland Revenue are all investigating Davies.' There is evidence that, during the months after Maxwell's death, the Special Office of the Inland Revenue did take an interest in Davies's earnings. But apart from that, Maxwell's equerry seems to continue much as before. Perhaps the CIA in Paris calls him less often. Whether he enjoys some sort of immunity, or other protection, is an interesting area for speculation. Whether truth is his only currency is open to doubt.

In August 1994, it was reported, in this case by the *Independent*, that:

> Seymour M. Hersh, and the publishers of his book *The Samson Option*, accepted 'substantial' libel damages in the High Court from Mirror Group Newspapers over suggestions the book made false allegations about the late press tycoon Robert Maxwell and a former senior journalist, Nicholas Davies.

# CHAPTER EIGHT

## 'I have chosen New York'

'Why are you buying a New York newspaper when the state of the city is so bleak?' asked David Sheff, a Contributing Editor of *Playboy*[1]. 'When else?' might have been the most truthful reply. Instead, Maxwell went into prophetic mode: 'New York will get its revival, and I will be here.' Maxwell was not prepared to flatter New York in the expected corny style until he had first flattered himself, but he eventually came forth with the obligatory formula. 'The city has lost confidence in itself,' he rumbled. 'People are departing. I say *enough*! New York still has something to say. That I have chosen New York is a vote of tremendous confidence in this city. It's the first good thing that New Yorkers have seen happen in a long time. But the fact is, New York is a giant, the biggest, loveliest, maddest town in the world.' Cue for a song: and later, sure enough, in Maxwell's *Daily News* office, he gave a demonstration of telephone terrorism in lining up immediate broadcasting rights for the song *New York, New York*, the essential musical backing for his inaugural television commercial. The price agreed was $50,000.

At that moment in the spring of 1991, Robert Maxwell was a new face to most Americans. He was viewed with suspicion, as all foreigners are who take over American assets – a process that is not even permitted in the television world, so that Rupert Murdoch had recently been obliged to apply for US citizenship

[1]Issue dated October 1991.

in order to further his interests there. Yet in himself, as an English-speaking Carpo-Ruthenian, Maxwell was a perfectly standard immigrant figure within the Five Boroughs. Instead of passing through the historic filter of Ellis Island, he had simply passed by it, in his yacht. He came, as ever, to play the role of saviour, and to make money.

And he came with more than forty years' experience of New York. His early dealings with Ferdinand Springer's publication business had taken him all over the world. In the first instance, he was not selling Springer's technical publications so much as reassuring customers abroad that it would be morally acceptable to take such material from a German source. American libraries had actually threatened to apply a boycott, and Maxwell's wife remembers him addressing 'four large gatherings in Atlantic City, Boston, Washington and New York', where he recommended the worldwide pooling of scientific data. His journeys to the United States became frequent – he claimed that one crossing, on the liner *United States*, had brought him a chance meeting with President Harry Truman – and more especially so after his acquisition of a large, and eventually controlling, share in the British Book Center in New York.

Maxwell opened a New York office there in 1952, an outpost of his primary business concern of the time, LMS, or Lange, Maxwell and Springer. (In setting up his businesses, Maxwell had a lifelong habit of taking over sets of initials which had already made themselves memorable in another sphere. LMS had been the London, Midland and Southern Railway; the British Book Center was the BBC, and the Marylebone Cricket Club was obliged to share its abbreviation with his latter-day umbrella company, the Maxwell Communications Corporation. The latter, especially, wrought an enjoyable revenge upon 'the Establishment'.) His early publishing partners saw no need for a New York office, but Maxwell was determined to challenge the existing American reprint houses on their own territory. By 1953, he was fully established as a small, but active presence in Manhattan.

It was at that date, we now know, that Maxwell first attracted the scrutiny of the American intelligence services. Specifically, it was the foreign counter-intelligence arm of the FBI that first began to investigate him in 1953. This information did not emerge until the spring of 1994, when a report in the *New York Observer*[1] revealed that some FBI file-material had been brought into the public domain 'in an unrelated civil case' (although nothing with Maxwell's name on it can confidently be called 'unrelated' to any matter that reaches the courts). The well-known investigative journalist Robert Parry reported that some twenty pages of FBI findings had been released in response to a request filed under the Freedom of Information Act by Mr William Hamilton, President of a Washington computer-software company that was in dispute with the US Government.

Like many such requests, Mr Hamilton's brought a tantalisingly fragmentary response. The reputed Freedom of Information enjoyed by the US citizen too often consists, in reality, of a freedom to know that information exists, and not much more. Nevertheless, the implied quantity of information amassed about Maxwell was interesting. Although the FBI's released pages were 'heavily censored' in the traditional manner, with thick black strokes of a Department of Justice official's pen, it was evident that Maxwell's name had come up 'at least nine times' in separate national security investigations mounted by the FBI. One biographical précis whose text came through relatively unobscured showed Maxwell to have been the target of an FBI investigation that began in 1953 and was pursued until 1961. Attached to the investigative campaign, the same summary said, were ten internal FBI reports and eight 'investigative memoranda'.

In one of his own 'Memoranda for the Record', drawn up in the course of his long legal battle, Mr William Hamilton (and his wife Nancy, co-signatory of the document) had said that: 'In June 1993, the FBI acknowledged in writing to INSLAW [Hamilton's company] that it has approximately 600 pages of investigative files on the late British publisher Robert Maxwell's involvement in the distribution of computer-software products.' This statement would appear to be based on a misunderstanding,

[1]Issue of 4.4.94.

but a perfectly pardonable one, since the FBI's initial reply[1] had informed Hamilton, in impeccable bureaucratese, that, 'Documents which appear responsive to your request consist of approximately 600 pages.' It subsequently became clear that the number of pages actually dealing with computer matters was very much smaller. Robert Parry's *New York Observer* article reported FBI officials as having said 'that the total Maxwell file numbers into the hundreds of pages, but only twenty pages related to Mr Hamilton's request'. Of the 580 pages withheld, little is known in detail, though many of them will inevitably contain standard Cold War trackings of Maxwell's East–West business movements.

The released pages yielded a great acreage of black ink, and only one moment of satisfaction for Mr Hamilton. On one page, the censor's marker, skating too hurriedly across the government's secrets, allowed one phrase to escape: 'computerised databases on behalf of the Soviets', it read. This reference apparently belonged to an FBI report, dated 13 June 1984, emanating from agents in Albuquerque, New Mexico, and concentrating on Maxwell's Pergamon International company. As Parry's article remarks, 'New Mexico is the home of highly sensitive US research facilities, including the Los Alamos nuclear laboratories.'

William Hamilton's interest in Maxwell arose in the course of his campaign to demonstrate that a software package of his design, called PROMIS, had been, in effect, stolen by the US Department of Justice, who had adapted and used it without due acknowledgement or recompense. This struggle for justice, and against Justice, began in 1983, and has taken Hamilton into all available corners of government documentation. His claims have been upheld by a US Bankruptcy Court, a US District Court of Appeal, and the House Judiciary Committee. The first event signalling Maxwell's involvement came in 1987, when two senior computer systems executives left their positions in the Justice Department of Edwin Meese and transferred to what Hamilton, in one of his narrative

---

[1]Signed by the Chief, Freedom of Information-Privacy Acts Section, Information Management Division.

memoranda, calls 'an extremely small US publishing company in McLean, Virginia'.

This Maxwell company went by the name of Pergamon-Brassey's International Defense Publishers, Inc., and employed, according to Dun & Bradstreet's official listings, only half a dozen people. The business of the company was listed as '100 per cent publishing'. Hamilton therefore questioned why both of the defectors from the Justice Department should have been computer experts – and why one of them, the JD's former Director of Computer Technology and Telecommunications, should have signed up with Pergamon-Brassey's as 'Vice President for Technical Services'. No such services were known to be supplied, and it would be ludicrous to claim that the company's own internal computer system would need two ex-Justice Department computer chiefs to service it.

The Chairman of the Pergamon-Brassey company was the former US Senator John G. Tower, a figure who did not need an involvement with Robert Maxwell to make him controversial. President Bush, in 1989, nominated Tower as Defense Secretary, but the proposal was voted down by the relevant committee. Bush insisted on placing Tower's nomination before the whole Senate, but the Senate's vote also rejected Tower, narrowly but definitively. It was the first time in history that the Cabinet nominee of an incoming President had failed to secure the necessary approval. Allegations against Tower ranged from the almost routine Washington rumours of drunkenness and sexual harassment to more elaborate narratives in which Tower's private consultancies drew benefits from contacts he had made as an arms-control negotiator under Reagan's Presidency.

Tower had been close to both the Intelligence and Defence communities for years. He acted both as poacher and game-keeper, beginning in 1981 as Chairman of the Senate Armed Services Committee, a post well suited to his twenty-year history as one of the Senate's 'uncomplicated' conservatives, as the American euphemism has it. Tower left the Senate in 1985, and, turning gamekeeper, served fourteen months as Reagan's chief arms negotiator in Geneva, involved in US–Soviet attempts to ban medium-range nuclear missiles. Resigning from that post, he returned to a profitable civilian version of his old trade. In what one of his obituaries called 'a prime example of the political "revolving door" syndrome, when leading figures in government regularly move between the private and public sector[s]', he established in Dallas a consultancy, Tower and Associates, which advised several of the largest American weapons manufacturers of the day. His opponents in 1989 argued that Tower could not act impartially in matters of military hardware procurement, when he had personally accepted $750,000 in consultancy fees in that very area. No instances of direct lobbying had been proved against him, although he had reportedly called up an Air Force administrator, a former associate, to enquire on a client's behalf about the way a certain contract was going.

It was also Tower who chaired the Senate Commission of Inquiry into the Iran-Contra affair – an appointment roughly equivalent in acceptability to Lady Thatcher's presiding over an investigation into supposed left-wing bias at the BBC. With the assistance of former Vice-Presidential candidate Ed Muskie of Maine, and General Brent Scowcroft, Tower produced a report in which Reagan and Bush, charged with a lack of awareness of what was going on under their noses, were sufficiently chided to keep the public initially content, though it very soon became clear that some of the Tower Commission's allegations of 'chaos' at the White House reflected the unincisiveness of its own methods as well as Reagan's lack of control. 'The Board was not established . . . as an investigative body, nor was it to determine matters of criminal culpability,' Tower's report pointed out, anticipating attack on these grounds. Col. Oliver North and Admiral Poindexter, two central figures in the scandal, had not even testified before Tower. His attempt to persuade the President to order them to do so, recorded in correspondence carefully displayed in Appendices to the report, had not been notably passionate. (North and Poindexter did testify, a few months later.)

Having given the world this perhaps not wholly impartial view of the activities of, among others, his fellow-Texan George Bush, Tower now worked indefatigably for Bush's election to the Presidency in 1988 – two favours in a row. Bush came back with the offer of the Defense Secretaryship, with humiliatingly negative results for both men. Not even a special FBI report, assembled as a character-reference for Tower, could secure him the job. The consolation prize provided by Bush was the Chairmanship of the Foreign Intelligence Advisory Board. This had been a fifteen-member panel, but Bush cut it to six and put Tower in charge. The *New York Times* reported that a more expert panel could imply 'an enhanced role for outside consultants in setting the direction of the American intelligence agencies'. The six-man board was constituted in July 1990.

Tower's new duties were not so onerous as to keep him from wreaking revenge on those he considered to have subjected him to 'a political mugging'. The following February, accordingly, Tower's book *Consequences* appeared, bringing reviews that spoke of 'barely disguised rage'. John M. Barry of the *New York Times* commented that, 'These pages seethe with ego and contempt,' adding that, 'Mr Tower seems to have cultivated enemies.' Tower embarked on a promotional tour for the book. In early April, he was on his way to a party organised by his literary agent on Sea Island, Georgia, when his twin turbo-prop commuter plane crashed in flames, two miles short of the runway at Brunswick, Georgia. All the passengers, including Tower's daughter Marian, were killed, seven months to the day before the death of Robert Maxwell.

An investigation by the National Transportation Safety Board returned the verdict that the failure of a 'severely worn part' in the Brazilian-made plane's propeller system caused the plane to spin out of control. This finding did not seem to accord with reports immediately after the crash, which had stated that the plane was 'a relatively new piece of equipment'. Suspicions about the accident were not widely voiced, since it is distasteful to speculate that any assassin could be so ruthless as to kill twenty-three people in order to bring about one specific death[1]; but such things have happened. Tower was still a very angry man, who knew a lot more about Iran-Contra than his report had passed on (as was admitted even by the text of the report itself). There must have been fears – whether or not they were

[1] From the Grim Irony department: among the passengers who died with Tower was a senior internist who was about to take up office as President of the American College of Physicians. His name was Dr Nicholas Davies.

acted upon – that Tower was about to perform a retaliatory mugging of his own. His friend President Bush declared himself 'among those who will sorely miss his advice, especially in the fields of arms control, national security and intelligence'.

This, then, was the figure Maxwell had placed at the head of his Pergamon-Brassey operation. Tower was no token presence on the Maxwell payroll. His salary has been quoted by several sources as $200,000 per annum. It has been assumed that the main service Tower was meant to provide in return for this handsome bung was the clearing of a private path for Maxwell to President Bush, with whom Tower continued to share occasional lunches à deux. But there is no evidence that Tower was successful in this quest, or even that he seriously attempted it. Bush, as a former CIA director, was at this stage comparable to his sometime KGB counterpart Andropov in his reluctance to deal with Maxwell. Yet Maxwell persevered with Tower, and, if Nicholas Davies is to be believed, made some enigmatic noises when Tower's plane went down. 'It was a great shame Senator Tower died like that,' Davies quotes Maxwell as saying. 'He was doing some very useful work for us.' Davies presents himself as reluctant to believe that Tower's death could have been anything but an accident. 'Don't ever jump to conclusions,' Maxwell is said to have advised. 'Things never look the way they seem.' [sic]

The relevance of Tower's experience to the Pergamon-Brassey combine is not far to seek. Brassey's, in its British form, was a long-established defence-industry publishing house. Most British readers have heard of Jane's, whose annually updated technical listings of planes, ships, guns and other hardware are available in popular forms. Brassey's was their major competitor in the same line. There was a moment in 1980 when Robert Maxwell could have controlled both sources simultaneously. He already owned Brassey's, and was due to absorb Jane's as part of his take-over of the British Printing Corporation; but days before the deal went through, BPC's chief executive sold off Jane's in an attempt to control the company's debts. Maxwell was reportedly 'spluttering with fury' when he heard about this.

One must bear in mind that the reporter here is Nicholas

Davies, in whose interest it is to connect Maxwell with arms specifications as a means of easing the pressure on himself. Even so, Davies is not wrong to emphasise that, if Brassey's and Jane's had been merged, or otherwise yoked under Maxwell's management, 'the knowledge contained in those books – and the top-secret sources they relied on for their accurate information – would have rested with Maxwell alone'. Davies considers that alarm would have been caused 'in security and defence circles in Britain and the West'; and yet in the United States, Maxwell the publisher had been allowed to get just as close to sensitive strategic and military information. He was paying a fat salary to a man who had chaired the Senate Armed Services Committee, ran a defence-industry consultancy business of his own, and wound up chairing the Foreign Intelligence Advisory Board – a man, moreover, who had successfully sat on some of the available intelligence about Iran-Contra. If anybody was potentially worth $200,000 a year to Maxwell, it was Tower.[1]

The fact that Maxwell was making inroads into classified information does not mean that simple vanity had ceased to number among his primary motives. American Presidents remained the one class of international leader (unless we count his shipboard meeting with Harry Truman) upon which he had failed to urge his person-to-person influence before the Reagan years; and even Reagan proved less available than Maxwell felt entitled to expect. Some amusing disclosures from the museum of the Reagan Presidency show Maxwell claiming such an entitlement through his Pergamon-Brassey output: specifically, an item on the company's publishing list bearing the title *National Security Strategy of the United States*, and otherwise known as the 'Little Blue Book'. A sequence of internal memoranda and letters, shuffled to and fro among Reagan's staff, shows Maxwell using this work as

---

[1] A footnote to Hamilton's Memorandum of 1 November 1993 further points out that another member serving with Tower on the Pergamon-Brassey board during 1988 was General Paul Gorman, who had headed the US Army Southern Command for some years under Reagan's Presidency: 'The Southern Command included such Central American countries as Nicaragua, El Salvador, Honduras and Costa Rica, which played prominent roles in the Iran-Contra affair.'

a lever with which to crank himself into the Presidential line of sight.

The subject first arises in late April 1988, when a letter arrives at the White House from Dr Franklin L. Margiotta, Colonel, USAF (Ret.), President and Director of Publishing at Pergamon-Brassey's in McLean, Va. It is addressed to no less a figure than Lt. General (as he then was) Colin L. Powell, the Assistant to the President for National Security Affairs. Margiotta encloses five copies of the book *National Security Strategy of the United States*, which claims Ronald Reagan as its author. In the final paragraph of his missive, Margiotta wonders if he might request the President to sign a copy ' – to the Chairman of our multinational corporation, Mr Robert Maxwell ... The President met Bob Maxwell at a luncheon organised by Charles Wick (USIA)[1] which brought international opinion and communications leaders to town to discuss ways of improving foreign views of America.' Margiotta goes on to recommend the wording of the possible note, to wit: 'Dear Bob, I sincerely appreciate your company's help in insuring that a much broader audience understands our national security strategy.'

Some days later, two researchers provided a memo to be sent to Powell, clarifying the current status of Robert Maxwell. It is interesting as a potted view of Maxwell from inside the security system, just before his acquisition of Macmillan, Inc. 'Mr Maxwell is a colorful figure,' said the staffers, 'serving as head of one of the ten mega-corporations in the world of communications.' (Maxwell was later to tell *Playboy* that he had 'decided to scale down, to be happy with the fifth or sixth place in the rank'.)

> He is the largest publisher of scientific and technical literature in the world [continued the research team] through such subsidiaries as Brassey's Defense [sic] Publishers (London) and Pergamon-Brassey's International Defense Publishers (US). He recently acquired *Armed Forces Journal, International*, installing John Tower as chairman of its board. Mr Maxwell

[1] United States Information Authority.

is also a former soldier, commissioned in the field during the
Battle of Normandy and subsequently awarded the Military
Cross by Montgomery, and a former member of Parliament.
He has met the President on at least one previous occasion at
a luncheon arranged by Charles Wick . . .

Since this somewhat ingenuous profile was seemingly calculated
to encourage a soldier like Powell to see nothing but merit in
Maxwell, it comes as no surprise to see its closing recommendation giving the nod to the Presidential book-signing:

> Even though Mr Maxwell is far removed from the 'Little
> Blue Book' [this was a serious underestimate of Maxwell's
> mobility, both of mind and body] the attempt by his stateside
> subsidiary to market it commercially is helpful from our
> perspective. It can only increase the availability and use of
> the document, and thus contribute to public understanding
> and consensus building. Whether or not it will be a profitable
> venture for Pergamon-Brassey's is yet to be seen. But, we
> should encourage the effort and forward a copy of the reprint
> for the President to sign and forward to Maxwell.

The two contributors initialled their work. What is striking
about their conclusion is that one can imagine the same
recommendation having been made in the same terms by their
counterparts in Moscow for at least three decades previously.

Colin Powell could do no other than pass on to the President
the recommendation that he sign, particularly as Margiotta's
request had apparently been reinforced in the meantime by
another from John Tower. Powell did suggest a shorter message:
'To Bob Maxwell, With thanks for your help in promoting
national security dialog, Best wishes.' But then the Powell
memorandum was countered the following day by another,
from Arthur B. Culvahouse, Jr., Counsel to the President,
who advised Rhett B. Dawson, Assistant to the President for
Operations, that: 'I respectfully disagree with Colin Powell's
recommendation that the President sign the 'little blue book'
[sic] reprint of National Security Strategy. Long-standing White
House policy strongly discourages Presidential autographs of

books and other such items . . .' Culvahouse recommended 'a nice letter of appreciation and perhaps an autographed photograph to Mr Robert Maxwell' instead.

A 'Dear Bob' letter was concocted ('Through efforts such as your firm's, we will be able to promote together – government and private sector – the public dialogue [sic] so vital to this nation's security'), but it apparently remained unsigned. The two original National Security Council researchers now had to backtrack to Colin Powell, explaining Culvahouse's objection, and enclosing the whole correspondence so far. A request for an autograph had grown into a file. The episode came full circle almost a month after its beginnings, when Colin Powell wrote to Frank Margiotta undertaking to tell the President about Pergamon-Brassey's effort to 'spread the word' (Powell's quotation-marks). 'As a matter of policy, however,' the President's National Security Assistant added, 'we don't ask the President to provide book inscriptions of the kind you requested.' And that was how Robert Maxwell failed to get the President's signed dedication, but received the consolation prize of a nice letter from Colin Powell instead.

Maxwell's aides in England remained convinced that Reagan felt some attachment to the British supplicant. The President had, after all, been insinuated into the 'Leaders of the World' series (a volume even less obtainable than its Eastern-bloc predecessors). So the producer of Thames Television wrote to the President's assistant Fred Ryan later that year, asking Reagan to record a filmed insert that might be played into a Robert Maxwell edition of *This Is Your Life*. The request was made 'in view of President Reagan's connection with Mr Maxwell over the years'. The hearts of the White House staff remained unmelted by this formulation. With Chinese courtesy, Ryan replied that the President was too busy, but: 'I know, though, he would want me to express his appreciation for your thoughtfulness in offering him this opportunity.'

These entertaining sidelights on another of Maxwell's strenu-ous courtships of a world leader were collected by William Hamilton; but one could sympathise with Mr Hamilton, if, with him, their hilarity quickly palled. Hamilton's interest in

Robert Maxwell's publications scarcely extended to books at all: what he still wished to know was why the tiny Pergamon-Brassey operation was collecting computer experts. He wanted to know if it had anything to do with the alleged pirating of his computer package PROMIS by the Justice Department – not an easy arm of government for an individual to fight. Luckily for Mr Hamilton, some information had been provided to him 'two and one half years before the FBI revealed the existence of investigative files': in other words, early in 1991. Unluckily for Mr Hamilton, his informant was Ari Ben-Menashe.

Such is the general distrust of Ben-Menashe that one could believe that he had been made the victim of a comprehensive and worldwide character-assassination campaign carried out by the CIA, Mossad and British Intelligence in concert, if it were not for the fact that individuals who have dealt with him also report that he is infuriatingly prone to lace his evidence with fantasy. Even Seymour Hersh, who has probably checked more of Ben-Menashe's assertions against the available realities than any other person, reports serious losses of patience with him. At the same time, Menashe's stories are so crammed with authentic detail, checkable personnel and plausible motives, that one is often forced to conclude that, give or take some rather plaintively obvious James Bondery, a lot of what he says hangs together. Only if he had been specifically briefed, and in minute detail, by some very tightly goal-directed disinformation agency could his version of events be worthless.

Ben-Menashe first gave Hamilton his story early in 1991, Hamilton says, at Cincinnati International Airport. He said that Maxwell and former US Senator John Tower, 'both of whom were still alive, had co-operated in the illegal dissemination of INSLAW's PROMIS software to the intelligence agencies of foreign governments on behalf of Allied intelligence'. The PROMIS programme itself was a kind of computer bloodhound: it could allegedly pick up the 'scent' of an individual from recorded traces – not just criminal records and banking histories, but evidences as apparently trivial as water-consumption and power-supply readings – and follow the person, once identified, around the world. In tracking organised crime, drug traffic, terrorism, military insurgency and counter-intelligence, the potential applications of such a programme were almost limitless.

Inevitably with Ben-Menashe, there was an Israeli connection. He went on to provide Hamilton with an affidavit in which he stated that an Israeli intelligence official called Rafi Eitan had obtained a copy of PROMIS while on a visit to the United States in the early Eighties. Hamilton's firm, INSLAW, had subsequently learned from photographic evidence that a man sent by the Justice Department to see a demonstration of PROMIS had been Rafi Eitan operating under a pseudonym. The 1992 Investigative Report of the House Judiciary Committee had established that a man using this pseudonym (Dr Ben Orr) had received from the Justice Department a fraudulently obtained copy of PROMIS in 1983.

INSLAW believes that the computer package was illegally acquired by the Justice Department in order to be used, and sold on, by the US intelligence agencies, particularly the National Security Agency (NSA). It further believes that the Israeli government was part of the marketing process that sold the programme to foreign governments. The departure of the computer experts who joined Pergamon-Brassey in Virginia is held to be an indication of Maxwell's involvement in this trade – a subject on which William Hamilton laid down a specific 'Memorandum for the Record', on 8 November 1993. In this, Hamilton records that he was told on 15 September 1993 that Maxwell had 'worked for Israeli intelligence since 1967', and that, 'British intelligence also provided support for Maxwell.' Hamilton was told on the same date that a campaign was currently under way to destroy US Customs records that might mention transfers of PROMIS. A list of five nations was provided, four of them in South America, to which it was claimed Maxwell himself had sold PROMIS.

The same source, almost a month later, informed Hamilton that Maxwell had made 'three separate sales of PROMIS in New Mexico, all to the Los Alamos National Laboratories and the Sandia National Laboratory'. The names of four law practices who were said to have handled the transactions were provided by 'our trusted source'. The informant was not named, but 'our trusted source' does not sound like Ari Ben-Menashe. That gentleman's version of the PROMIS story was by then in the public domain (for his book *Profits of War* had been issued in America in 1992). Ben-Menashe's account features, naturally, an extra twist, in that he insists the copies of PROMIS distributed around the world were bugged. He and Rafi Eitan between them had come up with the idea of fitting the programme with what computerites usually call a 'back-door' (Ben-Menashe calls it a 'trap-door'), a sort of algorithmic keyhole allowing those in the know, the suppliers, to log into the system anywhere in the world, and inspect, undetected, its operator's research. The security secrets of any country that took on PROMIS would thus stand open to the scrutiny of Israel and/or America. The Israelis' original test-version of the back-door was installed by a friend of his in California, Ben-Menashe says: a technician who was paid a $5,000 fee which, if all this is true, can only be called derisory. The Americans installed their own back-door independently.

Maxwell's worldwide contacts, and newly established status in Israel, made him the ideal distributor of PROMIS (bugged or not), according to Ari Ben-Menashe. The approach to Maxwell was made, he says, by Senator John G. Tower himself, in 1984, shortly before Tower retired from representative politics. What's more – and Ben-Menashe gives this part of the story the tag 'according to Maxwell' – the first contact between Tower and Maxwell had occurred as much as eight years before, when the Texan had approached Maxwell, asking that some private channels into Soviet intelligence be provided for Tower's friend George Bush, then head of the CIA. Maxwell had obliged, and Tower never forgot the favour. Menashe admits he does not know whether Maxwell knew of the 'back-door' in the exported software, a confession of ignorance so staggeringly rare that it almost lends his story a human depth.

And here we return to the FBI's files. It was in hopes of laying bare Maxwell's involvement with PROMIS – and with any luck, demonstrating also a connection between PROMIS and those Justice Department computer experts mysteriously lured down to Pergamon-Brassey's, where no declared computer work awaited them – that William Hamilton applied to the FBI for the release of its computer-related Maxwell data. That single interesting phrase 'computerised databases on behalf of the

Soviets' appears all the more alluring in the light of the other information Mr Hamilton has gathered. Ari Ben-Menashe has himself floated the idea that Maxwell sold PROMIS to the Soviet Union 'in the late Eighties', through one of his Israeli companies; though any alert posted by the FBI's Albuquerque station as early as 1984 obviously could not have referred to this transaction (or not, at least, to its accomplishment).

No businessman trading habitually with the Eastern bloc, and also making sporadic attempts to buy into the legitimate American business world, could have hoped to avoid attracting the attention of the American intelligence services. Within the United States, however, Maxwell helped to minimise the turbulence of his commercial life by remaining faithful to a tight enclave of advisers and representatives. Ellis Freedman was his perennial New York lawyer; Sheldon Aboff and Laszlo Straka were delegated board members in a number of Maxwell enterprises. They both turned up on the board of Pergamon-Brassey's International Defense Publishers, Inc. Between them, the three men put in a lifetime of service with Maxwell. Even after his death, Kevin Maxwell appointed Freedman and Aboff to the board of the New York *Daily News*, though they were soon forced off again when the extent of their links with Maxwell's money-juggling became apparent.

His history of acquisitions in America had been a fretful one. Attempting to find an early partner in the computer business in the late Sixties, Maxwell had fixed on an American company called Leasco, with whom he became locked in a long and very bitter reciprocal take-over battle. Out of this grew the demand for a Board of Trade (later Department of Trade and Industry) enquiry into Maxwell's business methods, and the adjudication pronouncing him unfit to run a public company. This wording would later be recycled, in lightly disguised form, by William Jovanovich, of Harcourt, Brace, Jovanovich, the publishers, for whom Maxwell put in a $2 billion take-over bid in 1987. Jovanovich called Maxwell 'unfit to control' Harcourt, Brace, citing his socialism, his Communist connections, and his undeclared sources of income. (That the Maxwell money-trail seemed often to disappear into the imponderable vaults of

Liechtenstein had now become widely known.) In an outburst of seemingly race-based snootiness which must have reminded Maxwell vividly of his treatment at the hands of 'Establishment' patricians in England, Jovanovich, who came of Serbian stock, remarked that, 'Mr Maxwell's dealings since he emerged from the mists of Ruthenia after World War Two have not always favoured shareholders.'

Maxwell retreated, as he had recently done in take-over raids on both Bell & Howell and the *Scientific American*. But in 1988 he was back, with an even bigger bid for the American publishers Macmillan. This time, Maxwell was forced up by competitive offers until he was paying over one-third more than he knew the company to be worth; but the hammer did finally come down in his favour at $2.6 billion. Why he should have compounded this frightening commitment by going on to buy the Official Airlines Guide for $750 million is a mystery, unless by any chance it is true that in 1988 he had secured a loan guarantee of national dimensions, direct from his friend Yitzhak Shamir in Israel. (Source: the ineffable Ari Ben-Menashe.)

Even yet, Maxwell was not the personal presence in the United States that he desired to be. But being a creature of habit and, in his strange, improvised way, even of system, he knew what to do. His appearance in the front rank of British notables had coincided with his acquisition of the Mirror Group in 1984. It had also brought him a kind of ambassadorial base for his operations, and a refreshed sense of empire which justified his private planes and helicopters. When a similar opportunity presented itself in America, he would grasp it. The New York *Daily News* take-over of 1991 was just what he had been looking for. The state of the paper satisfied all his habitual desires: it was not only failing dismally in the New York circulation battle, but at that moment it was not even on the streets, being paralysed by strike action. As *Playboy* rather misleadingly reported, the Tribune Company of Chicago, owners of the *News*, ended up paying Maxwell $60 million to take the paper off their hands. Various debts and liabilities came with the asset, of course, not to mention the enormous problem of the unresolved labour disputes; but at that, it was the kind of deal Maxwell enjoyed. His victim was sick and helpless. He promised to cure the sickness and restore strength. Unfortunately, his favourite technique was amputation.

Maxwell had bought himself not only into a paper but into the celebrity role of *Daily News* Publisher, vacated by Jim Hoge. Access to the realms of influence he had sought so long became immediately available. Invited to the Gridiron Dinner in Washington, where the nation's satirists meet their political prey, Maxwell finally got the chance to give President Bush the benefits of his analysis of global developments. Bush, never a man to match Maxwell in either fluency or sonority, was so browbeaten by him that on the photograph of the two men in conversation which Maxwell inevitably obtained, Bush sent 'warm greetings from Washington' to 'Sir Robert Maxwell'. The closest Maxwell had hitherto come to Bush was a conversation with his Secretary of State, James A. Baker III, which according to Baker[1] took place on 12 July 1990. The meeting was set up at the recommendation of the Secretary's namesake, Senator Howard Baker, whose law firm Maxwell had employed to oversee a share-launch of Berlitz, the international language-school.

James Baker at that moment had just returned from the G-7 Economic Summit in Houston, Texas, and was about to leave for Europe for meetings concerning German reunification. According to his records, the Maxwell meeting lasted forty-five minutes. He remembers 'very little about the conversation specifically, although I do recall he was concerned with the Bush Administration's policy toward Israel'. In Baker's judgement, Maxwell played 'scarcely any substantive role with regard to US policy toward Israel or any other issue' during his tenure as Secretary of State.

Naturally, that was not Maxwell's own view. His sense of his own importance was now subject to few restraints. He had asked his wife of forty-five years, probably the only person who regularly questioned his decisions, for a formal separation.[2] He

---

[1]Letter of James A. Baker III to Daniel Korn, dated 31 March 1994.
[2]Their separation was not widely publicised, but Maxwell only pretended to keep his bachelor habits private. On *Start The Week* (Radio 4, 7.3.88), he said: 'Unlike an ordinary person, for instance, I can't take a girl out to tea and hold hands without it being reported to the *Sun*.' 'Oh bad luck!' said Mary Soames, Churchill's daughter, in the background.

was sixty-seven years old, and in no mood to allow anyone to underestimate his contribution to world affairs. Maxwell was aware of the legitimate claims of modesty in the shaping of character; but he had always perceived a danger in this virtue. Twenty-five years before, he had sent his sixteen-year-old son Philip off on a tour of America, providing him as he went with an extraordinary portfolio of instructions on how to enjoy himself productively in the new world. Under the heading 'How to Make Friends Amongst Young and Old', he had recommended: 'Remember a listener is always more appreciated than a talker and avoid boasting. On the other hand, one must not fall into the other scale of being too self-effacing or too frightened to intervene in a conversation. Because I know that you do not suffer from this I have not found the need to stress it.' Somebody should have reminded him of his own advice before he started to talk to *Playboy*.

The magazine has many faults, but its journalistic instincts on this occasion were impeccable. The collection of material began in the spring of 1991, but the article, billed *Playboy*'s 'most interrupted interview ever', was not published until the October issue. Taping sessions began conventionally, if spectacularly, on Maxwell's yacht, the *Lady Ghislaine*, moored off Manhattan 'at the ritzy Water Club'; after which the scene moved quickly to the *Daily News* building. Next, Contributing Editor David Sheff moved on with Maxwell to Washington, for the Gridiron Dinner: 'Maxwell also had a number of meetings (with Turkey's president Turgut Ozal and Senator Patrick Moynihan, to name two)'. The following day, Sheff met up with Maxwell in London; and the day after, they flew on, in Maxwell's latest Gulfstream, to Israel. The interview continued at the King David Hotel in Jerusalem. ('The following day, between our interview sessions, Maxwell met with Prime Minster Shamir, Ariel Sharon, Moshe Arens, and other Israeli government members.') The occasion of the visit was the launch of the Russian-language newspaper, *Vremia*: 'But Maxwell soon headed back to his jet . . . there was business to be done in Paris, London, Quebec and Bonn, and the *Daily News* needed him in New York.' American reporters are not easily impressed by overstuffed schedules and cast-lists of celebrities, but this was exceptional.

Much of the published conversation sees Maxwell in fascinated close-up as the newspaper boss: his clumsily calculated but successful outbursts charm in the presence of his new staff; the alternating hard-soft voice in which he addresses union representatives and raw-material suppliers; his bulldozing of a route to the TV-ad rights for *New York, New York*; and, midway through that negotiation, the narcoleptic slumber into which the sixty-seven-year-old Maxwell[1] falls. But for once, the international dimension of his life does show through, sometimes aggressively. Calls are announced as coming in from Brian Mulroney of Canada (twice), Hans-Dietrich Genscher of Germany (Maxwell ostentatiously holds this call off in order to continue with the interview), and Ozal of Turkey. Maxwell fields some direct calls himself, including one which he answers in Russian, and *Playboy* translates as follows: 'I am going to Moscow to see my old friend. We have important things to talk about. Germany will play a small role, too. I want to speak with you about this in confidence. I'll call you.'

At least three Maxwell biographies were by now in the public domain, all of them suggesting in a casual way that he enjoyed contacts which readers would have expected to be available only to elected representatives. What was new here was the openness with which Maxwell now described his role in specific world events. 'I'll let you in on another secret,' he told Sheff. 'Remember the time when relations between the United States got so bad that James Baker said, in the House hearing, "Mr Shamir wants to talk peace: our telephone number is area code 202 . . . that's the White House switchboard." It was a most insulting moment. Soon after, Shamir sent me to America to see your new President to see what we could do about putting relations right. That has not been made public.' Pressed for more details, Maxwell said he had met Baker 'last autumn. I had two hours with Baker. It was a highly satisfactory meeting'.

Neither the length nor the date of the conversation accords

---

[1]His birthdate is commonly given as 10 June 1923, so that he was sixty-seven when this 'interrupted' interview began, in March 1991. Towards the end of the published text, however, he remarks, 'I'll be sixty-nine next June.' It is possible that the interview sessions had staggered on into the summer, so that Maxwell's sixty-eighth birthday was now in the past.

with the recollections of James A. Baker III, though its central theme sounds right. 'The most important thing I carried away,' Maxwell told his questioner, 'was that the security of Israel will never be traded by the United States. And I helped Israel be assured that, as a result of its restraint in the Middle East, the Soviet Union would be looking seriously at a peace treaty and working to improve relations. At the same time, all that would disappear if they interfered.' Even allowing for a measure of grandiosity on Maxwell's part, these were astonishing responsibilities for a private businessman to have assumed – or even claim to have assumed. But Maxwell was not in a mood to hold back. Asked how his negotiations with Gorbachev on the matter of Israel had begun, Maxwell outlined a simple bargain. About three years before, he said, 'I was invited to assist him with his economic and management problems. I asked why I should: I have enough to do. I was told the USSR would recognise Israel in twelve months.'

Since the Gulf War was newly won, it was natural to ask this unexpectedly frank Maxwell whether he had played any part in back-room diplomacy. Flinging wide the back-room door for the first time, Maxwell appeared to glory in his answer: 'Absolutely. My message was consistent: to urge Israel to stay her hand, be ready for the worst but give the President and his allies a chance to finish off Saddam Hussein. I was in touch with all the actors.' Challenged to give names, Maxwell replied: 'Bush to Assad [of Syria] to Gorbachev to Shamir. I met with them and spoke with them on the phone.' Double-checking sensibly, Sheff got Maxwell to repeat that he had advised Shamir not to retaliate against Iraq. 'I applied heavy pressure in that regard,' Maxwell confirmed, 'and it was taken very seriously.' This theme was picked up again by Sheff during his flight from London to Israel in the Gulfstream jet. 'Many governments in Europe called me to intercede with Shamir,' elaborated Maxwell this time.

Getting closer to matters where Maxwell's personal and business interests were involved, the *Playboy* correspondent asked about measures taken by Maxwell to soften the effect of Gulf War sanctions on certain third-party states, notably Bulgaria. Maxwell took credit here for persuading the German government to help Bulgaria out financially. 'Bulgaria is the only one that's public,' Maxwell continued obligingly. 'I intervened with Turkey to let them have some gas.' Aside from this revelation, Maxwell either deflected or ignored other questions concerning his evident contacts with the Turkish President. On this topic, he admitted he was being evasive. Within the interview as printed, the only other question Maxwell conspicuously swerves to avoid is: 'What kinds of business have you done with Gorbachev?' After a momentary diversion, he gives the bland reply, 'Raising capital.'

He also shrugs off the suggestion that it is his ownership of media outlets that accounts for his influence with world leaders. 'The fact is that they can talk to me and they know that I don't betray them; I don't use these sources to write stories.' (Until now, that had been largely true: but in this very interview, Maxwell was bizarrely exposing some of those sources in order to help someone else write a story.) Felix Sviridov, the head of Maxwell's Moscow office, agrees that the directness, speed and privacy of Maxwell's personal communications to, and on behalf of, political leaders counted for more than any public power he wielded in the shaping of opinion. In the transmission of any message entrusted to Maxwell, Sviridov says, 'Both sides knew that he was the person who a) had direct access to the author of that message, and b) that the message he was transmitting had not been doctored by anyone – in other words, it had not been doctored by either a Foreign Ministry or any other service of a country . . . They knew that their message reached the adversary exactly in that form in which it was originated.' This is somewhat to overestimate Maxwell's ability to abstain from comment – it is difficult to imagine him passing on any given outline without adding vivid touches of personal colour – but the general point stands: in the space between nations, there was room for Maxwell, in one of his favourite phrases, 'to be of service'.

One other unaccustomed note was struck in the *Playboy* interview: the echoing note of mortality. Was he more powerful than politicians, Maxwell had been asked. 'Yes,' he recklessly replied, 'except for the two or three highest people in an administration.' But those people are accountable, protested his interviewer: they are elected for finite terms. When Bush and Major had left their posts, Maxwell would still be there. 'Certainly not,' said Maxwell. 'I'll be sixty-nine next June. I, too, have a contract that expires one day – with the good Lord.'

The *Playboy* interview went on sale to Americans during September. By that time, Maxwell's contract was almost up.

# CHAPTER NINE

# Belly Up

The unclothed corpse of Robert Maxwell is adrift in the Atlantic. Borne on a gentle swell, he lies face-up to the dawning sky. The waters lap at the black dye of his hair. It is hard not to think of him as a giant baby; for if there is a motto for this scene, it is to be found in the book of Job, where it is written: 'Naked came I out of my mother's womb, and naked shall I return thither: the Lord gave, and the Lord hath taken away; blessed be the name of the Lord.' Neither in the biblical nor in the modern world, however, has the Lord invariably performed these functions unassisted. How much help He received in the case of Robert Maxwell is still a vexing question.

The year of 1991 had been one of most turbulent of the century. In almost every headline event, Maxwell had some direct and personal interest. Kuwait had been liberated from Saddam Hussein's forces on the last day of February. The World Economic Forum in Davos had taken place at the height of the Gulf War. The situation within the USSR belied the name of Union, as Lithuania and Latvia struggled to be free. Boris Yeltsin had called for Gorbachev's resignation in February. Tension within Yugoslavia was similarly rising: in late June, Maxwell, pursuing his new policy of advertising his political clout, published an MGN press release stating that, 'The President of Croatia, Dr Franjo Tudjman, has sought help of Publisher Robert Maxwell to publish a message seeking international support for Croatia's declaration of independence.' Older campaigns of Maxwell's were showing signs of paying off. In April, Yitzhak Shamir met Soviet Prime Minister Pavlov in London, expressing the hope that full diplomatic relations between their countries could soon be restored.

The following day, Maxwell announced the flotation of almost half the Mirror Group empire, claiming that the move was the redemption of 'a pledge I gave to the management and workforce when I took over the Mirror from Reed International some six years ago, namely that, as and when the company is re-equipped and is profitable on a sustained and growing basis, we will go public.' A BBC interviewer, Nick Clarke,[1] mentioned that it was 'said in the City' that Maxwell needed cash. Was there a cash element in the deal for the wider parts of his empire? Not for the wider parts, Maxwell assured him. 'There is a cash element in it for the Mirror Group itself.' The £250 million he expected to raise would be used to repay some bank borrowings, he said, because he would rather use equity than borrow. Only a week later came the issue of documents detailing the proposed sale of Pergamon Press, Maxwell's creation and, in earlier years, his public self. Nobody who knew Maxwell's commercial history could have taken this for an encouraging signal.

Maxwell was in a most strange situation. The wheels were falling off the chariot of his ambition, yet it was parked already at the centre of world politics. He had interceded with Shamir, helping, by his own account, to prevent wholesale Middle East war. Now, in one of his last international interventions, he helped preserve the democratic momentum in Russia. A Soviet hard-line coup, predicted months earlier by the former Foreign Minister Edvard Shevardnadze, unseated President Mikhail Gorbachev in August. Felix Sviridov was in Moscow at the time. 'On 19 August, I was driving to my office. I saw some tanks and military personnel carriers on the streets. I was surprised to see them, but I didn't think too much about it. Only when I came to the office I learned of the so-called coup happening, and I telephoned Bob Maxwell.' Unable to get through, Sviridov sat by the phone, which suddenly rang. 'He was telephoning me, so actually he learned about that whole thing earlier than his representative in Moscow.' Sviridov recalls a Maxwell interview

[1] *The World At One*, Radio 4, 17.4.91.

on the BBC World Service, '– at about 9 or 9.15 a.m. Moscow time. He was the first Western representative . . . to say the coup was unconstitutional.'

Sviridov received instructions from Maxwell to contact 'a number of leading personalities in the Soviet Union', to ask what was needed by way of international help. 'I managed to contact all the people he wanted except one.' (Shevardnadze, as it turned out, was in the 'White House' building, rather than his usual office.) The Maxwell telephone exchange had gone into urgent action. 'As a result of these efforts of ours, during the first two days, Bob Maxwell managed to organise telephone conversations between Mr Yeltsin on the one side and a number of Western leaders on the other side.' Mitterrand, Kohl and James Baker III were among those who responded.

In former days, Maxwell himself would have kept quiet about all this. But what had once been 'back-door' diplomacy on his part was now placed by Maxwell on the front porch. His large *Mirror* article 'Why The Hard Men Failed'[1] left readers in no doubt that he himself had succeeded, in telephonic concert with Boris Yeltsin. 'On Tuesday afternoon,' he confided, 'I received an urgent message from him, shortly before he was called by John Major. Yeltsin wanted me to alert the Prime Minister and the White House to the imminent danger he was in, which I did.' He had spoken to 'a Yeltsin aide for about ten minutes', Maxwell said.

The plotters, he judged, had overlooked 'what is still the key element in Soviet life, the Communist Party itself'. If Gorbachev, as rumoured, was ill and unable to continue as leader, the Party wanted to hear it from his own lips; and so it stalled for time, depriving the coup of its impetus. 'During yesterday and Tuesday,' Maxwell continued, 'in a series of phone calls from the Soviet Union, and especially from Mr Yeltsin's office and from Alexander Yakovlev, formerly Mr Gorbachev's closest adviser and friend, all these events were unfolded to me.' But it was the active part of Maxwell's programme that must have caused dismay, especially in the White House. 'I, in turn,' he boasted, 'passed details to General Brent Scowcroft, President Bush's

[1] 22.8.91.

National Security Adviser, and to Downing Street.' Scowcroft (a member of John Tower's Iran-Contra investigative triumvirate) will not have been pleased to see this. Confidential briefings of security staff are not the sort of material that the Americans like to see paraded in a tabloid newspaper.

The same issue of the *Mirror* carried an aggrandising squib about the Downing Street contact. 'Prime Minister John Major discussed the failed Soviet coup with *Mirror* Publisher Robert Maxwell for ten minutes yesterday. A grateful Mr Major thanked Mr Maxwell for passing "new important information" to him.' Not much more than two months later, Major was confirming the truth of this, as part of his obituary tribute to Maxwell: 'During the attempted Soviet coup this August, he was able to give me valuable insights into the situation in the Soviet Union because of his many contacts,' he said. This had indeed been the last service Maxwell performed directly for the United Kingdom.

Moscow was undergoing a transition for which Maxwell had long worked. Having been one of those most tirelessly active in introducing capitalism into the Communist system – inserting the profit-motive as if it were a self-replicating virus – he now watched the Russian body politic in the throes of the resulting fever. It was still conceivable that this paradoxically liberating infection might be overcome, and the system returned to its former glum, semi-paralysed condition. Maxwell had to take this possibility into account. He was at his most seriously analytical when he faced the TV cameras and gave his interpretation of the latest developments. He dared not throw away all his work in Moscow by rejecting the hardliners' intervention out of hand. Some of them, like KGB Chairman Kryuchkov, and Valentin Falin, were very well known to him, and might yet end up in charge of a lingering Soviet Union.

So Maxwell allowed the instigators of the coup a plausible rationale, and admitted the possibility that their improvised regime might be ratified at the polls. 'What these people are against,' he argued, 'is political and economic chaos; and if the Soviet people by vast majority will agree with that, then they may be given a chance. But in my opinion, they will come up against the problems of the Soviet Union – that if you want to run a major country scientifically and technologically based, then you've got to give people freedom, you've got to give them incentives.' This had been his credo all along. Putting out perfunctory biographies of the Communist leaders had given those involved, if nothing else, an inkling of the joys of selling.

Even after the coup had subsided, opinion remained highly fragmented in Moscow, but in certain circles Maxwell's reputation was still strong. Some of his friends had backed Gorbachev's return, and prospered. Among them was Boris Pankin, who, from Czechoslovakia, was the first Ambassador to declare his opposition to the Emergency State Committee in whose name the coup was mounted. Pankin had known Maxwell since 1974; in 1977, he had helped the publisher organise the first Moscow Book Fair, at which Israel was represented long before the *détente* had been attempted. Maxwell's *Daily Mirror* was quick to point out Pankin's uniqueness among the Soviet envoys in declaring himself for Gorbachev, and predicted a reward. Sure enough, Pankin earned a spell as Foreign Minister in Gorbachev's post-coup administration.

Maxwell, who had been in touch with Pankin during the August confusion, made much of him that autumn, inviting him both to Maxwell House in September, and then on to the *Lady Ghislaine* in the same month. The yacht by now was moored once again in New York, while a meeting of the UN General Assembly was in progress. (It was the session at which, late in November, Boutros Boutros Ghali, Deputy Prime Minister of Egypt, was made Secretary-General.) Susan Baker, wife of James, was running coffee mornings at the Whitney Museum of Art, for the spouses of the delegates. Maxwell, for his part, held a large reception on his yacht, where the guests of honour were Pankin and Genscher.

At the meetings both in London and New York, Boris Pankin recalls, Maxwell's favourite topics were discussed: Middle East peace, and the resumption of Soviet–Israeli relations. Pankin himself, along with James Baker, now went on from New York to conduct during October an intense bout of shuttle diplomacy in Jerusalem, setting up Middle East peace talks to which Israel and the Palestinians eventually agreed. In the last weeks of Robert Maxwell's life, many filaments of his diplomatic web were being suddenly pulled together. Pankin signed an agreement with David Levy, the Israeli Foreign Minister, taking the first step towards resumption of full diplomatic relations. Just twelve days before Maxwell's disappearance, the Israeli embassy in Moscow reopened, after nearly twenty-five years. At the end of October, the Madrid Conference began, and Israelis faced Palestinians, angrily, across a table. The plane that had brought Yitzhak Shamir to Madrid was Maxwell's Gulfstream.

As political satisfactions deepened, Maxwell's commercial embarrassments multiplied. A journalistically thorough investigation into his finances and methods of management had been undertaken by the BBC's *Panorama* programme, which aired on Monday, 23 September. It did not raise the topic of pension funds; in spite of which Maxwell, to whom an advance viewing of the programme had not been granted, volunteered a defence against charges of pension-mismanagement in the previous day's *Sunday Mirror*. Reaching into the tattered grab-bag of Communist-era abuse, he called his piece 'The Jackals of the BBC'.[1] Their programme, he claimed, had:

> . . . sought to discover 'facts' about Mirror Group's pension funds and when they were told these 'facts' didn't exist, it lost interest . . . I am concerned about needless anxieties which the programme may cause to pensioners in our Group. For some months, a lawyer and a small group of pensioners have claimed their pensions should have been higher. They haven't a case . . .

It took an almost unbelievable gall for Maxwell, knowing what he knew, to put this argument across; but shortage of nerve was never his problem. Writs against the BBC, targeting chiefly its allegation that Maxwell had set up his bingo game to cheat his *Mirror* readers, satisfactorily postponed consideration of any material *Panorama* had amassed.

\* \* \*

[1] Winston Churchill, it is true, also favoured 'jackals' as a term of contempt.

To be a dedicated Maxwell-watcher had now become a bigger job than being Maxwell. All his lives were becoming public, and there were investigators at work in the sundry trails of wreckage he was leaving all over the world. High-level officers were leaving his organisation. His Deputy Chairman at Maxwell Communications, Jean-Pierre Anselmini, resigned early in October, and at the month's end, the President of Macmillan also went. Between the two events came the volley of writs with which Maxwell greeted the publication on 20 October of Seymour Hersh's book *The Samson Option*, with its arms-dealing allegations. Speaking to a BBC interviewer[1] from New York, Maxwell expressed himself with care rather than fluency, and appeared to be reading his initial statement from a written sheet: 'I am sure your listeners will be aware that the allegations contained in the motion by these two irresponsible MPs are vehemently denied, and writs for defamation have been issued against the publisher of the book in England, Faber & Faber, and its author, Mr Seymour Hersh.' The allegations themselves had remained non-reportable in Britain, until the MPs Rupert Allason and George Galloway raised the matter in sufficient detail under House of Commons privilege, on 22 October. The Nicholas Davies 'Ohio' furore followed immediately, and on 28 October, the *Mirror* Foreign Editor was fired.

It was on 23 October that Maxwell, speaking from New York, had demonstrated his extreme agitation over the Israeli allegations by threatening to 'hang up and stop this interview' if a BBC radio questioner[2] did not stop spreading 'these libels'. Maxwell was speaking from his now customary penthouse suite at the Helmsley Palace Hotel, where, on that visit, he had held a consultation of a kind he had never troubled to arrange before. His visitor was Jules Kroll, founder of the company Kroll Associates, which from an office on Third Avenue runs one of the most discreet and wide-ranging private investigation services in the United States. The meeting is a topic upon which Mr Kroll declines to be interviewed, although he has remarked

[1]Martin Dawes, *The World At One*, Radio 4, 23. 10.91.
[2]ibid.

privately on 'the bizarre nature of the case'. Evidently Maxwell's old suspicions about enemies in 'the Establishment' – not to mention the muck-raking journalists whose activities he seemed to regard, perhaps not always without cause, as an extension of the Establishment's own – had been augmented by new fears.

According to the only detailed, albeit second-hand, report of the meeting's progress, supplied by 'one of the participants',[1] Kroll was already well supplied with information on Maxwell, as he had compiled a large dossier on the publisher for William Jovanovich, as part of Harcourt, Brace, Jovanovich's successful effort to stave off Maxwell's take-over bid of 1987. The 'very solemn' Helmsley Palace meeting, says the source, lasted two hours. Maxwell felt under attack. He identified enemies in both business and politics, and asked Kroll to identify the promoters of what he felt to be an orchestrated campaign of defamation. 'It's one thing for people to speculate whether I'm overleveraged [financially] or if I can make this payment or that payment,' he is quoted as saying. 'But this is going far beyond that.' Maxwell, for his part, undertook to supply Kroll with a memorandum detailing events he considered 'suspicious and unexplained'. His notes for such a document were presumably among the large stock of paperwork Maxwell took with him on the lonely voyage from which he did not return.

One of the last of his international contacts to meet Maxwell in a purely social way was his old friend Leonid Zamyatin, who was preparing to leave his ambassadorial post in London. It was, Zamyatin believes, 'some thirteen or fifteen days before he flew to Gibraltar'. Their conversation was pleasant, friendly: 'very bold from his point of view'. Maxwell said it was his dream to merge the Macmillan publishing empire with that of McGraw-Hill, and he 'had now bought all the appropriate companies'. Zamyatin detected no change from the old Maxwell. 'I didn't notice any kind of depression.' His ambition at that moment seemed centred on America: 'to live and work there a little'. Maxwell had told his *Daily News* readers in Manhattan

---

[1] Article by Edward Klein, *Vanity Fair*, March 1992. There were reportedly two other parties to the meeting, besides Maxwell and Kroll. For fear of being bugged, as his own London employees had been by him, Maxwell conducted the conversation on the patio of his suite.

that, if he had emigrated to the United States instead of England, he would have run for Mayor of New York; and he had actually told his wife that he had emigrated to the wrong country.[1] But he would never see America again.

On 30 October, the *Lady Ghislaine* was moored at Gibraltar, waiting to sail to New York, where most of the crew had been taken on just a few months before. The Captain, Angus J. Rankin, had himself joined the vessel only in May 1991. Although he is a resident of Pocahontas, Arkansas, Captain Rankin's accent betrays a British origin. He is a burly and unsmiling man; and though it is no part of an officer's duty to conform to a stereotype of clean-cut eagerness, something about Rankin, as seen in interview footage, tends rather strikingly the other way. This also was the initial reaction recorded by Dr Elisabeth Maxwell (*A Mind of My Own*). 'He was tall and rather stout,' she writes, 'in uniform, but casually so, not giving the spruce naval appearance of previous captains. Some of the crew gave me the same impression. The boat did not seem quite "ship-shape" to me.' Nor did Dr Maxwell care for Rankin's manner. 'The Captain did not know me, yet he immediately adopted a familiar way of talking about Bob, which I did not like at all because it didn't ring true, familiar as I was with Bob's loathing for intimate conversation.' But Dr Maxwell concedes that both she and the ship's complement were under stress at that moment, so she does not dwell on the matter.

Considering that eleven crew members were on board the *Lady Ghislaine* to conduct Maxwell's last voyage, remarkably little has been heard of their side of the story. Once permitted by the Spanish authorities to leave their last port of call, they dispersed with impressive speed and have not been heard from since. It is unusual, in these days, to find a body of people so uniformly resistant to the attractive financial inducements normally offered in such cases by the tabloid press. Only Captain Gus Rankin has remained contactable, and his version of events now emerges for the first time.

When a message came through that Maxwell wanted to be

[1]ibid.

called because he was planning to come to the boat, Rankin says he was disinclined to believe it. 'My first reaction was to call one of the secretaries to find out if this was for real, which I did. And she said, "'Well, if he said call, call him," which I tried to do.' Rankin couldn't get a response that night, but called the operations managers for Maxwell's aircraft instead. 'And they said, yes, they had repositioned the aircraft to leave at an early hour the following morning.'

Early next day, Rankin called Maxwell again and received his confirmation '– that he would like to go with us out to Madeira. He was trying to get rid of a cold that he'd had for quite some time – which had been an ongoing conversation, trying to get to the boat for a month or so.' Rankin explained that they would have to leave by a certain hour in order to arrive in Madeira in time to get fuel for the continuing journey to New York. 'And he said whatever schedule I wanted to maintain was fine by him.' Maxwell arrived on time, and apparently in a good mood. Because the yacht had been prepared for its Atlantic crossing, a lot of luxuries had been packed away, and some of the normal interior staff were not on duty, but this didn't seem to bother Maxwell either. 'When he arrived on the boat he just brought his normal stuff and quite a lot of papers;[1] showed the stewardess from the plane around the boat, who was new; and gave instructions for the plane to leave for Madeira right there and then.' The *Lady Ghislaine* left Gibraltar 'within an hour or so' of the owner's arrival.

It was a two-day trip to Madeira. If a desperate and suicidal Maxwell was on board, he had his chances to get it all over with on the way. Instead he emerged at Funchal looking remarkably like his normal self. 'Somehow,' Rankin says, 'the press knew that we were arriving with him before we arrived.' It would be interesting to know how this happened. At all events, photographs were taken – the last of Maxwell alive. He is seen in his latterly habitual baseball cap, and, more forebodingly perhaps, a dark jacket and glasses. The most apocalyptic desire

---

[1] Five or six suitcases of papers were sent back to London by Betty Maxwell, on the instructions of her son Kevin. The Spanish authorities apparently did not request a viewing of these papers. There was a shredder on board the *Lady Ghislaine*.

Maxwell expressed that day, however, was to go swimming. By permission of the harbour-master, Rankin took the *Lady Ghislaine* out to an appropriately uninhabited island called Desertus, where Maxwell did indeed swim for 'about ten minutes', in Rankin's recollection; but it was too cold. They returned to Madeira where, that evening, a crew member took Maxwell ashore. He visited the Casino, with $3,000 in hand. The briefness of his stay suggests limited enjoyment.

Rankin says he and the crew had been expecting Maxwell to return to London the following morning; but instead, he 'said that he'd like to stay a couple of extra days and go somewhere else and we discussed the options, which is why we went to Tenerife'. This was another overnight trip. The next day, Maxwell again went swimming. Before they all returned to Santa Cruz, he announced that he was leaving the following morning, and asked 'if it would be possible that night if we could take the boat out, because he slept better on the boat at sea if it was calm, rather than just sitting in port'. Maxwell said that in the morning he would then release the crew to sail on to Bermuda and New York. He would eat ashore that night.

As he did so, the Anglo-Israel Association was convening in London under the impression that it was to be addressed by Robert Maxwell. In the event, his son Ian read the speech, which had been worked out between them over Maxwell's satellite telephone. 'Of all nights that my father would have wished to have been present, this, I think, would be it,' Ian Maxwell told the gathering. Speaking for his father, he said:

> The Jewish population of my homeland was almost entirely wiped out by the Nazis. I was one of the lucky ones. At sixteen I escaped a death sentence and joined the Czech army in France and then Britain, before the Holocaust began. Six million other Jews, including my father, my mother, my grandfather, three sisters and a brother, were not so lucky. My family died in the gas chambers of Auschwitz, the most infamous monument to man's inhumanity to man.

As these words were being spoken, their author was smoking a Havana cigar in a hotel in Santa Cruz – an odd choice of pleasure if Maxwell was suffering, as he sometimes had, from shortness of breath, or indeed a cold. He returned to the boat 'about a quarter to ten, ten o'clock'. Rankin had decided '– that Los Cristianos would be a good place to drop him off because it was only like about a twenty-minute drive to the airport instead of an hour or so's drive from Santa Cruz . . . So to make up the time to get to Los Cristianos, to keep a reasonable amount of speed on the boat, to keep it stable although it was calm that night, flat calm, we decided to take . . . [sic] our course was set to go round the north end of Gran Canaria, staying about five miles offshore all the way around, and end up in Los Cristianos after nine o'clock the following day.' Rankin himself soon went off watch. 'At midnight I turned it over to the mate and they followed the course.'

At the time he went to bed, Maxwell had been wearing a nightshirt, much the most comfortable sleeping attire for a man of his bulk. (The garment was later found on the floor of his state room.) He received a late telephone call from his son Ian, who let him know how the Anglo-Israel speech had gone. It is known that a further call came in, from Rabbi Vogel, one of a number of Lubavitcher rabbis (several of whom were also 'present', as it was a conference call) who were agitating for sacred Jewish texts to be exported from Russia. The previous April, Rabbi Berel Lazar of the Lubavitcher Hasidic Community in Brooklyn had visited the Soviet Union, with the aim of securing the release of 12,000 sacred and historic volumes held in the Lenin Library. Maxwell's last two communications with the outside world, therefore, dealt intimately with the Jewish past he had for so long denied.

Gus Rankin came back on watch at 8 a.m. He estimates the boat was twenty-five miles from Los Cristianos at that point. They anchored off the town about nine-forty-five 'and then waited for Mr Maxwell to appear'. When a phone call came in about ten-thirty, Rankin advised that Maxwell was still in his cabin. The caller didn't feel he needed to be disturbed. Then a more urgent call came in at eleven o'clock. Rankin gave the same reply, but this time it was imperative that Maxwell be roused. 'That's when we first got the inkling that he wasn't there.'

Suspecting a medical problem, he says, Rankin went 'down through the office to try to make entry through the bathroom that adjoined his [bedroom] and that was locked'. He took with him the ship's chef, who was an instructor in resuscitation techniques. 'We then went around to the aft entrance, a sliding door, knocked on there and tried to get a response.' There was none. The door was locked, so Rankin used his pass key, '. . . expecting now to see somebody either passed out on the bed or on the deck or something. And nobody inside – rather strange feeling!' The bed had been slept in, and clothes were scattered about: 'There was fruit, bowls of fruit, some eaten, some not' (a typical Maxwell scene). Rankin now organised a thorough search of the vessel, '. . . which we did several times, to the point of opening up drawers. I mean strange what one does in these circumstances.' While these bizarre and repeated manoeuvres were under way, no notification of a man overboard had yet been made.

At one point, a black-haired figure was spotted swimming near the beach; looking through binoculars, Rankin couldn't swear it was not Maxwell. 'We put a boat over the side to go over and have a look and see if it was him; and just before the boat got there, the man walked out on to the beach and one could tell it wasn't Maxwell.' The mate was rowing the boat. Having failed to contact the local radio station ashore, Rankin instructed him to 'go in and speak to the harbour authorities and tell them what we suspected, that he had gone missing during the night'. In the meantime, Rankin says, he and the crew fell to sorting out who had seen or spoken to Maxwell last. It was then that it emerged that at 4.25 a.m., the second engineer had received a request from Maxwell for the air-conditioning to be turned up. This was not a telephonic request: both men had been taking the air towards the stern of the vessel, and had spoken face to face. Half an hour later, Maxwell allegedly asked for the cooling system to be turned down again. No later message from him is reported.

Eventually the *Lady Ghislaine* 'put out an SOS through the Sat[ellite]-Comm[unication] system'. (An international marine rescue system is co-ordinated from Stavanger in Norway.) More than an hour had passed between the discovery of the empty stateroom and the successful transmission of a message to the outside world. Rankin went in and spoke to the port captain at

Los Cristianos, and an effort was made to estimate where the vessel had been at 5 a.m. which was the latest stated time at which Maxwell had been alive. A message went out to ships in the vicinity. In an effort to inform the family, Rankin also called Maxwell's offices in London. 'By chance I spoke with Brian Hull, who was one of the airplane captains; and his suggestion was, because he knew the family a lot better than I did, that the person to speak to would be Kevin Maxwell.' He called Kevin, who asked him to call again in ten minutes; when he did, Kevin and Ian were together to receive the news.

Rankin presumes that someone intercepting the Sat-Comm message had passed it on to the media, because calls now started to come in from reporters. The first such call, he believes, originated in New York. By the time BBC radio located the *Lady Ghislaine*, one of the two female crew-members had been deputed to fend off enquiries: 'I can't make any comment, I can't tell you anything, I'm sorry. I've strict orders not to tell anything. I'm just sitting answering the telephone, so [sic] the Captain is really busy. None of us here are allowed to . . . to tell anything.' Apart from a couple of inconsequential shouted remarks from ship to shore while the *Lady Ghislaine* lingered in port, that was the last anyone heard from the crew-members.

The police had arrived to inspect Maxwell's stateroom. They taped up a safe they found there, to which Rankin had no key. Later, when Betty Maxwell arrived, she first insisted on a private interview with Rankin, during which he gave it as his belief that her husband had committed suicide. This theory she rejected. In Maxwell's cabin, she went straight to the hiding-place of the key, and opened the safe: it was empty. Dr Maxwell's inspection of the room should have been taken as a minor, if helpful and humanly necessary, stage in its examination for forensic purposes. Instead, amazingly, it was taken by the local police as the signal for the whole investigation of the site to be wound up. As Captain Rankin has it: 'The room was left intact until Mrs Maxwell was there, spoke to the police, did whatever there was – and at that point, the police gave permission for the room to be cleaned up.' Rather icily, Rankin re-emphasises, 'The *police* gave that permission.'

The damage caused by that decision has been importantly,

if almost inadvertently, underlined by Dr Iain West, the Guy's Hospital pathologist who in view of Maxwell's £20 million personal insurance policy, was called in by Lloyd's of London to give an independent opinion on the causes of death. Dr West did not examine the body until it had arrived, in a semi-embalmed condition, in Israel for burial; but for these purposes, the pathologist was also required to take into account whatever circumstantial information could be deduced from the environment of the deceased immediately before death. 'I gather,' says Dr West in this connection, 'the boat was handed over to the relatives very quickly . . . I think the deck was washed down. We lost a crime . . . a potential crime scene.' The slip of the tongue is revealing of doubts. In spite of the fact that Dr West has tended all along to favour – very narrowly – the theory of suicide, it is clear he wishes that all the potential evidences of crime had been preserved for assessment.

The insurance report prepared by a British firm of loss adjusters is, in fact, much the most thorough investigation yet made of an incident in which Scotland Yard might have been expected to take a more lively interest, since Maxwell was a British citizen lost under circumstances whose vagueness certainly aroused suspicion from the start. It is believed, for example, that not until Dr West entered the case were sea-water samples collected, against which to check whatever liquid had been ingested or absorbed by Maxwell's body. (Such findings may often conclusively indicate drowning as the cause of death, though in this case they did not.) On the other hand, there were aspects of life aboard the *Lady Ghislaine* which were never examined by anybody. Nicholas Davies has stated, for example, that Maxwell had taken to keeping guns on board, which he referred to cryptically, when checking they were in place, as 'vegetables'. If these existed, they would surely have been of interest to an investigating police force: but they were never mentioned.

One almost painfully traditional aspect of this case is that theories purporting to solve it must contend with those classic symptoms of mystery, locked doors. As Maxwell was retiring for the night, he asked the stewardess to lock his main stateroom door from the inside, and leave the area through his bathroom, into the area described by Rankin as the 'office'. Later Rankin himself found that bathroom-office door to have been locked from the inside 'because that's the only way to lock it'. The main door, aft, was also found to be locked. It was equipped with a key that would lock it from either side; but since there was nobody in the room, it was inevitably deduced that Maxwell had gone out on the aft deck at some time after 5 a.m., taking the key with him. Whatever process accounted for Maxwell's ending up in the sea had taken the key, too.

'There was a presence of mind,' Gus Rankin reasons. 'Closing the door, locking it, taking the key out and having that presence of mind at that point to do that. There'd be no reason to lock the door from the outside if he were planning to go back in. And why take the key? Was this done to maybe keep us crew members to think [sic] that he was still inside? I think so.' Well, yes: clearly anybody who locked the door had the motive of postponing as long as possible the world's awareness of the emptiness within. It is not a pattern of action that particularly points to Maxwell as its perpetrator.

If Maxwell's entry into the water had been a violent one, would it have been heard? Rankin says emphatically not. 'The boat was moving along at about 13½, 14 knots; and that doesn't seem fast by driving standards, but you drop a can over the side and see how fast it disappears from you, it disappears rapidly. Plus you've got the noise of engines, the turbulence of the water and you've got a crew pretty much forward on the boat. With closed doors, they're not going to hear it all.' Once over the side, the 22-stone Maxwell was on his own. Rankin even suggests that his second order to the Second Engineer was a ruse to secure his privacy. 'I think maybe the air-conditioning call to the wheelhouse – you know, "Can you change it back" – might have been the way of keeping the engineer away from the aft deck again, if he might go back there.'

Almost nobody who knew Maxwell believes that he would have committed suicide: but a completed suicide, by definition, is not something that numbers among the observable habits of an individual in his lifetime. True, suicides usually talk about the idea here and there beforehand – sometimes for years, and sometimes habitually – as if to test the reaction of friends, and also perhaps their own reaction as well. Spoken aloud, an idea moves one small step nearer to its fulfilment. But among Maxwell's colleagues and intimates, only Nicholas Davies has described a scene in which the Publisher gave voice to self-destructive impulses. It occupies the first two pages of his book, *The Unknown Maxwell*. We are told it was 'a damp Sunday afternoon'; Maxwell had a cold; his new paper the *European* was disappointing him; he had no friends. 'Sometimes,' he allegedly ruminated, 'I think I should just end it all, throw myself out of the window.' But it is not in this maudlin mood that suicides find the paradoxical strength to go through with it. And indeed, even Davies himself doubts whether Maxwell 'had the courage to take his own life by silently slipping over the edge of the *Lady Ghislaine* and swimming until exhaustion overcame him'.

If the body had not been recovered, many friends of Maxwell's (including Davies)[1] would have been able to convince themselves that he had 'done a Stonehouse'[2] and staged an escape from his old identity. How such a vast and notorious figure could have accomplished this disappearing act is a question to stretch even a spy-novelist's imagination, but anything that is possible nourishes some believers. As the events of 5 November 1991 turned out, speculation was reasonably short-lived. It was at dusk just after 5.30 p.m. local time, and not quite four and a half hours after the first search helicopter reached the zone of operations, that a Spanish Air Force plane – a Hercules in the first reports, later a Fokker – spotted the body in the sea, some twenty miles south-west of Gran Canaria. Less than forty-five minutes later, the body was winched aboard a helicopter and flown to the airport at Las Palmas. It was formally identified later that evening by Dr Betty Maxwell and her eldest son Philip.

The Spanish pathologists, like the police, seem to have gone about their work with only a limited range of suspicions in mind. Their most prudent act was to send samples of the inner organs

---

[1] 'When I first heard about his death, I thought well, well, well, he's decided to just disappear, to hide himself somewhere else in the world.' Nicholas Davies, *Mann Über Bord*, German TV programme, 10.9.94.

[2] Former Labour Minister (1925–88) disgraced in 1974 after a business scandal, and an attempt to fake suicide.

to Madrid for analysis; there proved to be no significant toxins in Maxwell's system. Traces of a cold remedy had been found, although nobody on the *Lady Ghislaine* had noted signs of a particularly virulent cold. It may have been that Maxwell was one of the many who use such medicines as sleeping-draughts. His widow had now questioned Captain Rankin for a second time. 'I felt a sense of malaise that is difficult to describe or explain,' she records. 'Nothing was suspicious in his answers and yet Bob's death still made no sense to me.' No note, no statement to the world had been left behind. But there was little time to ponder these matters, since it had now been determined that the body, if it were to be buried in Maxwell's purchased plot on the Mount of Olives, needed by Jewish religious law to arrive in Israel before dusk on the Friday of that week, in time for the Sabbath. This timetable was met, at considerable cost to the thoroughness of procedures in Tenerife.

It was on the Saturday, in Tel Aviv, that Dr West, his wife, Dr Vesna Djurovic (another forensic pathologist from Guy's Hospital), and some Israeli colleagues were enabled to perform their own post-mortem examination, at the Institute of Forensic Medicine. A video recording of the process was made, and subsequently leaked to the magazine *Paris-Match*. In Tenerife, the importance of the case had only slowly dawned on local officials: here, it was understood in its full notoriety, not to mention its large potential cost to Maxwell's insurers. But the state of the remains was far from ideal. 'Remember,' says Dr West, 'I'm looking at him after the body's been embalmed, and been embalmed in such a way that the tissues became very fixed by formalin, and therefore minor injuries could easily be missed.'

Bearing that in mind, says Dr West, 'We're left with basically four options.' First, there were signs of incipient heart and lung disease which were potentially lethal: but if Maxwell had died of either, 'I would have expected him to have fallen on the deck and remained there, so I think that's by far the least likely.' Then again, Maxwell could have fallen overboard accidentally: but the sea was not rough, there were no abrupt changes of course, and 'one would have to do something quite active to fall over'. The third option, says Dr West, is suicide: 'And clearly the problems that he had at that time could cause a person to kill themselves.'

The fourth option is murder. 'In order to demonstrate that, at least from a pathology point of view, one's got to have injuries which are suggestive or even characteristic of an assault. Now whilst some of the injuries could have occurred during an assault, I could see nothing which indicated there had been an assault.' This determinedly non-controversialist stance of Dr West's would later emerge as an area of disagreement between him and his Israeli colleagues. Unfortunately, the possibility of violence involved the very category of evidence most clumsily, and efficiently, obscured by the Spanish post-mortem, and indeed the contemporaneous efforts of the police. 'I don't think the Spanish police investigation was particularly thorough, so a lot of the evidence which could have assisted in saying whether we were dealing with a suicide or a homicide wasn't gathered.' West was therefore left in the position of being unable to rule out the murder theory. 'I've got no positive evidence of homicide so it remains a possibility, one which one simply can't exclude.'

As for the manner of Maxwell's entry into the water, the most indicative evidence found by West here was 'a tear of a fairly large muscle in the back of the shoulder blade, not caused by impact but caused by violent stretching of that muscle'. This damage is consistent with Maxwell's '. . . holding on to something and his body suddenly dropping so that the shoulder takes all his weight, even for a relatively short time. He wasn't particularly fit, so that the muscle wouldn't be able to cope with this sudden violent wrenching; it would simply split.' Since Maxwell 'was clearly alive when the muscles received the damage', this injury suggests that Maxwell clung briefly to some projecting part of the vessel, such as the rail, but was unable to hold on.

Some suicides, Dr West says, do take the process by degrees. 'People do that going off bridges, coming out of high buildings: some will go straight or jump straight through the window or from the windowsill, others will lower themselves over the windowsill or over a bridge parapet into the water.' So it is conceivable that Maxwell's entry into the sea was voluntary and gradual, until the moment when he dropped and was wrenched away into the wake of the *Lady Ghislaine*:

Some people seem to take quite a long time before they either jump into the water or even sometimes change their mind and come back out. If they're jumping, they may well be preparing themselves and it may well be at this stage that he slipped, whilst hanging on to the rail, and he's held on long enough to tear his muscles. He could have lowered himself over the side, that's another possibility, and changed his mind, tried to swing himself back up, which again could explain this pattern of muscle damage we've got.

To cause the tears, Maxwell would have needed to be hanging on by his left hand: he was indeed left-handed.

At the same time, it does not seem particularly likely that a man who swam well and to whom swimming was a pleasure – one in which he had recently indulged – would have chosen such an anti-instinctive way to die. Neither does Maxwell appear to have made any preparations whatever for the moment of his departure. Suicides who are otherwise sane commonly nerve themselves up with a large intake of alcohol, but Maxwell's organs (though an incipient cirrhosis of the liver was noted) gave no evidence of any such ingestion. Betty Maxwell re-emphasised at her sons' trial her astonishment at the lack of any final note or message. It must have been a dark night of the soul indeed if Maxwell merely walked out on deck, locked his door, and dropped first the key, and then his life, into the ocean.

From the point of view of an assassin, it was necessary only to get Maxwell into the water. Like Captain Rankin's dropped can, he would soon be left far behind: a 22-stone man, alone in a cold sea at night. Maxwell would not go quietly, so it would be necessary to hit him first: an injury noted in the area of the right ear – with bruising severe enough to survive the embalming process – went unexplained, as did a curious bruise on the shoulder. As Dr West admits, 'I can't explain the patterned injury on the back of the shoulder, this little, relatively superficial bruise which has left a pattern of some sort of fabric on the surface of the skin.' But if Maxwell was assaulted within his stateroom, there were a good many fabric-covered surfaces against which he could have fallen heavily enough to sustain an impact bruise of this kind. West, while deploring the sketchiness

209

of the Spanish detective work, does not seem to have explored this rather elementary line himself.

It is imaginable that a Maxwell thus assaulted could have recovered sufficiently to resist being bundled into the sea, and hung on long enough to tear his shoulder-muscles. Then either his attackers, or the pain of his injury, loosened his grip. After that, he was lost – or so an assailant would be entitled to assume. But Maxwell, returned to consciousness by the cold slap of water, had one more hope. His shoulder injury would have made it impossibly painful for him to swim, and besides, there was nowhere to swim to in the dark: but if he could float for long enough on the 'flat calm' waters, day would break and he might be spotted. So he lay on his back in the water and waited for sunrise. The combination of agony and fear a man in that position would suffer is uncomfortable to imagine.

This was not a northern sea, but the month was November, and after just ten minutes of swimming on a recent day, the water had been judged too cold. So it was while the floating Maxwell waited that hypothermia overcame him. The posture in which his body was found, face-up to the sky – most unusual in a person supposedly drowned – may well have been the one in which he died. Since the classic symptoms neither of drowning nor of disease-induced heart failure were found in his remains, the probability is strong that Maxwell died of reduction in body temperature – effectively, of exposure. Buoyant with body-fat, he continued to float.[1] Above all, his outspread posture in the water indicates that, far from seeking death, he was doing the only thing he could to survive.

Who wanted Maxwell dead? Almost everyone had some reason to wish him out of the way. As Rupert Allason has it, 'The number of people who would have been willing to undertake that particular exercise must be able to form a queue right round the entire block.' They included such seldom-mentioned candidates

[1] Bodies 'can float, as one pathologist put it, "where there is plenty of wind or fat".' *Guardian*, 12 November 1991. It should be said that the same article discourages speculation about Maxwell's face-up posture when found: '"It just depends on whether someone has a fat stomach or a fat bum," says Professor Bernard Knight of Cardiff Royal Infirmary.'

as the Iranians, whose erstwhile leader, Ayatollah Khomeini, Maxwell had insulted in a speech to the headquarters staff of the UK Land Forces of the British Army.[1] 'Let us deal with the barbarian in his own coin, the only coin that so diseased and underdeveloped a mind can understand, the coin of a price on his head.' He had nominated the sum of $10 million. In New York, more recently, some of the mob-run trade unions had taken less than kindly to Maxwell's 'rationalisation' of the *Daily News* workforce. Nicholas Davies reports 'a senior mob person' as saying: 'If you go on acting like this with us, you're going to end up in the East River with your throat cut.' Maxwell was still updating the list of his enemies for submission to Jules Kroll.

The international political community had particular reasons to be alarmed by Maxwell's recent activities. Many nations held information on him, but only recently had the evidence begun to be drawn together – notably by Maxwell himself. Seymour Hersh's allegations, backed by the yet more alarmist testimony of Ari Ben-Menashe, were newly in the public domain. Yitzhak Shamir had rebutted those parts of the story that implicated him, although Maxwell's own swaggerings in *Playboy* again suggested close links between the two men. Maxwell had claimed that his policy and Shamir's were identical, that he had represented Shamir in talks with James Baker, that he had been instrumental in cooling the Israeli response to Iraqi missile attacks. How much more of Israel's private business was he prepared to reveal? His writs against Hersh and his publisher, and Allason and Galloway, would be defended: dangerous witnesses would be brought to court. But the death of the litigant would close the cases.

There were yet more possibilities. In the conventional business world, there are not many creditors who feel so strongly about unpaid debts that only the death of the debtor will give satisfaction; but in his money-laundering activities, Maxwell was dealing with a new generation of post-Communist trader, practising a capitalism that took little account of traditional business ethics (an adaptable concept at best), and still had access to Cold War methods of enforcement. Maxwell's empire

[1]Reported in the *Daily Mirror*, 17.2.89.

was a shambles of high-interest obligations: if a debt had been called in, and it was discovered that Maxwell had 'adopted' the funds and committed them elsewhere in his empire, some old friends might have turned against him, definitively.

The KGB, the old Central Committee of the Communist Party, and the former Bulgarian government all had interests here, and between them, in the past, they had worked up some picturesque ways of doing away with undesirables. One that particularly impressed itself upon the British consciousness was the stabbing of the Bulgarian defector Georgi Markov with a poison-tipped umbrella, on Waterloo Bridge in September 1978. It is interesting that nobody in the former Eastern bloc appears to believe that Maxwell met a natural end. As Stanislav Sorokin of the KGB has declared, 'I think it was a contract killing performed very professionally to look like suicide.'[1] Felix Sviridov's formulation is that 'somebody helped him to die'.

But to do that, one had to keep up with Maxwell's erratic and often improvised movements. It was the British themselves who were now tracking him most assiduously. Investigative reporters for the *Financial Times* revealed on 15 June 1992 that, at the time of Maxwell's death, a full intelligence report was prepared for the Joint Intelligence Committee. 'The JIC,' it explained, 'which is part of the Cabinet Office, co-ordinates and assesses information from Britain's intelligence services, including M.I.5 and M.I.6.' From the detailed information and interpretation supplied by Lord Howe's office on Maxwell's visit to Moscow after the Korean airliner incident, it is clear that thorough records had always been kept on his movements abroad. But these had now been augmented by a variety of electronic surveillances made necessary – and possible – by the latest developments in communications technology.

It fell to Mr Robin Robison, a former administrative officer for the JIC, to reveal in the same report that Government Communications Headquarters (GCHQ), the Cheltenham intelligence centre, was keeping a close watch on Maxwell in 1989, two years before his death. Mr Robison, who had been spurred to make these disclosures by his Quaker principles,

[1] *Mann Über Bord*, 10.9.94.

said: 'The sigint (signals intelligence) I saw in the autumn of 1989 included intelligence data on Robert Maxwell taken from telephone conversations and faxes intercepted in Israel and the Mediterranean, probably from his yacht, the *Lady Ghislaine*.' Mr Robison recalled that the information had been variously distributed, according to content, among the offices of the Prime Minister, cabinet ministers, and officials he identified as representing the Bank of England.

In late 1989, the most politically active and exciting phase in Maxwell's career had only just begun, with the fall of the Berlin Wall. It is inconceivable that GCHQ's surveillance can have relaxed at this point: it will have intensified, not only because Maxwell's activities were becoming intrinsically more interesting month by month, but because the surveillance methods themselves were becoming more formidably cute. Where Maxwell himself was stuffing his employees' telephones with clumsy and discoverable bugs, the eavesdroppers on his own affairs were able to aim lasers at window panes, and read speech from the vibrations of the glass. An international network of monitoring stations meant that Maxwell's communications could be intercepted wherever his transports took him. Moreover, national security did not need to be at issue in order to justify the deployment of surveillance methods. Among the bodies licensed by the Interception of Communications Act of 1985 to authorise phone-tapping had been the Department of Trade and Industry – the enemy who had once judged Maxwell unfit to exercise stewardship of a public company.

First reports of the government listening-posts' involvement were amplified by the *Guardian*, who reported[1] that communications from the Maxwell yacht '– were intercepted by GCHQ, with the help of British submarines, after a tip-off from the CIA in the late Eighties that he was suspected of being involved in arms deals. His conversations were sent by low frequency transmission to GCHQ's outstation at Edzell on Tayside, Scotland.' This information came evidently from a different source, since it was presented as 'corroboration' of Robison's disclosures. These evidences of collusion between

[1] 18.6.92.

the CIA and the British intelligence services may have been the beginning of the end for Maxwell, certainly in a commercial sense. In a way it is surprising that his credit, which was being busily withdrawn at the time of his death, was allowed to endure so long. Between the Americans and the British there was agreement: Maxwell was embarrassing everybody.

Motive for a face-saving homicide, therefore, is embarrassingly abundant. The practicalities of the matter are not necessarily complex either. Three schemes suggest themselves for getting the victim into the sea. A person or persons unknown on the vessel itself could have done it; strangers could have boarded the boat stealthily and carried out the operation without the crew's knowledge; or the whole event could have taken place by arrangement, with the crew turning a blind eye. The latter scenario has the advantage, from the crew's point of view, of enabling them to offer a convincing plea of ignorance when questioned by port authorities, police and insurance investigators, all of whom did take their turn in checking the stories of the ship's complement.

Only one complete and detailed blueprint for a Maxwell murder has been published, by the journalist Kevin Cahill in the April 1993 edition of the American magazine *Business Age*. 'How and why Robert Maxwell was murdered' chooses the stealthy-boarding option, fingers a rogue element in Mossad as the executioners, and altogether betrays the heavy influence of Ari Ben-Menashe. The narrative postulates a pair of contracted Mafia killers brought from Catania in Sicily, and shadowing the *Lady Ghislaine* in a 40-foot motor cruiser – waiting, by night, 'for Maxwell to come out on the afterdeck'. When he did ('locking the doors of the stateroom behind him, something he is never known to have done before'), the assassins supposedly 'moved in for the kill'. The method of assault is perhaps plausible: Cahill nominates a military hard-rubber cosh and an air-injection into a vein from an empty syringe, any minute lesion from which would probably have been missed by the Spanish pathologists, and would have been disguised by the beginnings of decomposition four days later, when West's post-mortem team got to work.

But the account is encrusted with bizarre novelistic detail. Maxwell is described as 'on the satellite phone, talking' at the moment of attack, although nothing has since been heard from the person on the other end of the line. Overnight calls, in any case, were being withheld from Maxwell: it was only when Macmillan of New York insisted on being put through to the stateroom the following morning that his absence was discovered, or admitted. Again, it is recorded that Maxwell, when attacked, 'laughed as he fell back' – an eerily poetic notion, perhaps, but a symptom of invention.

Captain Angus Rankin ('Augustus' in the *Business Age* scenario) dismisses the idea of a boarding-party at sea – even one with the kind of training our own Special Boat Service receives. 'Without being detected? I would say not possible, because even if there isn't somebody on the aft deck, we do have other equipment for detecting other boats . . . One of the reasons for having radar is to detect other vessels that come at various ranges but in particular those that come within a certain range, and the instructions to the crew were: any vessel that comes within five miles of this boat I am to be called – I, the Captain, am to be called. Nobody called me.' Rankin also dismisses the persistent rumour that there exists a satellite photograph showing another boat alongside the *Lady Ghislaine*. 'That's the first I've ever heard about a satellite photograph – and why would somebody be taking a satellite photograph of the boat? Does that mean they're taking satellite photographs of all boats as time goes on? I don't know . . .' As Captain Rankin is aware, the presence of Robert Maxwell on board his vessel answers these questions in advance.

The British attitude to all these events has been strangely passive. Not so the French. *Paris-Match*, having received from Israel the eighty-minute video of the second, four-hour autopsy – evidently from a source who felt the proceedings called for a third opinion, and a non-British one – made it the subject of a very large report in their edition of 9 January 1992. Their coverage included both still-frame images from the video, and photographs taken in the laboratory. To have published these was, from the Maxwell family's point of view, an unfeeling act, and one for which the magazine was made to pay damages to the widow. But in quoting the soundtrack of the video at considerable length, *Paris-Match* was keen to emphasise that Dr West had displayed 'a tendency to minimise every question raised by his Israeli colleagues'. That the Israelis had reacted more excitedly to the progress of their findings is indeed evident from the transcript of the tape. That West made, and continues to make, more cautious expressions of opinion is understandable in view of his responsibility to the insurers in a £20 million adjudication. (Either accident or murder would activate the insurance policy: suicide would invalidate it.)

The conviction *Paris-Match* reached, in consultation with experts of its own who saw the tape (but nothing but the tape), was that Maxwell had been attacked before death, and possibly violently beaten. The nose and one ear showed signs of impact, and on the body were found several haematomas – swellings containing blood – which are the body's common response to heavy blows. (Only a living body can react in this way, which makes nonsense of a suggestion emanating from the Spanish enquiry that such injuries were the consequence of rough treatment as Maxwell's corpse was winched from the sea into a helicopter.) Professor Louis Roche, a former President of the International Academy of Forensic Medicine, drew attention to three such haematomas. 'They are not very serious in themselves,' he commented, 'but they prove that there was trauma' (the term used was '*un traumatisme*') before death.

Defending their conclusions in the following week's issue, *Paris-Match* stated that they had now consulted Dr Birtolon Levy, the Hungarian-born pathologist who had taken part in the Tel Aviv post-mortem. He had told them somewhat enigmatically that, 'It wasn't the Holy Ghost who did what was done to Maxwell.' According to a 'reliable but confidential source', *Paris-Match* added, Dr Levy had expressed himself more forcefully in the immediate aftermath of the examination. 'What is certain,' he was reported as saying, 'is that, if they hadn't hit him, Maxwell would still be alive today.'

This controversy was revived in mid-November 1995, at the London trial of Ian and Kevin Maxwell. Dr Jehuda Hiss, Director of the Forensic Institute in Tel Aviv and another of the team assisting West, pointed out in court that, if Maxwell had jumped voluntarily into the sea, 'obviously neither the lacerations nor the haematoma would have been present'. Even if he had suddenly changed his mind and tried to cling on to the vessel, those particular injuries remained hard to account for. 'For these reasons,' Dr Hiss concluded, 'it is my opinion that it is unlikely the deceased committed suicide. It is more likely that he fell involuntarily into the sea either as a result of accident or homicide.'

On the same day,[1] a statement from Dr Jane Ward, a Lecturer in Physiology at Guy's and St Thomas's Hospitals, was read into the proceedings, raising the possibility that Maxwell had suffered 'micturition syncope', a condition which causes men, in particular, to faint while urinating. Maxwell was in the habit of relieving himself over the side of the boat at night (and, if his employees are to be believed, over the side of the *Mirror* building during the day).[2] But such a theory would seem to be subject to the same drawbacks as those cited by Dr West as making a heart attack an unlikely cause: 'I don't think that he would have dropped from disease and then fallen into the water, he would have ended up on the deck, and I don't think once he's on the deck he could simply roll into the sea.' Dr West, who had visited the yacht, had gone further: Maxwell would have needed to do 'something quite active', he said, in order to fall over the side. And in the unlikely event that Maxwell did faint and then toppled over the rail, his impact and muscle injuries are still to be accounted for. All in all, murder remains the one explanation which no medical expert is able to set aside.

Jacques-Marie Bourget, the journalist collating the *Paris-Match* coverage, had himself visited the Canaries, during the period when the crew of *Lady Ghislaine* was under orders from the local magistracy not to leave the islands. On 13 November, eight days after the discovery of the body, he happened to overhear a person using a public telephone.

[1]*Daily Telegraph* report, 15 November 1995.
[2]'When he landed by helicopter on the roof of the *Mirror* Building in Holborn he would often urinate over the edge and say, pointing at people ten floors below, "Look, I'm pissing on them and they don't even realise it."' *Maxwell Stories*, by Sam Jaffa: Robson Books, 1992.

Apparently addressing a superior in rank, the speaker first remarked on the badness of the line: 'It's quite a business phoning from here. You've got to be very careful.' Apparently the atmospherics then settled down. 'It's a public call-box,' the caller explained. 'The line's protected.' Then, answering a question from the other end of the line: 'We've done our job. The "other one" pissed about a bit, but everything's fixed now.' More speech from the recipient of the call. 'Don't worry,' the caller replies. 'It's a shambles here, like in Africa. The Spaniards do and say any old thing. They stick to you a bit, but they're not really effective. Never fear. All lights are green. Goodbye, sir.'[1] The caller is identified by Bourget as a member of the crew of the *Lady Ghislaine*.

Bourget is also one of the few to take an interest in the previous career of Captain Gus Rankin. His suggestion is that Rankin had behind him something of an adventurous career ('*une belle carrière d'aventurier*'). Bourget refers to a period of ten years or so previously, when Rankin, he alleges, might have been found shuttling to and fro between Malta and Libya – where, he reminds us in the same sentence, Edwin Wilson and Frank Terpil 'worked'. This is to stir up very murky waters indeed. Edwin P. Wilson and Frank E. Terpil were rogue defectors from the CIA, who, in 1981, were discovered to have been running guns and large tonnages of explosives to Colonel Gadhaffi's Libya, and also setting up training schools which passed on new-world techniques in assassination and terrorism.

The reporter who broke the story of Wilson and Terpil in the *New York Times* was none other than Seymour M. Hersh. And there are one or two other shudder-making coincidences in their double career. Wilson was lured to New York in June 1981, and arrested. While the case against him was being prepared, a key witness in the prospective trial, Kevin P. Mulcahy, was found dead outside his motel room in Virginia. An autopsy failed to discover a cause of death, but, in a familiar pattern, a medical

---

[1] A re-translation back from the French, which was given as follows: '*Nous avons accompli notre boulot. "L'autre" a un peu fait le con, mais tout est arrangé maintenant ... N'ayez pas peur. Ici, c'est le bordel, comme en Afrique. Les Espagnols font et disent n'importe quoi. Ils sont un peu collants, mais pas vraiment efficaces. N'ayez crainte. Tous les feux sont au vert. Au revoir*, sir [sic].'

examiner later ruled out foul play. Wilson was found guilty just the same, though a technical error would have brought him a surprisingly modest sentence if he had not conspired, while in jail, to liquidate two of his prosecutors and five of their witnesses. Terpil, meanwhile, an equally vicious operator, simply disappeared. In 1983, a judge ordered that his house be sold to pay back taxes. Terpil's house, which made nearly half a million dollars, was in McLean, Virginia, headquarters of Pergamon-Brassey's International Defense Publishers, Inc.

Jacques-Marie Bourget finally met Gus Rankin on the harbour at Palma, by the mooring of the *Lady Ghislaine*. He tried to show him a copy of the *Paris-Match* autopsy edition, but the Captain would not look at it closely. No doubt sensing that the interview was not destined to be a long one, Bourget went for broke: 'The "Company", the CIA, does that mean anything to you?' 'Negative.' 'And Frank Terpil, Ed Wilson, do those mean anything?' 'Negative. Never heard of them. Bullshit.'[1] 'Talk to me about Maxwell, tell me something about him.' Rankin grinned. 'He's well off where he is,' he replied. Behind him, a chorus of sailors, hired in New York that spring, laughed.

Englishmen of a common-sense disposition are trained up in the ways of William of Ockham, or Occam, whose proposition, known as 'Occam's Razor', states that entities should not be multiplied unnecessarily: in other words, that, when theories contend, we should favour the simplest, or at least, the one which demands the introduction of the fewest unknowns, variables and novelties. When it comes to Maxwell's death, his Chief of Staff, Peter Jay, is an Occamist. 'It appears to me that he had a heart attack,' he says, 'which appears to me to be a very common reason for death.' On another occasion, Jay had put it more flatly: 'The man most likely in the world to have a heart attack – had one.' He now stands almost alone in this belief.

My guess would be that Maxwell travelled alone to his yacht because he was asked to do so by a contact who told him

---

[1] The world 'Bullshit' is given by Bourget in the original, and also translated (as *Foutaises*). The rest of the dialogue here is again my re-translation from the French.

there was a solution – the one solution left – to his otherwise career-ending problems of debt. A meeting would take place in the Canaries, the venue to be decided once Maxwell was down there. This climactic tête-à-tête was put off once (hence the morning of bad temper and agitation Maxwell was observed to suffer) while final arrangements were made for an operation that had been mounted in a hurry. Having no choice, he obediently extended his stay among the islands. It strikes me as most likely that whoever put him overboard was already on the vessel when it left port. If, later, another vessel did come alongside, it was to take supernumerary persons away. Maxwell had gone, beaten down in his own cabin, dragged out to the aft deck and dumped in the sea – hanging on at the last moment and tearing a muscle as his shoulder took the whole weight of his dangling body. He floated till he died. The 'locked-door mystery' is no mystery once one accepts that it wasn't Maxwell who locked it. His key followed him into the sea.

The Secret Intelligence Service had created this monster long ago. It would have been very neat, very British, very circular, if they had finally delivered him up. But so far, the only evidence suggesting confirmation of that theory is the tiny word 'sir' in an overheard telephone call reported by a French journalist. It suggests an official hierarchy, a quasi-military structure. But maybe New York mobsters expect, these days, to be called 'sir' too.

The fate Maxwell suffered was not beyond his own imagining, if we are to judge by the front page of his own *Daily Mirror* on 19 August 1991, less than three months before. That day we were treated to one of the *Mirror*'s old-fashioned, outraged exposés, this time of a 'timeshare conman' who had been cheating holidaymakers. 'THROW HIM TO THE SHARKS', the headline said.

# Epilogue

In England, at the corporate offices and in the newsrooms, shock and dismay at the loss of the 'Man Who Saved The *Mirror*'; in the worldwide communities of diplomacy and secret intelligence, and above all within M.I.6 and the CIA, almost universal satisfaction and relief. There is no better indicator of the difference between the two worlds in which Maxwell moved.

His acquaintances at first were caught in a whirlpool of humbug. How to escape the ritual obeisances when a man lies dead on some foreign mortuary slab and his family weeps? This is not the place to tax those who supplied their sound-bite tributes by repeating the words they chose to utter, and would wish, within days, that they had withheld. One anecdote told by the then President Herzog of Israel stands for all:

> I asked Mrs Maxwell at a certain stage for copies of the messages and cables that she received after he passed away. And I got that file – she sent me a file, and it was quite unbelievable. And at one stage I was approached by a certain very prominent peer in the United Kingdom who said to me, 'I can't understand why you honoured him at his funeral.' And I said, listen, whatever I said was nothing compared to what *you* wrote her . . . From Russia, from France, from America, from all over the world, all the political leaders of all parties, I saw these messages and

I just couldn't get over it. I then realised I'd been very very modest in what I'd said.

Even as Maxwell was being laid to rest on the Mount of Olives, the backlash was winding up. Once again, home news predominated, with the discovery of the pension fund losses, and the general sense of liberation at the thought that nothing one said about Maxwell would ever again be countered by a libel writ. At the level of international politics, Israel at the funeral had declared itself in Maxwell's debt (in a manner of speaking), but nobody even in Israel seemed keen to specify why. In Russia, news immediately emerged of a list of Western firms classified as 'friendly', and eligible for priority payments from the Soviet Communist Party. It was no surprise to find the *Morning Star* newspaper (formerly the *Daily Worker*) on the list, and only a little more shocking to find Pergamon Press nominated.

The fact that Maxwell had been toying with publishing a public-relations magazine for the KGB – he had discussed the possibility with Kryuchkov – was received rather as a symptom of the quaint confusions of post-Gorbachevian Russia than as an act of treachery on the Publisher's part. The Communist Party's clandestine money-deals had now been formally banned by Boris Yeltsin, and their known export channels closed. Three leading figures implicated in those, notably the one-time Interior Minister Boris Pugo, had committed suicide after the failure of the August coup. An enquiry into the history of the 'friendly firms' was now promised – by Boris Pankin, one of Robert Maxwell's closest Russian friends. In an amusingly parallel move in London, a trusted city figure was appointed to sift through the remains of the Maxwell empire and see what assets could be rescued for the bereft pensioners of the Mirror Group. The man chosen was Sir John Cuckney, formerly of M.I.5 – so there would be no embarrassments there.

In spite of a general closing of ranks, to avoid admitting undue contact with Maxwell, some oddities continued to emerge. The *Observer* brought up the unexpected name of Arthur Scargill, who, it said, had received a telephone call on 5 November 1991, giving him the news of Maxwell's death and tipping him off that, '. . . if he, his union, or its pension fund had any connection with the Mirror Group, he had exactly forty-five minutes to do something about it. The death was announced forty-five minutes later.' Mr Scargill has privately confirmed the truth of this report, without naming his informant, but indicating that the person was of such standing as to convince him immediately a) that the report was true, and b) that the security services were involved. Scargill himself had been no friend of Maxwell, who on taking control at the *Mirror* had failed to back the miners in their strike action, and in his role as employer always gave Margaret Thatcher credit for dealing roughly with unions who had 'behaved badly'. Scargill himself had ended up with few friends in high places: yet somebody close to security sources felt that this was one pitfall from which he should be preserved.

No particular 'fix' upon Maxwell's international dealings emerged in the memoirs published after his death. Tom Bower extended his heroic grapplings with the account books of the Maxwell empire, 'following the money' without weighing the political consequences. Nicholas Davies's mock-horrified and semi-besotted account of Maxwell's way of working included an inept defence of Davies's proven dealings with Ari Ben-Menashe, whose own book, in turn, over-exerted itself in implicating Davies and demonising Maxwell. Davies knew more than most about Maxwell's demeanour in Eastern Europe, however, and his account of the 'King of Bulgaria' period was, in its time, a revelation. Roy Greenslade's book *Maxwell's Fall* marked the rare entry into this field of a writer whose reactions to Maxwell still bore the stamp of immediacy; but again, Maxwell's monstrous behaviour at the *Mirror*, seen in close-up, blotted out his overseas dimension.

Even now, it is difficult to step back from all the complications of Maxwell's career and assess what he was aiming for, what his programme was. He claimed to be guided, if not by principle, then at least by a humane instinct: 'I can be both human and ruthless,' he told Russell Harty in 1988.[1] 'If you want to build a global communication empire in a short period of time, you have to be ruthless; and at the same time, coming from a very poor background, I've never lost my feeling of responsibility and care for my fellow human beings.' He referred continually

[1] *Start The Week*, Radio 4, 7.3.88.

to the poverty of his beginnings, but these dips into a reservoir of compassionate memory were obligatory pieties. Maxwell's occasional humanitarian crusades – Africa, Chernobyl – were almost invariably marked by crude displays of showmanship, indicative of his desires for approval and simple attention. Like many grandiose narcissists, he took pleasure from playing a munificent, Father Christmas role. (And how appropriate it was that such a Narcissus should have chosen the *Daily Mirror* as his organ of opinion.)

Everywhere in the psychoanalytic literature of narcissism, one meets with descriptions of personality-types which seem to have been modelled on Robert Maxwell. I quote, almost at random, from a paper by W. W. Meissner:[1]

> The exhibitionism, pride in prowess, show-offishness, and the often counterphobic competitiveness and risk-taking in the service of narcissistic exhibitionism are quite familiar. Such individuals tend to be self-centred, and to have an exorbitant need for approval and admiration from others – particularly admiration. Their relationship with others often has a quality of arrogance and contempt . . .

This particular quality leads on to a more specific, and more dangerous personality type, in whom:

> . . . the contempt for others, the implicit notion that they have potential value only in terms of their exploitability or manipulability in the service of self-enhancement, the high value often placed on putting something over on others or getting away with something, even though that may involve deceptive or even dishonest practices, all carry the narcissistic stamp of this sort of personality . . .

These manipulative characteristics, all present to a marked degree in Maxwell, indicate 'a somewhat more pathological

[1] 'Narcissistic Personalities and Borderline Conditions' (Meissner), from *Essential Papers on Narcissism*, ed. Andrew P. Morrison, M.D., New York University Press, 1986.

level' of the condition, Meissner says. At the same time, 'strong inner resources' are commonly present; and what all narcissistic personalities have in common is 'a capacity for charm and the ability to entertain, flatter, and influence others'.

Maxwell was of course not deluded in reckoning himself to be an extremely able individual. His early circumstances had also obliged him to develop a striking adaptability, aptly symbolised by his freedom to move among languages. Whether, by the end of his life, Maxwell really had any 'home' language, any set of linguistic tools of which he was completely and instinctively the master, is an interesting question, and perhaps a clue to the seeming directionlessness of his internationalism. As the political dimension of his activities developed, it was as if he could not believe in the reality of national borders, knowing that he, as an individual, was already a living embodiment of their dissolution.

It was fortunate for the world that Maxwell's personality, being of its nature deeply resentful of efforts to restrict or control it, was predisposed to resist tyrannies, and to promote the kind of political freedoms that would leave him free to act. 'Freedom for Maxwell', very broadly speaking, entailed freedom for his fellow human beings, though this was happy accident rather than idealism. He understood tyrants very well, being one himself; and he knew from his own *modus operandi* that to talk to the top man in a totalitarian state (such as his own empire) is to confine tiresome negotiations to a single table. The process also contributed a steady input of the self-flattery Maxwell required – for it is another characteristic of the advanced narcissist that his sense of specialness can be satisfied only by the company of those who in the eyes of the world are similarly special, however deeply he may despise them in his heart. Maxwell knew what manner of men Brezhnev and Zhivkov and Ceauşescu were, but he was unable to resist seeking their company.

The sense of limited time to which Maxwell often referred caused him to accelerate all his programmes of ambition through the Eighties. In Israel, he found at last a sympathetic entity, a nation-sized projection of himself, into which he could pour some of the narcissistic overflow. He continued to be used by regimes of East and West as a sort of universal adaptor, allowing a flow of power in either direction, or both – a flow from which a fraction was always diverted into Maxwell's own batteries.

But where the Cold War had needed its freelances, the new, chaotic world was merely confused by them. The last recommendation made to President Reagan by John Tower's Special Review Board in 1987 had been: 'We recommend against having implementation and policy oversight dominated by intermediaries. We do not recommend barring limited use of private individuals to assist in United States diplomatic initiatives or in covert activities. We caution against use of such people except in very limited ways and under close observation and supervision.' John Tower was becoming rather too obvious a freelance himself. In 1991, his time was called, and so was Maxwell's, in all probability by an international committee of those who had used him, but did not care to hear him tell the world how much.

William Hazlitt once wrote: 'The love of liberty is the love of others; the love of power is the love of ourselves.' But Robert Maxwell, though he offered employment to so many of the type, had no time for scribblers.

# Selected Bibliography

Badash, Lawrence. *Kapitza, Rutherford and the Kremlin*. Yale University Press, 1985.

Ben-Menashe, Ari. *Profits of War: Inside the Secret US–Israeli Arms Network*. Sheridan Square Press, New York, 1992.

A. M. Biew, *Kapitsa: the Story of the British-trained Scientist who Invented the Russian Hydrogen Bomb*. Frederick Muller Ltd, 1956.

Boag, J. W., Rubinin, P. E., and Shoenberg, D. *Kapitsa in Cambridge and Moscow*. North-Holland, 1990.

Bower, Tom. *Maxwell: The Outsider*. Aurum Press Limited, 1988. Revised edition, Mandarin Paperbacks, 1992.

Davies, Nicholas. *The Unknown Maxwell*. Sidgwick & Jackson Limited, 1992. Pan Books, 1993.

Dorril, Stephen. *The Silent Conspiracy*. Mandarin, 1993.

Gordievsky, Oleg. *Next Stop Execution*. Macmillan, 1995.

Greenslade, Roy. *Maxwell's Fall*. Simon & Schuster, 1992.

Haines, Joe. *Maxwell*. Macdonald and Co., 1988.

Hersh, Seymour. *The Samson Option*. Faber & Faber, 1991.

Hoy, Claire and Ostrovsky, Victor. *By Way of Deception*. Bloomsbury, 1990.

Jaffa, Sam, *Maxwell Stories*. Robson Books, 1992.

James, W. Martin, (III). *A Political History of the War in Angola*. Transaction Publishers, New Jersey, 1992.

Loftus, John and Aarons, Mark. *The Secret War Against the Jews*. St Martin's Press, New York, 1994.

Maxwell, Elisabeth. *A Mind of My Own: My Life with Robert Maxwell*. Sidgwick & Jackson, 1994.

Milne, Seumas. *The Enemy Within*. Verso, 1994.

Parry, Robert. *Trick or Treason: The October Surprise Mystery*. Sheridan Square Press, New York, 1993.

Robinson, Jeffrey. *The Laundrymen*. Simon & Schuster, 1994.

Sampson, Anthony. *The Arms Bazaar*. Hodder & Stoughton, 1977. Revised edition, Coronet, 1988.

Stokes, Gale. *The Walls Came Tumbling Down*. Oxford University Press, 1993.

Thompson, Peter and Delano, Anthony. *Maxwell: A Portrait of Power*. Bantam Press, 1988. New paperback edition, Corgi, 1991.

Woodward, Bob. *Veil: The Secret Wars of the CIA 1981–1987*. Simon & Schuster, 1987.

Other biographies of interest (see Chapter One) are:

Wasserstein, Bernard. *The Secret Lives of Trebitsch Lincoln*. Yale University Press, 1988.

Wyatt, Will. *The Man Who Was B. Traven*. Jonathan Cape, 1980.

The best short account of the Lynskey Tribunal is given by John Gross in *Age of Austerity*, ed. Philip French and Michael Sissons, Oxford University Press, 1963.

# Sources and Acknowledgements

This book arises out of research into Robert Maxwell's unpublicised activities gathered from all over the world, over a period of more than two years. More than one hundred interviews were undertaken at a preliminary stage and some testimony was also given off-the-record, by sources who cannot be named, but whose authority to speak on the matter in question is not in doubt. Additional research materials included transcripts, interview notes, reports and documentary items ranging from Maxwell Communications Corporation Annual Reports to photocopies of faxes itemising orders for millions of dollars' worth of firearms. I am grateful to Touch Productions, of London, for making this material available. All parties quickly realised that the book could not be put before the public until the trial of Robert Maxwell's sons, Kevin and Ian, was concluded, for fear of prejudicing the outcome of those proceedings.

The following interviewees testified in English (for brevity's sake I omit their titles here): Mikhail Lyubimov, Oleg Gordievsky, Oleg Kalugin, Dzhermen Gvishiani, Valery Boldin, Felix Sviridov, Yitzhak Shamir, Chaim Herzog, Ariel Sharon, David Kimche, Saul Zadka, Uri Dan, Desmond Bristow, Stephen Dorril, Rupert Allason, Tam Dalyell, Peter Jay, David Hooper, Nicholas Davies, Gus Rankin, Iain West. The testimony of these individuals is reproduced as given, with a very small number of silent corrections – as when a witness, caught up in a long statement, mixes up tenses, or a native Russian speaker typically omits the definite article before a noun. Since linguistic expertise played no small part in Robert Maxwell's story, from first to last, it would be appropriate here to thank all foreign-born witnesses for their excellent English. The testimony of Leonid Zamyatin and Vladimir Kryuchkov was given in Russian, and that of General Jaruzelski in Polish.

In the writing of the book to a strict deadline, I was grateful to Nigel Newton, Managing Director of Bloomsbury Publishing, for some timely advice at an early stage. To work with Editorial Director Liz Calder has been an ambition of mine for some years, and I'm only sorry such a pleasurable collaboration was so brief. My copy editor, Mary Tomlinson, did wonders in as little time as anyone has ever been given for such a job. There was no opportunity to go in search of outside expertise, but fortunately, I was able to call upon highly appropriate cottage-industry resources within the family. My father, a former Principal Inspector of Taxes well used to investigating the likes of Maxwell, was able to explain to me some outstanding features of his commercial strategy; and my son Steffan knows more about the computer and defence industries than is good for a teenager. I thank them both; but my most heartfelt gratitude goes to my wife, for her patience and good advice.